KU-791-061

KITCHIN'S ROAD TRANSPORT LAW
1979

A SUMMARY OF THE LEGISLATION AFFECTING THE CONSTRUCTION, EQUIPMENT AND USE OF MOTOR VEHICLES

Edited by JAMES DUCKWORTH

OF MOTOR TRANSPORT

UNIVERSITY LIBRARY
2 4 MAY 1979
NOTTINGHAM

LONDON
BUTTERWORTHS
1979

THE BUTTERWORTH GROUP

ENGLAND:
   Butterworth & Co. (Publishers) Ltd.
   London: 88 Kingsway, London WC2B 6AB

AUSTRALIA:
   Butterworths Pty. Ltd.
   Sydney: 586 Pacific Highway, Chatswood, NSW 2067
   Also at Melbourne, Brisbane, Adelaide and Perth

CANADA:
   Butterworth & Co. (Canada) Ltd.
   Toronto: 2265 Midland Avenue, Scarborough, M1P 4S1

NEW ZEALAND:
   Butterworths of New Zealand Ltd.
   Wellington: 77–85 Customhouse Quay

SOUTH AFRICA:
   Butterworth & Co. (South Africa) (Pty.) Ltd.
   Durban: 152–154 Gale Street, Durban

U.S.A.:
   Butterworth (Publishers) Inc.
   Boston: 19 Cummings Park, Woburn, Mass. 01801

© Butterworth & Co. (Publishers) Ltd. 1979
First published 1941
Twentieth Edition 1979

All rights reserved. No part of this publication may be reproduced
or transmitted in any form or by any means, including photocopy-
ing and recording, without the written permission of the copyright
holder, application for which should be addressed to the publisher.
Such written permission must also be obtained before any part of
this publication is stored in a retrieval system of any nature.

ISBN 0 406 26471 6
ISSN 0308 8987

This book is sold subject to the Standard Conditions of Sale of Net
Books and may not be re-sold in the U.K. below the net price
fixed by Butterworths for the book in our current catalogue.

UNIVERSITY OF NOTTINGHAM
WITHDRAWN
FROM THE LIBRARY

KITCHIN'S
ROAD TRANSPORT LAW 1979

PREFACE

The steady stream in 1978 of new legal requirements and changes to existing requirements which directly affect the operation of goods and passenger vehicles has meant that a further 22 pages have had to be added to the 1979 edition of Kitchin.

The most important changes in the last 12 months are in the law controlling drivers' hours of work. The E.E.C. law was applied to national transport operations within Britain last January and Regulations were made which phase-in its full application over a three-year period. Instead of removing the British law from those drivers newly affected by the E.E.C. law, further complicated Regulations were made to 'harmonise' the British law with that of the E.E.C. Still further Regulations were made exempting various national transport operations from the E.E.C. law and the Regulations which gave exemption from the British law to drivers meeting special needs were re-made. Consequently the chapter on drivers' hours law has been re-written and substantially enlarged.

The move to the E.E.C. law has also resulted in a revision of the chapter on drivers' records. The section on E.E.C. tachograph law has been brought up to date to take account of minor changes made to these rules last December and to explain why these rules are not yet enforced in Britain.

Revision and enlargement of the p.s.v. licensing chapter has followed the passing of the Transport Act 1978. The Act provides new law for non-p.s.v. community buses, makes changes to road service licensing and widens the circumstances under which paid car-sharing can be free of p.s.v. licensing. The conditions of fitness for vehicles used under the Minibus Act 1977 are now included in the appropriate chapter.

This edition also incorporates the consolidating Motor Vehicles (Construction and Use) Regulations 1978 and the changes they introduce. These include stricter bans on the mixing of tyres of different structures, duties to maintain seat belts and anchorage points and the important provision of treating, for some purposes, a converter dolly and semi-trailer combination as a single trailer.

Changes which the 1978 Act made to the powers of vehicle examiners and the distances which vehicles can be taken for examination or weighing are included. New Regulations dealing with the fitting and use of rear fog lamps and the use of dynamic axle weighing machines are also explained. Opportunity has also been taken of re-writing the section on tests for three-year-old vehicles to provide more detail and, in particular, to describe the duties of examiners and their liability for damage.

November 1, 1978.   J.D.

SYSTEM OF REFERENCE

The purpose of this book is to enable the layman easily to understand the various Acts and Regulations affecting the construction, equipment and operation of vehicles. The legislation is presented in summarised form, and if it is desired to consult a particular Act, Regulation or Order the special system of reference used gives the official titles and thus facilitates further elucidation. The extent to which the material is compressed necessarily means that some of the more detailed points of the law are omitted.

Each point of law is identified by reference to the appropriate Act, Order or Regulation. For example 1017/78/13(1) means paragraph 1, Regulation 13 of Statutory Instrument No. 1017 of 1978, the full title of which will be found at the head of the section. In succeeding references to the same Orders or Regulations in the same or following sentences, the references are often abbreviated to, for example [13(1)].

Since the beginning of 1948 the general title Statutory Rules and Orders has been replaced by Statutory Instruments. References in this book to Regulations issued before 1948 therefore denote S.R. and O. and not S.I. numbers.

Copies of the Acts, Orders and Regulations mentioned in the book may be ordered through any bookseller or obtained direct from H.M. Stationary Office.

In this edition the law is stated as at November 1, 1978.

CONTENTS

DEFINITIONS AND GENERAL NOTES

Road Traffic Act 1972
Motor Vehicles (Construction and Use) Regulations, **No. 1017/78**

Section 190 of the Road Traffic Act 1972 places motor vehicles into various basic classes according to their description and unladen weight.

A motor car is a mechanically propelled vehicle, not being a motor cycle or invalid carriage, which is constructed itself to carry a load or passengers and the unladen weight of which (a) if constructed solely for the carriage of not more than seven passengers and their effects does not exceed 3 tons; (b) if constructed or adapted for the conveyance of goods or burden does not exceed 3 tons; or (c) in any other case does not exceed $2\frac{1}{2}$ tons.

A heavy motor car is a mechanically propelled vehicle, not being a motor car, which is constructed itself to carry a load or passengers and the unladen weight of which exceeds $2\frac{1}{2}$ tons.

A motor tractor is a mechanically propelled vehicle which is not constructed itself to carry a load, other than water, fuel, accumulators and other equipment used for the purpose of propulsion, loose tools and loose equipment, and the unladen weight of which does not exceed $7\frac{1}{4}$ tons.

A locomotive is a mechanically propelled vehicle, described in the same way as a motor tractor, and the unladen weight of which exceeds $7\frac{1}{4}$ tons.

If a motor vehicle is constructed so that a trailer can be partially superimposed on it whereby a substantial part of the weight of the trailer is borne by the vehicle then that vehicle is deemed to be constructed itself to carry a load [190(9)].

For the above purposes a crane, dynamo, welding plant or other special appliance or apparatus which is a permanent or essentially permanent fixture on a motor vehicle does not constitute a load or goods or burden but is deemed to form part of the vehicle [190(10)].

A motor vehicle is a mechanically propelled vehicle intended or adapted for use on roads. A trailer is a vehicle drawn by a motor vehicle [190(1)].

In the High Court Case of *Newberry* v. *Simmonds*, [1961] 2 Q.B. 345; [1961] 2 All E.R. 318 it was held that a motor car from which the engine had been removed was still a mechanically propelled vehicle. A vehicle licence was required for a van with a defective engine which was being towed—*Cobb* v. *Whorton*, [1971] R.T.R. 392. But in *Smart* v. *Allan*, [1962] 3 All E.R. 893 a vehicle was held not to be a mechanically propelled vehicle since it had no gearbox and the engine was so defective that there was no likelihood of it being repaired.

In three cases, *MacDonald* v. *Carmichael*, 1941 S.C.(J.) 27, *Daley* v. *Hargreaves*, [1961] 1 All E.R. 552 and *Chalgray* v. *Aspley* (1965), 109 Sol. Jo. 394 it was decided that a dump truck, though used on a road, was not a motor vehicle because it was not 'intended or adapted for use on roads'. Similarly in *Burns* v. *Currell* [1963] 2 Q.B. 433; [1963] 2 All E.R. 297 a go-kart was held not to be a motor vehicle. On the other hand, in *Childs* v. *Coghlan* (1968), 112 Sol. J. 175 a Euclid earthscraper was held to be intended for use on roads since it was too large to be carried and to get from site to site had to be driven on the road.

A motor vehicle can change from one class to another if a reconstruction takes place. In *Keeble* v. *Miller*, [1950] 1 K.B. 601; [1950] 1 All E.R. 261, where a heavy motor car was converted into a locomotive, it was ruled that 'constructed' meant constructed at the material time and not originally constructed. A vehicle chassis on delivery was held not to be a motor tractor in *Millard* v. *Turvey*, [1968] 2 Q.B. 390; [1968] 2 All E.R. 7 when it was said that 'constructed' meant constructed when completed.

An articulated vehicle is a motor car or heavy motor car with a trailer superimposed on it so that when the trailer is uniformly loaded not less than 20% of the weight of its load is borne by the drawing vehicle [1017/78/3(1)]. When coupled-up an artic is treated as a motor vehicle and trailer [Act 1972/191].

A composite trailer is a combination of a converter dolly and a semi-trailer [1017/78/3(1)]. A converter dolly is a trailer with two or more wheels designed to enable a semi-trailer to move without any part of its weight being superimposed on the drawing vehicle and which is not itself part of the semi-trailer or drawing vehicle [3(1)]. A semi-trailer is a trailer which is constructed to form part of an articulated vehicle [3(1)]. A composite trailer is to be treated as a single trailer for the purposes of Regulations 73 (overall length); 86(1), (2) (old weight limits); 87 (train weight limits); 89(3) (newer weight limits); 137 (restriction on number of trailers); and 101 (brake maintenance) of the Motor Vehicles (Construction and Use) Regulations 1978 [3(6A)].

A dual-purpose vehicle is a vehicle not over 2040 kg unladen weight which is constructed or adapted to carry both passengers and goods and is either (a) so constructed that all its wheels can be power-driven or (b) constructed with a permanent roof, and behind the driver's seat has a row of transverse seats with backrests for two or more, in prescribed positions, and windows of minimum sizes [1017/78/3(1)].

A goods vehicle is a motor vehicle or trailer constructed or adapted for the carriage of goods. The carriage of goods includes the haulage of goods [Act 1972/196].

For particular purposes different definitions are given and these will be supplied in the relevant chapters. In *Plume* v. *Suckling* [1977] R.T.R. 271 a motor coach with most of its seats removed and adapted to carry domestic equipment and a stock car was, for speed limit purposes, held not to be a passenger vehicle but to be a goods vehicle.

The unladen weight of a vehicle is to be taken as its weight, inclusive of the body and all parts (the heavier being taken where alternative bodies or parts are used) necessary to or ordinarily used with the vehicle when working on a road but not including the weight of water, fuel or accumulators used to supply power for the propulsion of the vehicle, loose tools and loose equipment [Act 1972/194]. It was held in *Cording* v. *Halse*, [1955] 1 Q.B. 63; [1954] 3 All E.R. 287 that a cattle container carried on a platform truck was not an alternative body and was excluded from unladen weight. Specified items can be deducted *for taxation purposes only* and these will be dealt with in the chapter on vehicle excise licensing.

The majority of traffic offences can be committed only on a road. A road is defined as any highway and any other road to which the public has access, including bridges over which the road passes [Act 1972/196].

Some traffic laws apply only to the 'driving' of a vehicle and they are generally straightforward. But many others relate to a person who 'uses' or 'causes' or 'permits' a person to use it.

The person driving a vehicle 'uses' it and an employer 'uses' it when it is driven on his business by an employee—*Green* v. *Burnett*, [1955] 1 Q.B. 78; [1954] 3 All E.R. 273. Where a vehicle is driven by a person other than an employee of the owner the owner is not then using it—*Crawford* v. *Haughton*, [1972] 1 All E.R. 534; [1972] 1 W.L.R. 572. A car-hire firm was not using a car which was hired out—*Carmichael & Sons* v. *Cottle*, [1971] R.T.R. 11—and a truck operator was not using a vehicle driven by an agency driver on his business—*Howard* v. *G. T. Jones & Co., Ltd.*, [1975] R.T.R. 150—nor when he hired a vehicle with a driver—*Balfour Beatty & Co., Ltd.* v. *Grindley*, [1975] R.T.R. 156. In *Mickleburgh* v. *B.R.S. (Contracts) Ltd* (1977) R.T.R. 389

the owners of a vehicle hired out with a driver for three years were held to be using it when overladen by the hirers who had control of its day-to-day operations.

In *Elliott* v. *Grey,* [1960] 1 Q.B. 367; [1959] 3 All E.R. 733 it was ruled that a broken-down vehicle parked in the street was being 'used' and required insurance. But this case was not followed in *Hewer* v. *Cutler,* [1974] R.T.R. 155 which involved an immobilised car parked without a test certificate. The court based its decision on the mischief aimed at by the test certificate requirement.

A person 'causes' a vehicle to be used if through some express or implied instruction, or through some position of authority, he causes another person to use it—*Houston* v. *Buchanan,* [1940] 2 All E.R. 179. To cause the use of an overloaded lorry a person must have knowledge of the facts constituting the offence—*Ross Hillman, Ltd.* v. *Bond,* [1974] Q.B. 435; [1974] 2 All E.R. 287.

To 'permit' use a person must have knowledge of what is alleged to have been permitted or must have been closing his eyes to the obvious not caring whether it happened or not—*James & Son* v. *Smee,* [1955] 1 Q.B.78; [1954] 3 All E.R. 273. Also, in *Grays Haulage Co., Ltd.* v. *Arnold,* [1966] 1 All E.R. 896; [1966] 1 W.L.R. 534 it was held that the mere fact than an employer does not take steps to prevent an employee committing an offence does not mean that he has 'permitted' it. This was followed in *Knowles Transport, Ltd.* v. *Russell,* [1975] R.T.R. 87 when it was held that knowledge of irregularities after they had occurred did not impute the knowledge required for permitting. Proof of knowledge by a responsible officer of a company of a vehicle's deficiency is required for permitting use of a vehicle with an insecure load—*P. Lowery & Sons, Ltd.* v. *Wark,* [1975] R.T.R. 45.

If a person can be charged with causing or permitting an offence he should not be charged with aiding and abetting it—*Carmichael & Sons* v. *Cottle,* and followed in *Crawford* v. *Haughton,* [1972] 1 All E.R. 534; [1972] 1 W.L.R. 572.

CONSTRUCTION OF VEHICLES

Road Traffic Act 1972, as amended by *Road Traffic Act 1974*
Motor Vehicles (Construction and Use) Regulations, **No. 1017/78**
as amended by:
  Motor Vehicles (Construction and Use) (Amendment) Regulations, **No. 1233/78**
  Motor Vehicles (Construction and Use) (Amendment) (No. 2) Regulations, **No. 1234/78**
  Motor Vehicles (Construction and Use) (Amendment) (No. 3) Regulations, **No. 1235/78**
  Motor Vehicles (Construction and Use) (Amendment) (No. 4) Regulations, **No. 1263/78**
Transit of Animals (Amendment) Order, **No. 750/31**
Transit of Horses Order, **No. 335/51**
Transit of Calves Order, **No. 1228/63**
Agriculture (Tractor Cabs) Regulations, **No. 1072/67**
Transit of Animals (Road and Rail) Order, **No. 1024/75**

BRAKES—MOTOR VEHICLES

For heavy motor cars and motor cars in general, different standards of braking are laid down for vehicles first used on or before January 1, 1968, from those first used after that date [1017/78/59, 64 and 4th Sched.]. In both cases, the vehicle must be equipped with an efficient braking system with two means of operation or with two efficient braking systems each with its own means of operation. But one braking system with one means of operation is sufficient if it is a split braking system. In the event of the failure of any part, other than a fixed member or a brake shoe anchor pin, there must still be braking capable of being applied to not less than half the number of the vehicle's wheels sufficient 'under the most adverse conditions' to bring the vehicle to rest within a reasonable distance [1017/78/59(1 to 3), 64 (1 to 3)].

Special provisons apply to heavy motor cars first used before August 15, 1928, to steam wagons and to motor cars first used before January 1, 1915, as well as to works trucks equipped with one braking system with only one means of operation [1017/78/59, 64].

Dealing first with pre-1968 heavy motor cars (other than works trucks and pedestrian-controlled vehicles) and motor cars (other than those not exceeding 1525 kg unladen, dual-purpose vehicles, works trucks and pedestrian-controlled vehicles), and which are goods

5

vehicles, rigid four-wheelers must have a main brake (footbrake) efficiency of at least 45% and a secondary brake efficiency of at least 20%. On such vehicles with more than four wheels or which form part of an articulated vehicle the footbrake efficiency must be at least 40% and that of the secondary brake 15% [59(6)(7) and 64(6)(7)]. The secondary brake is usually the hand-brake but any other method of application, including a dual-line split footbrake, which gives the required efficiency in the event of failure of one-half of it, is permissible.

All heavy motor cars and motor cars (other than works trucks and pedestrian-controlled vehicles) first used on or after January 1, 1968, whether goods or passenger vehicles, must have a main brake efficiency of at least 50% and a secondary brake efficiency of 25% [59(5) and 64(5)].

Once a Department of Transport plating certificate has been issued for a motor vehicle, the efficiencies it has to attain have to be achieved by the vehicle when operating at its design gross weight. If no design weight is shown on the plate, the legally permitted gross weight figure is to be used instead [1017/78/152]. The design gross weight in some cases is higher than the legal limit and, although the vehicle cannot be operated at the higher design weight, the brakes have to match it.

Parking brakes for pre-1968 vehicles must be capable of being set to prevent at least two wheels—or one wheel on three-wheelers—from revolving. On motor vehicles first used on or after January 1, 1968 direct mechanically actuated brakes must hold a vehicle on a gradient of 1 in 6·25 without the assistance of stored energy—e.g. vacuum or compressed air—and must be independent of the main braking system. Spring-brake chambers are perfectly acceptable [1017/78/13].

Specific braking efficiency figures are not applied to locomotives or motor tractors. Locomotives first used before June 1, 1955, must have brakes which act upon all but the steering wheels, and which can bring the vehicle to rest within a reasonable distance. Other locomotives and all motor tractors must be equipped with one or more braking systems with two means of application. The application of one means must not affect or operate the pedal or hand lever of the other means of operation. In the event of failure, brakes must still be capable of being applied to at least half the number of wheels sufficiently, under the most adverse conditions, to bring the vehicle to rest within a reasonable distance [50, 51 and 55].

On locomotives first used from June 1, 1955, no braking system is allowed which is rendered ineffective by the non-rotation of the engine [51(4)]. The same rule applies to other vehicles first used on or after April 1, 1938—motor tractors [55(3)], heavy motor cars [59(11)] and motor cars [64(11)].

If a vehicle first used on or after October 1, 1937, is equipped with a braking system which embodies a vacuum or pressure reservoir, there must also be a warning device so placed as to be readily visible to the driver from the driving seat in order to indicate any impending failure or deficiency in the vacuum or pressure system. This does not apply to vehicles not exceeding 3050 kg unladen with a vacuum system dependent on engine induction provided that, despite a failure of the vacuum, the brakes are sufficient to bring the vehicle to rest within a reasonable distance [14].

Braking efficiency is defined as the maximum braking force capable of being developed by the application of the brakes, expressed as a percentage of the weight of the vehicle including any persons (excluding fare-paying or other travelling passengers) or load carried in the vehicle [3].

BRAKES—TRAILERS

Every trailer made before January 1, 1968, with an unladen weight of more than 102 kg (or agricultural trailer over 102 kg irrespective of when it was made) must be equipped with brakes which can be applied, while being drawn, to at least two wheels if it has not more than four wheels, or to at least four wheels if it has more than four wheels and, in any case if made after April 1, 1938, to at least half its wheels. Except for trailers with overrun brakes, these brakes must be capable of being applied by the driver of the drawing vehicle or by a person on the trailer. On semi-trailers permanently attached to tractive units, it must be possible to set brakes to prevent at least two wheels from revolving when not being drawn. Parking brakes on other trailers must be provided to prevent at least two wheels from turning [1017/78/75(1)].

Trailers over 102 kg unladen (other than those with overrun brakes) built after January 1, 1968, must have brakes capable of being applied to all wheels by the driver of the drawing vehicle when he applies the system giving maximum efficiency—almost invariably, the footbrake. In the event of the failure of any part, other than a fixed member or a brake shoe anchor pin, of the braking system of either the drawing vehicle (excluding the means of operating a split braking system) or the trailer, brakes must still be capable of being applied to at least two wheels of the trailer (or one wheel of a two-wheeler) by the driver of the drawing vehicle when he uses one of the braking systems which the law requires it to have. For parking, every trailer must have brakes which can be applied to at least two wheels by a person standing on the ground. These parking brakes must be able to hold the trailer on a gradient of 1 in 6·25 by direct mechanical action without the assistance of stored energy [75(2)].

The foregoing requirements on trailer brakes do not apply to: (a) any land implement or land implement conveyor drawn by a motor vehicle; (b) street cleansing trailers carrying no load other than necessary gear or equipment; (c) any broken-down vehicle drawn by a motor vehicle in consequence of the breakdown; (d) any agricultural trailer made before July 1, 1947, when drawn by a motor tractor or a land tractor if its unladen weight is not over 4070 kg, is the only trailer drawn and if it travels at not more than 10 m.p.h. [75(4)].

Trailers built on or after April 1, 1938, must have brakes that are not rendered ineffective by the non-rotation of the engine of the drawing vehicle [75(5)].

COMPENSATOR

Every motor vehicle or trailer with more than four wheels and every semi-trailer with more than two wheels must be provided with a compensating arrangement to ensure that all the wheels remain in contact with the road surface and will not be subject to abnormal variations of load. But, in the case of a motor vehicle, a steerable wheel on which the load does not exceed 3560 kg is excluded [1017/78/11].

DOOR LATCHES AND HINGES

Passenger and dual-purpose vehicles first used on or after July 1, 1972, must be marked with an approval mark indicating that the vehicle's door latches and hinges meet specified burst-proof requirements. This does not apply to vehicles adapted to carry more than seven passengers, first used before June 3, 1977, to a vehicle adapted to carry more than eight passengers first used on or after June 3, 1977, a vehicle which is dual-purpose only by reason of its four wheel drive, a home-made vehicle, a vehicle which does not have doors or has only sliding doors, a vehicle made before January 1, 1972, or a vehicle of a named make and model [1017/78/15].

FARM TRACTOR CABS

It is unlawful for a person to sell a new tractor, or let one on hire, for use in agriculture in Great Britain unless it is properly fitted with a safety cab which is approved for use with that tractor and which bears specified approval marks [1072/67/4(a)]. New safety cabs must not be sold or hired for use in British agriculture unless approved and marked [4(b)]. 'New' means not previously sold for agricultural use [2]. A person must not let on hire a tractor for use in British agriculture which is not fitted with an approved safety cab [4(c)].

An employer of an agricultural worker must ensure that every tractor driven by the worker in the course of his employment is properly
fitted with an approved safety cab, and, as far as is reasonably practicable, ensure that every safety cab fitted to a tractor driven by the
worker is approved for use with that tractor [5(1)]. An agricultural
worker must not drive a tractor in the course of his employment, and a
person must not cause or permit him to do so, unless it is properly fitted
with an approved and marked safety cab [5(2)]. Neither may he drive
a tractor fitted with a cab not approved for use with that tractor [5(3)].
Exemptions from these requirements are provided for tractors used for
work in hop-gardens, hop-yards and orchards and in buildings of a
size where it is not practicable to have a safety cab on the tractor
[5(4)].

The restrictions in Regulations 4(c) and 5 did not apply to a tractor
bought for agricultural use before September 1, 1970 until September 1,
1977 [1(2)].

An agricultural worker employed to drive or maintain a tractor
fitted with an approved safety cab must report to his employer any
occasion when the tractor overturns, any damage caused to the cab
or its securing devices or any defect in any windscreen wiper fitted [6].
The Minister of Agriculture may issue certificates exempting particular
cases or particular persons from any of these Regulations [8].

FUEL TANKS

Except for vehicles marked with a designated approval mark, motor
vehicles first used on or after July 1, 1973, and not made before
February 1, 1973, must be constructed so that any tank containing
petrol to propel the engine or ancillary equipment is made only of
metal, it is in a position as to be reasonably secure against damage and
any leakage of liquid or vapour is adequately prevented (except where
a pressure-relief device is fitted) [1017/78/19].

HEIGHT

The maximum height of a public service vehicle is 4·57 metres
[1017/78/10].

No height limit is laid down for goods vehicles or their loads.

HORNS, GONGS, SIRENS, BELLS

Every motor vehicle, except works trucks and pedestrian-controlled
vehicles, must be fitted with an instrument capable of giving audible
and sufficient warning of its approach or position. Gongs, sirens, two-
tone horns and bells are prohibited except on motor vehicles used

solely for fire-brigade, ambulance, salvage corps or police purposes, motor vehicles owned by the Forestry Commission or local authorities and used sometimes for fire-fighting, vehicles used for bomb disposal, blood-transfusion service vehicles, vehicles used for coastguard service, mine rescue vehicles owned by the National Coal Board; RAF mountain rescue vehicles and RNLI lifeboat-launching vehicles [1017/78/29].

In addition to a horn, a mobile shop may be fitted with sound instruments (e.g. chimes on an ice-cream van) to warn potential customers of its presence [29(6)].

On vehicles first used on or after August 1, 1973, the sound emitted by a horn must be continuous and uniform and not strident [29(2)].

LAMPS AND REFLECTORS

Motor vehicles must be fitted with front and rear lamps and red rear reflectors so that they can be driven on a road during the hours of darkness without contravening the statutory provisions, but excluding provisions relating to projecting loads or to vehicles drawing or being drawn by another vehicle. Headlamps must comply with anti-dazzle requirements. A lamp is not treated as a lamp for these purposes if it is painted over, masked or not equipped with wiring and the Regulation does not apply to a vehicle which is not fitted with any lamp [1017/78/41].

LENGTH LIMITS [1017/78/9, 73]

Type of Vehicle	Max. length (a)		
	metres	ft	in
Articulated (b)	15	49	$2\frac{1}{2}$
Drawbar trailer (c)	7 (e)	22	$11\frac{1}{2}$
Drawbar trailer (c) and (d)	12 (e)	39	$4\frac{1}{4}$
Public service vehicles	12	39	$4\frac{1}{4}$
All other motor vehicles	11	36	1

(a) Overall length excludes any driving mirror, starting handle, any hood when down, any Post Office letter box (305 mm allowed), any telescopic fog lamp when extended, any ladder forming part of a turntable fire escape fixed to a vehicle, any container to hold a seal issued for Customs clearance, and any snow-plough fixed in front of a vehicle. A tailboard which is not essential to support a load or a container which is lifted on or off from time to time with goods inside is not included [3(1)].

(b) There is no overall length limit for an articulated vehicle constructed and normally used for the conveyance of indivisible loads of exceptional length. This is subject to the condition that all the wheels of the vehicle are equipped with pneumatic tyres or, if solid-tyred, the speed of the vehicle does not exceed 12 m.p.h. [9(1) Proviso]. 'Indivisible' means a load which cannot without undue expense or risk of damage be divided into two or more loads for conveyance on a road [3(1)]. A load which can be carried within a vehicle of standard length is not of exceptional length—*Cook* v. *Briddon,* [1975] R.T.R. 505.

(c) Excluding trailers constructed and normally used to carry indivisible loads of exceptional length, land implements, all semi-trailers, broken-down vehicles, and trolley vehicles in course of construction or delivery. Nor does the limitation apply to any trailer which is a drying or mixing plant for the production of asphalt or bitumen or tar macadam and used mainly for the construction, repair or maintenance of roads, or to any road planing machine so used, provided the overall length of vehicle and trailer does not in any case exceed 18·3 metres [73(2)]. A composite trailer comprising a converter dolly and a semi-trailer is to be treated as one trailer for this purpose [3(6A)].

(d) The 12-metre trailer length applies to trailers with four or more wheels where the distance between the centre of area of contact with the road of the foremost and rearmost wheels is not less than three-fifths of the trailer's overall length and provided that the unladen weight of the drawing vehicle is 2030 kg or more [73(1) Proviso].

(e) Excluding drawbar and drawbar fittings [73(3)].

MAKER'S PLATE

Heavy motor cars and motor cars first used on or after January 1, 1968, other than passenger vehicles, dual-purpose vehicles, land tractors, works trucks and pedestrian-controlled vehicles, must be fitted with a maker's plate. Trailers made after the same date and which are over 1020 kg unladen weight must also have a maker's plate, except for plant trailers not over 2290 kg unladen, a pneumatic-tyred living van trailer not over 2040 kg unladen, works trailers, trailers used abroad before being brought into Great Britain and specified land and municipal trailers. A trailer which is a converter dolly made on or after January 1, 1979, must also have a maker's plate [1017/78/42(1)].

Locomotives and motor tractors first used on or after April 1, 1973, other than land locomotives, land tractors, industrial tractors, works trucks, engineering plant, pedestrian-controlled vehicles and vehicles made before October 1, 1972, must be fitted with a maker's plate [42(1)].

The plate must contain information required under (a) Schedule 2 of the Construction and Use Regulations, (b) the Annex to E.E.C. Directive 114/1976 or (c) that Annex as amended by E.E.C. Directive 507/1978. The plate of a vehicle first used after October 1, 1981 must conform to either (a) or (c) [42(2)(2A)].

Schedule 2 states that the plate on a motor vehicle must contain the maker's name, vehicle type, engine type and power (not for vehicles made before October 1, 1972, or for petrol-engined vehicles), chassis or serial number, number of axles, maximum design weight for each axle, maximum design gross weight, maximum design train weight (only if constructed to draw a trailer), maximum permitted axle and gross weights (not for vehicles made before October 1, 1972, locomotives or motor tractors). The plate on a trailer must contain the maker's name, chassis or serial number, number of axles, maximum design axle weight, maximum weight designed to be imposed on drawing vehicle (semi-trailers), maximum design gross weight, maximum permitted axle weight (not for trailer made before October 1, 1972), maximum permitted gross weight (not the trailer made before October 1, 1972, or a semi-trailer), year of manufacture (except trailer made before April 1, 1970) [42(2) and 2nd Sched.].

The E.E.C. Directive requires similar information but the weights recorded on the plate are to be the maximum weights permitted in Great Britain where these are less than design weights [42(3) (4) (5)].

Certain passenger and dual-purpose vehicles made on or after October 1, 1979 and first used on or after April 1, 1980 must be fitted with a plate which contains the maker's name, vehicle identification number and the approval reference number of either the vehicle's type approval certificate or the Minister's approval certificate [43].

MIRRORS

Vehicles adapted to carry more than seven passengers (excluding the driver), goods vehicles, and dual-purpose vehicles must be fitted with two mirrors. One of these must be fitted externally on the offside and the other either internally or externally on the near side of the vehicle. They must show traffic to the rear and on both sides rearwards. Motor cycles with or without sidecarriers, land locomotives and pedestrian-controlled vehicles are excluded, as are also works trucks if the driver can clearly see traffic to the rear. No mirror need be carried on any vehicle hauling a trailer provided that a person carried on the trailer can signal the driver concerning other vehicles to the rear. On all other vehicles (e.g. private cars) one mirror fitted internally or externally is required [1017/78/23]. No offence is committed where a mirror is temporarily obscured by a load—*Mawdsley* v. *Walter Cox* (*Transport*), *Ltd.*, [1965] 3 All E.R. 728; [1966] 1 W.L.R. 63.

Internal mirrors fitted to vehicles first used on or after April 1, 1969, must have their edges protected by some material such as will minimise cuts resulting from passengers striking the mirror [23(3)].

Stricter requirements as to rear view mirrors apply to (a) two-wheeled motor cycles made from April 1, 1978 and first used from October 1, 1978; (b) Ford Transit vehicles made from January 10, 1978 and first used from July 10, 1978; and (c) every other motor vehicle made from December 1, 1977 and first used from June 1, 1978 [24(1)].

Such a vehicle (other than an excepted vehicle) which is a motor tractor, an agricultural or forestry tractor, a locomotive, a works truck or a vehicle with a design speed not over 16 m.p.h. must be fitted with at least one exterior mirror on the offside of the vehicle [24(2)]. An excepted vehicle is a two-wheeled motor cycle with or without sidecar, a motor vehicle drawing a trailer which carries a person who can tell the driver about traffic to the rear, a works truck if the driver can easily obtain a clear view to the rear, a pedestrian-controlled vehicle and a vehicle chassis being driven from its manufacturer to its bodybuilder [24(8)].

A vehicle to which the stricter rules apply and which is a passenger, goods or dual purpose vehicle, but is not a vehicle referred to in the last paragraph or an excepted vehicle, must be fitted with at least one interior mirror and one offside exterior mirror. If an interior mirror does not provide an adequate view to the rear a nearside exterior mirror must be fitted. Where mirrors are fitted on both sides externally an interior mirror is not necessary if it would provide no rear view [24(3) (4)].

Mirrors fitted to vehicles to which Regulation 24 applies must (a) be marked with a designated approval mark; (b) be fixed to remain steady under normal driving conditions; (c) an exterior mirror must be visible through a side window or through a part of the windscreen swept by the windscreen wiper; (d) where the bottom edge of an exterior mirror is less than 2 metres above the road it must not project more than 20 cm beyond the width of the vehicle or, if the vehicle draws a wider trailer, 20 cm beyond the width of the trailer; (e) an interior mirror must be capable of being adjusted by the driver in his seat; (f) except for a spring-back mirror, an exterior mirror on the driver's side must be capable of being adjusted by the driver in his seat, but this does not prevent a mirror being locked in position from outside the vehicle [24(5)].

NOISE

Every motor vehicle, first used after April 1, 1970, must be constructed to pass the appropriate noise measurement test undertaken by prescribed noise meter and used in specified conditions.

Excluding motor cycles, maximum sound levels, in decibels, are:

Class of vehicle	Decibels
Goods vehicles first used on or after January 1, 1968, and plated by the maker for a gross weight over 3560 kg	89
Goods vehicles not over 3 tons unladen, other than above	85
Motor tractors, locomotives, land tractors, works trucks and engineering plant	89
Passenger vehicles for more than 12 passengers	89
Any other passenger vehicles	84
Any other vehicle not listed above	85

Exceptions are motor vehicles going, by appointment, to be noise tested or mechanically adjusted for noise, vehicles returning from noise testing or mechanical adjusting for noise, and road rollers [1017/78/31 and 9th Sched.].

OVERHANG

'Overhang' of a vehicle (not to be confused with overhang of a load) is the distance between the rearmost point of the vehicle (excluding any Post Office letter box, for which 305 mm is allowed, any hood when down, any luggage carrier on a motor car seating not more than seven passengers excluding the driver, any expanding or extensible contrivance forming part of a turntable fire-escape fixed to a vehicle and trailer coupling fittings (305 mm allowed) on a public service vehicle constructed to draw a trailer), and (a) in the case of a two-axled or twin-steered three-axle vehicle, the centre of the rear axle, (b) if it has three or four axles (the front one or two of which respectively are steering axles), a point 110 mm behind a line midway between the two rear axles, (c) in any other case, a point on the longitudinal axis of the vehicle, being the point from which a line, if projected at right angles, will pass through the centre of the minimum turning circle of the vehicle [1017/78/3(1)].

For heavy motor cars and motor cars, overhang is limited to 60% of the wheelbase, measured from the centre of the front wheels to (a), (b), or (c) above, as the case may be. Overhang on motor cars with a wheelbase not exceeding 2·29 metres and first used before January 1, 1966, may be increased by up to 76 mm [58, 63].

This general statement is subject to the following exceptions:

The heavy motor car overhang limit does not apply to vehicles first used before August 15, 1928; to works trucks, street cleansing, refuse disposal or gully emptying vehicles or to rear-end tippers if the overhang is not more than 1·15 metres [58]. The motor car overhang limit does not apply to such vehicles first used before January 3, 1933, to works trucks or to ambulances or street cleansing vehicles and gully and cesspool emptiers [63].

In calculating the overhang of heavy motor cars which are special road-repair machines, incorporating road-heating plant, the length of such plant may be ignored [58].

The overhang of a motor tractor must not exceed 1·83 metres [54].

No overhang limit is prescribed for a locomotive or a trailer.

POWER TO WEIGHT RATIO

Diesel-engined locomotives, motor tractors, heavy motor cars and motor cars first used on or after April 1, 1973, and which are required to be fitted with a maker's plate must be so constructed that the engine power figure given on the plate indicates that the engine produces at least 4·4 kilowatts for every 1000 kg (i.e. 6 b.h.p. per ton) of the design train weight given on the plate or, if not shown, the design gross weight [1017/78/44]. This does not apply to heavy motor cars or motor cars made before October 1, 1972, or to any vehicle made before April 1, 1973 and which is powered by a Perkins 6·354 engine.

If the vehicle's engine also drives ancillary equipment which is used, or is likely to be used, when the vehicle is moving on a road faster than 5 m.p.h. the engine power must not fall below the minimum ratio when the equipment is being used [45].

REVERSING GEAR

Every vehicle weighing over 410 kg unladen must be fitted with a reversing gear [1017/78/21].

SAFETY GLASS

The glass of windscreens and all other outside windows of passenger vehicles and dual-purpose vehicles first used on or after January 1, 1959, must be of safety glass. On goods vehicles (other than dual-purpose vehicles), locomotives and motor tractors first used on or after January 1, 1959, the glass of windscreens and all windows in front and on either side of the driver's seat must be of safety glass. In all other cases, except for glass fitted to the upper deck of a double-decker, the glass of windscreens and other outside windows facing to the front of any motor vehicle must be of safety glass. If the inside surface of any glass at the front of the vehicle is at an angle of more than 30 degrees to the longitudinal axis of the vehicle, it is deemed to be facing to the front [1017/78/25]. 'Safety glass' is glass so constructed or treated that if broken it does not fly into fragments likely to cause severe cuts [3].

More stringent requirements apply to (1) caravan trailers made from December 1, 1977 and first used from September 1, 1978 and (b) motor vehicles and other trailers made from December 1, 1977 and first used from June 1, 1978 [26(1)]: Apart from the following exceptions, such vehicles must meet the requirements that (a) the windscreen and all other windows which are wholly or partly in front of or on either side of the driver's seat must be made of specified safety glass and (b) all other windows must be made of either specified safety glass or safety glazing [26(2) (3)]. Specified safety glass is glass which complies with British Standard Specification No. 857 or No. 5282 and safety glazing is material, other than glass, which is so constructed or treated that if broken it does not fly into fragments likely to cause serious cuts [26(12)].

The windscreen and other windows in security vehicles may be made of either safety glass or safety glazing [26(4)]. The windscreens of motor cycles not fitted with an enclosed driver's cab may be fitted with safety glazing [26(5)]. Windscreens or other windows in front of or alongside the driver's seat which are fitted temporarily to replace broken windows need not be of specified safety glass but must be of safety glazing and be fitted only while the vehicle is driven or towed to a place where new windows are to be permanently fitted or to complete the journey involved [26(6)]. The windows, other than windscreens, of engineering plant, industrial tractors, land tractors and land locomotives wholly or partly in front of or alongside the driver's seat may be of specified safety glass or safety glazing [26(7)]. So also may the windows of any driver's compartment inside a public service vehicle [26(7A)]. Motor vehicles and trailers which have not been fitted with permanent windows and are being taken to a place where they are to be fitted may have temporary windscreens or windows of specified safety glass or safety glazing [26(8)]. Specified safety glass and safety glazing fitted to vehicles must generally meet technical requirements as to light transmission [26(9)]. The requirements of Regulation 26 do not apply to vehicles fitted with certain French glass [26(10A)].

SEAT BELTS

Subject to the exceptions detailed below, seat belts and anchorage points must be fitted for the driver's seat and the 'specified passenger's seat' on every motor car registered on or after January 1, 1965 [1017/78/17].

No anchorage points are required for any seat which is one with integral seat belt anchorages [17(3)].

Belts are not obligatory for vehicles used under trade plates, when being delivered to dealers or buyers or in certain vehicles for the disabled [17(4) (4A)].

For these regulations, a specified passenger seat means the forward-facing front passenger seat if there is only one passenger seat or if there are two or more forward-facing front passenger seats, bench seats or otherwise, the one farthest from the driver's seat [17(9)].

Exceptions are: (a) goods vehicles (other than dual-purpose vehicles) exceeding 1525 kg unladen or built before September 1, 1966 or registered before April 1, 1967; (b) a passenger or dual-purpose vehicle for 13 or more passengers: (c) a land tractor; (d) a works truck; (e) an electrically propelled vehicle; (f) a pedestrian-controlled vehicle; (g) a vehicle on which purchase tax has been remitted and not again become payable; (h) a vehicle built before June 30, 1964; (i) a foreign-based vehicle brought into Great Britain while being driven to its new British base or to a place where anchorage points and belts will be fitted or (j) a vehicle made after October 1, 1979 and first used after April 1, 1980 [17(2)].

In the case of a motor car first used on or after April 1, 1973, the seat belts (other than a restraining device for a young person or a lap belt with shoulder straps) must be capable of being engaged and released by the wearer with one hand, there must be a device for securing the belt when not in use so that parts of it which touch the wearer do not lie on the floor, the belt can be removed easily from the device and it either adjusts automatically when worn or can be adjusted with one hand. These additional requirements do not apply to a vehicle made before October 1, 1972, or to the specified passenger's seat in a goods vehicle over 915 kg unladen if that seat is a bench seat for more than one passenger [17(7)].

SELLING DEFECTIVE VEHICLES OR PARTS

It is unlawful to sell or supply, or to expose for sale, or to offer to sell or supply, any vehicle not complying with the C. and U. Regulations respecting brakes, steering gear or tyres or construction, weight or equipment of vehicles or maintenance of parts or accessories, or as respects lamps or reflectors which are necessary when the vehicle is used on a road during the hours of darkness [Act 1972/60]. Nor must a vehicle be altered so that its use on a road would entail a breach of the regulations regarding construction, weight or equipment [60(2)].

A person will not be convicted of any of these offences if he proves that a vehicle was sold for export, or that he had reasonable cause to believe it would not be used on a road in Great Britain, or that it would not be used until it had been put into proper condition [Act 1972/60(4)].

A contract of sale will not be invalidated merely because these provisions are contravened [60(5)]. (But an innocent buyer may be able to discharge the contract through the seller's breach of condition or claim damages for breach of condition or warranty.)

It is an offence for a person to fit, or cause or permit the fitting of, a part to a vehicle if by such fitting the vehicle would contravene the C. and U. Regulations [Act 1972/60A(1)]. If a person who sells or supplies, or offers to sell or supply a vehicle part (or causes or permits the same) believes that it is to be fitted to a vehicle he commits an offence if the part could not be fitted without the vehicle contravening the C. and U. Regulations [60A(3)]. It is a defence to both offences for a person to prove that the vehicle was to be exported or he had cause to believe that the vehicle would not be used on British roads or would not be so used until put into a proper condition [60A(2), (4)].

The provisions of this Section do not affect the validity of a contract (e.g. sale or repair) or rights under it [60A(8)].

SILENCER

A vehicle propelled by an internal combustion engine must be fitted with a silencer, expansion chamber or other contrivance suitable and sufficient for reducing noise caused by the escape of exhaust gases from the engine [1017/78/30].

SMOKE, ETC.

Every motor vehicle must be so constructed that no avoidable smoke or visible vapour is emitted from it [1017/78/33].

Any excess fuel device fitted to a diesel engine in any motor vehicle, other than a works truck, must be in such a position that it cannot readily be operated by any person on the vehicle. An excess fuel device which, after the engine has started, cannot feed the engine with excess fuel or increase smoke emission is, however, permitted [34].

Crankcase vapours on a petrol-engined vehicle first used on or after January 1, 1972, must not escape into the atmosphere otherwise than through the engine's combustion chamber. This does not apply to vehicles with a two-stroke engine or to vehicles made before July 1, 1971 [35].

Petrol-engined vehicles first used on or after November 10, 1973 (or later dates for specified vehicle models), must be marked with an approval mark showing that the vehicle complies with a European agreement on the emission of gaseous pollutants by the engine. The requirement does not apply to vehicles made before September 20, 1973; to vehicles weighing over 3500 kg (laden or unladen); to vehicles with less than four wheels which weigh not more than 400 kg or which cannot exceed 30 m.p.h.; or to specified Ford vehicles first used before January 1, 1977 [36].

Diesel-engined vehicles first used on or after April 1, 1973, must be constructed so that the engine is one of a type for which there has been issued, on behalf of the Secretary of State, a type test certificate in accordance with a prescribed British Standard Specification indicating that the smoke emitted does not exceed specified limits. The requirement does not apply to vehicles made before October 1, 1972; vehicles made before April 1, 1973, and propelled by a Perkins 6·354 engine; or to a land tractor, land locomotive, industrial tractor, works truck or engineering plant which, in each case, is propelled by a diesel engine having not more than two cylinders; or to a vehicle fitted with a designated approval mark [37].

Vehicles using solid fuel must have an efficient appliance to prevent the emission of sparks or grit, and ashes must not be allowed to fall on to the road [38].

SPEEDOMETERS

Speedometers are compulsory on all vehicles first used on or after October 1, 1937, except on vehicles which cannot or must not exceed 12 m.p.h., invalid carriages and works trucks. The instrument must indicate to the driver, within a margin of accuracy of plus or minus 10%, if and when he is driving in excess of 10 m.p.h. [1017/78/18].

SPRINGS

Motor vehicles and trailers must have 'suitable and sufficient' springs between each wheel and the chassis frame, but the following are exempt: (a) any vehicle first used on or before January 1, 1932, (b) any motor tractor not exceeding 4070 kg unladen, if fitted with pneumatic tyres,(c) any land locomotive, land implement, land implement conveyor, agricultural trailer or trailer used solely for the haulage of felled trees, (d) any rail-shunting motor tractor not exceeding 4070 kg unladen, used on the road only when crossing from one part of the rail track to another, (e) motor cycles, (f) mobile cranes, (g) works trucks or works trailers, (h) any pneumatic-tyred vehicle not exceeding 4070 kg unladen, designed and mainly used for work on rough ground or unmade roads, provided it is not driven or drawn at more than

20 m.p.h., (i) pneumatic or solid-tyred vehicles, not exceeding 4070 kg unladen, used only for road sweeping and not driven or drawn at more than 20 m.p.h., (j) pneumatic-tyred pedestrian-controlled vehicles and (k) any broken-down vehicle which is being drawn as a result of a breakdown [1017/78/12].

STEERING COLUMN

Passenger and dual-purpose vehicles (including goods vehicle derivatives) first used on or after July 1, 1972, must be marked with an approval mark indicating that the vehicle has a protective steering mechanism meeting prescribed standards. The requirement does not apply to a vehicle adapted to carry more than seven passengers first used before June 3, 1977, a vehicle adapted to carry more than eight passengers first used on or after June 3, 1977, a vehicle which is dual-purpose only by reason of its four-wheel drive, a home-made vehicle, a vehicle with steering adapted for a disabled driver, a forward control vehicle (as defined), a vehicle made before January 1, 1972, or to a vehicle of a named make and model [1017/78/16].

TYRES

Locomotives and motor tractors may be either pneumatic- or solid-tyred. For land locomotives and land tractors there are special provisions [1017/78/52, 56]. Recut pneumatic tyres must not be used on a motor tractor under 2540 kg unladen unless the wheel has a rim diameter of at least 405 mm [56(2)].

Heavy motor cars must be pneumatic-tyred, but solid tyres may be used for (a) vehicles first used before January 3, 1933, (b) heavy motor cars weighing over 4070 kg unladen and used mainly over rough ground or unmade roads, (c) and also for vehicles used solely for street cleansing, or the collection or disposal of refuse, gullies or cesspools, or (d) turntable fire-escapes, tower wagons and works trucks [60].

Motor cars must be pneumatic-tyred but solid tyres may be used on motor cars not over 1020 kg unladen, works trucks, electrically-propelled goods vehicles not over 1270 kg unladen weight, vehicles used solely for street cleansing or the collection or disposal of refuse, gullies or cesspools and on motor cars first used on or before January 2, 1933. Recut pneumatic tyres must not be fitted to any motor car except an electric goods vehicle or a goods vehicle of 2540 kg or more unladen weight and with a wheel rim diameter of 405 mm or more [65].

All trailers except water carts used for road rollers, land-implements, agricultural trailers, horse and cattle trailers, and specific furniture trailers built before January 15, 1931, must have either pneumatic tyres or tyres of 'soft or elastic material' [77].

Trailers constructed after January 1, 1933, and drawn by a heavy motor car or motor car must be pneumatic-tyred [78(1)]. Pneumatics (recut or otherwise) or solids may be used on works trailers, special municipal vehicles, trailers drawn by solid-tyred heavy motor cars, water carts used for road rollers, land implements, agricultural trailers drawn by land tractors and broken-down vehicles [78(3)]. Outside these categories, recut pneumatics must not be fitted to any trailer not exceeding 1020 kg unladen, any trailer constructed to carry only plant or apparatus permanently affixed to it and which, in total, does not weigh more than 2290 kg or any trailer which is a living van and does not exceed 2040 kg unladen weight [78(2)].

When a plating certificate has been issued for any vehicle, that vehicle must be equipped with tyres which are designed to be strong enough and are maintained adequately to support the legally permitted axle weights [1017/78/154].

A pneumatic tyre is defined as a tyre which is provided with, or together with the wheel forms, a continuous closed chamber inflated to a pressure substantially exceeding atmospheric pressure, capable of being inflated and deflated without removal from the wheel or vehicle and, when deflated and under load, the sides collapse [3(1)].

VEHICLES FROM ABROAD OR GOING ABROAD

Any vehicle which complies with paragraphs I, III, and VIII of Article 3 of the International Convention relative to Motor Traffic (concluded at Paris on April 24, 1926) or with Article 21 and paragraph (1) of Article 22 of the Convention on Road Traffic (concluded at Geneva on September 19, 1949) and Part I, Part II (as far as it relates to indicators and stop lamps) and Part III of Annex 6 to that Convention if brought temporarily into Great Britain by a person resident abroad is exempt from specified C. and U. Regulations [1017/78/4(7)]. These are Regulations 8 to 79 except for Regulations 9, 47, 48, 49, 53, 57, 62, 70, 73 and 74 which still apply.

A British motor vehicle bought by a visitor from abroad or by a person about to be resident abroad and which is zero-rated for value added tax purposes is exempt from Regulations 8 to 79 except for Regulations 9, 47, 48, 49, 53, 57, 62 and 70 [4(8)].

Vehicles proceeding to a port for export are exempt from Regulations 9 to 12, 14 to 21, 23 to 26, 30 to 80, and 98 [4(3)].

VEHICLES—FIRST REGISTERED OR FIRST USED

Some regulations refer to a date of first registration and others to a date when the vehicle was first used. The date a vehicle is first used is the earlier of (a) the date it was first registered under the Vehicles (Excise) Acts and (b) the date it was manufactured in the case of vehicles previously owned by the Crown or by visiting forces, vehicles used abroad before being imported into Great Britain, vehicles used on land before being registered and vehicles used on trade plates (except demonstration and delivery) [1017/78/3(2)].

VIEW TO THE FRONT

The design and construction of every motor vehicle must be such that the driver can have a full view of the road and traffic ahead [1017/78/22].

WHEELS

A minimum rim diameter of 670 mm is laid down for wheels not fitted with pneumatic tyres, but this limit does not apply to special municipal vehicles, land implements, works trucks, works trailers, mobile cranes, pedestrian-controlled vehicles, vehicles first used on or before January 2, 1933, and trailers built before January 1, 1933; to any wheel of a motor car first used on or before July 1, 1936, if the diameter of the wheel plus tyre is not less than 670 mm; to any broken-down vehicle which is being drawn by a motor vehicle as a result of the breakdown nor to an electrically-propelled goods vehicle not over 1270 kg unladen [1017/78/20].

Twin wheels are counted as one for the purpose of the Regulations (except Regulation 108) if the distance between the centres of the areas of contact between such wheels and the road surface is less than 460 mm [3(5)].

'Close-coupled', in relation to a trailer, means that the wheels on the same side are unsteerable when in motion and that the distance between their areas of contact with the road surface is not more than 1 metre [3(1)].

WIDTH

The overall width of a locomotive must not exceed 2·75 m [1017/78/48]; a motor tractor, 2·5 m [53]; a heavy motor car, 2·5 m [57]; and a motor car, 2·5 m [62].

Pneumatic-tyred trailers can be up to 2·5 m wide if drawn by a locomotive, or a pneumatic-tyred tractor or heavy motor car provided that, in no case, the trailer edge does not exceed more than 305 mm outwards beyond the edge on the same side of the drawing vehicle. The same width is permitted for a semi-trailer forming part of an articulated vehicle of which the tractive unit is a motor car the unladen weight of which exceeds 2030 kg [74(1), (2)].

Otherwise, except for land implements, trolley vehicles in tow and broken-down vehicles, for all of which the width limits do not apply, the maximum trailer width limit is 2·3 m.

'Overall width' excludes driving mirror, any direction indicator, any snow-plough fixed in front of the vehicle, any tyre distortion caused by weight, front corner or side marker lamps, containers to hold seals for Customs clearance, and, in respect of vehicles registered before January 2, 1939, an allowance of 105 m for any swivelling window in the driver's cab. A container which is lifted on or off from time to time with goods inside is excluded [3(1)].

WINDSCREEN WIPERS AND WASHERS

One or more automatic windscreen wipers must be fitted to every vehicle unless the driver can see clearly to the front of the vehicle without looking through the windscreen, such as by opening the windscreen or looking over it. The wipers must clean the windscreen to enable the driver to see clearly the road in front on the near- and off-sides of the vehicle as well as ahead [1017/78/27].

On vehicles required to have wipers there must also be windscreen washers capable of clearing, with the wipers, the area of windscreen swept by the wipers. Land tractors, stage carriages and vehicles incapable of exceeding 20 m.p.h. are exempt [28].

WINGS

Heavy motor cars and motor cars must have wings to catch, as far as practicable, mud and water thrown up by the wheels *unless adequate protection is afforded by the bodywork*. This requirement does not apply, however, to the rear wheels of a motor car or heavy motor car when forming part of an articulated vehicle used solely for carrying round timber, to a vehicle in an unfinished condition proceeding to a works for completion or to a works truck [1017/78/61, 66].

The same requirement applies to trailers, but only to the rear wheels if the trailer has more than two wheels. Trailers used for round timber, unfinished trailers proceeding to a works for completion, land implements, land implements conveyors, living vans, water carts, fire pumps, trailers drawn by a vehicle which is restricted to a maximum of 12 m.p.h. or less, and any broken-down vehicle being drawn in consequence of the breakdown are exempt [79].

SPECIAL EXEMPTIONS

Road rollers, land tractors, vehicles proceeding to a port for export, pedestrian-controlled vehicles, certain vintage vehicles, towing implements and vehicles and trailers not used on the highway, are subject to a number of special exemptions. A vehicle being used on a statutory test by a person authorised to carry out the test is exempt from construction requirements, weight limits and maintenance regulations [1017/78/4, 6].

Where a type approval certificate or certificate of conformity has been issued in respect of a vehicle's conforming to certain E.E.C. directions regarding construction the vehicle is exempt from corresponding requirements of the C. and U. Regulations [5, 5A].

LIVESTOCK WAGONS

Vehicles used on a highway, road or lane: (a) for hire for the carriage of animals; (b) for carrying animals owned by a dealer or in connection with the trade or business of a dealer; or (c) for the conveyance of animals belonging to two or more owners, must comply with additional requirements.

The floor of the vehicle must have battens or other footholds, and there must be no projections inside the body likely to cause suffering to the animals being carried. If a wheel arch intrudes, it must be specially shielded. The vehicle must have either a fixed roof or one that can be used when required by weather conditions; the roof *must* be used during the carriage, between November 1 and April 30 (inclusive), of sheep last shorn within the preceding 60 days [750/31]. Constructional details for vehicles used for carrying calves are laid down [1228/63].

Similar provisions apply to the carriage of horses ('horse' includes ass, mule and jennet) except that there is no fixed period during which a roof or other protective covering must be used. All that is demanded is that 'any horse carried by road shall be protected against suffering due to exposure to the weather' [335/51/10, 13].

Unless there is a side door, other than one used for loading horses, there must be facilities for inspecting the interior from the outside at a height of not more than 4 ft 6 in [750/31/5(5) and 335/51/10(3)].

Horse-boxes designed to carry more than one horse must have a movable partition, at least 4 ft 6 in high, which can be placed from side to side and securely fixed across the vehicle [335/51/10(3)].

Additional requirements on loading ramps, partitioning, feeding, watering and disinfection of vehicles used for carrying farm animals or horses are consolidated in the Transit of Animals (Road and Rail) Order 1975. This new Order also prescribes stricter construction requirements which are to apply to all animal-carrying vehicles in two stages. From August 1, 1976 they applied to vehicles not used before that date to carry animals and from August 1, 1980 to animal-carrying vehicles of any age [1024/75/1(2)].

DANGEROUS GOODS

Petroleum (Consolidation) Act 1928
Deposit of Poisonous Waste Act 1972
Explosive Substance Order No. 11, No. 1129/24
Petroleum-Spirit (Motor Vehicles, etc.) Regulations, No. 952/29
Petroleum (Mixtures) Order, No. 993/29
Petroleum (Compressed Gases) Order, No. 34/30
Gas Cylinders (Conveyance) Regulations, No. 679/31
Gas Cylinders (Conveyance) Regulations, No. 1594/47
Packing of Explosives for Conveyance Rules, No. 798/49
Packing of Explosives for Conveyance Rules, No. 868/51
Petroleum-Spirit (Conveyance by Road) Regulations, No. 191/57
Conveyance of Explosives Byelaws, No. 230/58
Petroleum (Carbon Disulphide) Order, No. 257/58
Carbon Disulphide (Conveyance by Road) Regulations, No. 313/58
Petroleum-Spirit (Conveyance by Road) Regulations, No. 962/58
Gas Cylinders (Conveyance) Regulations, No. 1919/59
Carbon Disulphide (Conveyance by Road) Regulations, No. 2527/62
Petroleum-Spirit (Conveyance by Road) (Amendment) Regulations, No. 1190/66
Petroleum (Carbon Disulphide) Order, No. 571/68
Radioactive Substances (Road Transport Workers) (Great Britain) Regulations, No. 1827/70 and 1522/75
Corrosive Substances (Conveyance by Road) Regulations, No. 618/71
Poisons Rules, No. 726/71
Petroleum (Inflammable Liquids) Order, No. 1040/71
Inflammable Liquids (Conveyance by Road) Regulations, No. 1061/71
Inflammable Substances (Conveyance by Road) (Labelling) Regulations, No. 1062/71
Deposit of Poisonous Waste (Notification of Removal and Deposit) Regulations, No. 1017/72
Petroleum (Organic Peroxides) Order, No. 1897/73
Organic Peroxides (Conveyance by Road) Regulations, No. 2221/73
Radioactive Substances (Carriage by Road) (Great Britain) Regulations, No. 1735/74

COMPRESSED GASES

The provisions of the Petroleum (Consolidation) Act 1928, referring to the labelling and conveyance of petroleum spirit, have been adapted to apply to the carriage of the following gases when compressed in

26

metal cylinders: air, argon, carbon monoxide, coal gas, hydrogen, methane, neon, nitrogen, oxygen [34/30]. All cylinders used for the conveyance by road of any of these gases must comply with the provisions of 679/31, 1594/47 and 1919/59.

Recommendations have been made by the Home Office as regards the carriage of other gases, such as sulphur dioxide and ammonia. Details are obtainable from the Inspector of Explosives, Horseferry House, Dean Ryle Street, London, S.W.1.

CORROSIVE SUBSTANCES

The corrosive substances to which the following rules apply are those chemicals listed in the Petroleum (Corrosive Substances) Order 1970 [618/71/2(1)]. Apart from specified exceptions, any vehicle carrying a

The prescribed notice. It must be 7·9 in square when displayed on a vehicle and 3·9 in square when used on a container [618/71/Sched. 1]. It should be black and white, as shown here.

corrosive substance must display the prescribed notice at the front and rear [3(1)]. In addition, a tanker carrying corrosives must display a notice at each side of a tank, or compartment of a tank, indicating the nature of the contents [3(2)]. Any container carrying more than 1 kg (2·2 lb) of corrosives, other than a freight container of more than 512·1 cub. ft or a tank of a tanker, must be marked with a notice indicating its contents [4 and 11]. Generally, persons engaged in carrying, loading or unloading corrosives must ensure that none is spilt [5]; no explosives or article capable of causing fire or explosion by spontaneous combustion should be on a vehicle carrying corrosives [6]; a fire extinguisher should be carried on the vehicle [7]; and the owner of the vehicle must provide a copy of the rules for drivers to read [8].

Exceptions to the need to display the prescribed notice, and from regulations 5 to 8, are given to vehicles (other than tankers) which carry (a) no more than 500 kg (1102·5 lb) of corrosive substance and either no specified highly corrosive substance is carried or, if they are carried, are contained in receptacles of a prescribed construction or (b) more than 500 kg of corrosives but no highly corrosive substance is carried and all other corrosives are carried in prescribed receptacles [10]. Exceptions are made from the above rules (except the carriage of explosives, etc.) in the case of a vehicle brought temporarily into Great Britain which complies with an international agreement and containers carried by such a vehicle [12]. Corrosive substances contained in certain types of battery are excluded [13].

ORGANIC PEROXIDES

The Petroleum (Organic Peroxides) Order 1973 specified about 60 organic peroxides to which certain parts of the Petroleum (Consolidation) Act 1928 and the following regulations apply.

A person engaged in the carriage of any organic peroxide must take reasonable precautions to prevent fire or explosion and to prevent spillage. Except where specified small quantities are carried, no person may smoke or carry a naked flame in or in the immediate vicinity of the vehicle and a suitable and efficient fire extinguisher must be carried on the vehicle [2221/73/3–6].

There may not be carried on a vehicle conveying organic peroxides a portable light capable of igniting inflammable vapour, explosives, radio-active substance, any substance which on contact with water is liable to give off inflammable gas nor any substance capable of causing fire or explosion by spontaneous decomposition. Except where a small quantity of an organic peroxide is carried, no oxidising or corrosive substance may be carried on the vehicle unless it is carried in a separate compartment or is so secured that none of it will come within 2 metres of the organic peroxide [7]. An organic peroxide may not be carried if something has been added to it so that the resulting mixture is more liable to give rise to fire or explosives [8]. Only specified organic peroxides may be carried in a tank wagon [9]. A receptacle, other than a tanker, which contains any organic peroxide must comply with specified construction requirements [10, 11]. Critical temperatures must be observed [12] and vehicles and containers used for conveying organic peroxide must bear prescribed warning notices [13–15]. An employer must ensure that his employees are acquainted with the contents of the regulations [16].

The provisions of Regulations 7 to 14 and 16 do not apply to a vehicle engaged in international transport and brought temporarily into Great Britain which carries organic peroxide in accordance with the A.D.R. Agreement [18].

EXPLOSIVES

Regulations made by the Home Secretary as to the conveyance of explosives in any 'carriage' [1129/24] must be read in conjunction with the Home Office document 'Conveyance of Explosives on Roads' which lays down conditions as to vehicle construction and use.

Subject to compliance with the foregoing Regulations, the Government gives the haulier an indemnity against any accidental damage, including any claims for damage suffered by third parties, provided that no additional payment is charged because of the nature of the commodity. Three further conditions of the indemnity are that the damage must not have been caused or contributed to by any negligence of the haulier or his servants; that the damage is not 'war damage', and that the damage is not covered by any policy of insurance.

Certain exemptions affecting the conveyance of explosives under Government control, as covered by the Explosives Act 1875/97(5), have been extended to explosives carried in connection with a Government contract. Packing requirements for the conveyance of explosives are laid down in 798/49 and 868/51.

The mixtures of detonators with other explosives in the same load is controlled [230/58].

FUEL STORAGE

If not more than 3 gal of petrol is stored in securely closed glass, earthenware or metal vessels containing not more than 1 pt each

[Act 1928/1(1)], the only conditions to be observed are that there must be attached to or displayed near the vessels a label stating 'Petroleum Spirit: Highly Inflammable' and giving the name and address of the owner, or, if the spirit is on sale, of the vendor [Act, 5(1)]. For the keeping of any quantity over 3 gal a licence must be obtained from the local authority, except as indicated below.

Persons keeping and using petrol for motor vehicles (but neither wholly nor partly for sale) must either obtain and comply with the terms of a local authority licence or, instead, comply with Regulations No. 952/29, the main provisions of which are as follows:

Only leakproof metal vessels may be used for storage [952/29/2], and each (except vehicle fuel tank) must be labelled 'Petroleum Spirit: Highly Inflammable' [4]. The storage place, unless it is in the open, must be effectively ventilated and have an entrance into it direct from the open air [5(a), (b)]. A suitable fire-extinguisher or supply of sand must be ready to hand [5(c)]. Any storage place attached to a house or other building where persons 'assemble for any purpose' must be separated therefrom by a substantial fire-resisting partition without any opening such as a door [5(d)]. If the fuel is stored in not more than two 2-gal cans (in addition to the vehicle tank) it is, however, permissible to have in this partition a self-closing fire-resisting door [5(d)(ii)]. If the storage place is inside a building it must not be under any staircase or other means of exit unless suitably partitioned off [5(e)].

Not more than 60 gal of petroleum spirit, including that contained in any vehicle fuel tank, may be kept in any one storage place [6(a)], and any two places not more than 20 ft apart occupied by the same occupier are counted as one [6(b)]. In no case may the fuel be kept in vessels larger than 2 gal capacity apiece (except vehicle fuel tanks) unless the storage place is more than 20 ft from any building, highway or public footpath and unless provision has been made to prevent the fuel from flowing out of the storage place in the event of fire [7(1) (a), (b)]; in addition, the local authority must be notified that it is proposed to keep petrol in vessels of more than 2 gal each, and this notice must be renewed in January each year [7(1)(c), (2)]. Similar notice is required if the storage place is within 20 ft of any building or of any stack of timber or other inflammable material and it is intended to keep in it more petrol than that in any vehicle tank plus two 2-gal cans [8].

Special provisions apply to the storage of petroleum spirit used for engines in connection with road-making or repair [13].

INFLAMMABLE SUBSTANCES

An inflammable substance for the following rules is one of the chemicals listed in the Petroleum (Inflammable Liquids) Order 1971, or a solution or mixture of such chemicals, and which gives off an inflammable vapour at a temperature below 23°C (73°F) [1062/71/3].

Except for the carriage of small quantities detailed below, any vehicle carrying an inflammable substance must display a prescribed 'inflammable' notice to the front and rear. A tanker must, in addition, carry a notice on each side of the tank, or compartment of a tank, indicating the nature of the contents (except when petroleum spirit is carried) [1062/71/4]. The 'inflammable' notice need not be displayed on a vehicle (other than a tanker) not carrying acetaldehyde or carbon disulphide if (a) the total quantity of inflammable substances carried does not exceed 500 kg (1102·5 lb), (b) containers holding more than 1 kg (2·2 lb) of inflammable substance (other than petroleum spirit) are marked with the 'inflammable' notice and their contents (unless exempt) and (c) containers holding more than 1 kg of petroleum spirit are marked with the 'inflammable' notice. The notice is not required on a vehicle which does not carry acetaldehyde or carbon disulphide if the inflammable substances are contained in receptacles holding less than 1 kg and which meet prescribed construction requirements [7]. A container need not be marked if it holds less than 1 kg and meets the construction requirements, unless it holds acetaldehyde or carbon disulphide. The contents of a container need not be marked on receptacles of prescribed construction holding not more than 2·5 litres (4·4 pt). Markings are not required on metal containers holding not more than 5 litres (1·1 gal) of inflammable substance, other than acetaldehyde. An 'inflammable' notice is not required on a metal container holding not more than 5 litres of petroleum spirit or any container holding spirit for human consumption and not including any other inflammable substance [8]. If a substance is corrosive as well as inflammable a 'corrosive' notice must also be displayed on the vehicle or container which requires an 'inflammable' notice [9]. A container for these purposes does not include a freight container of more than 512·1 cub. ft [2(1)].

The following additional rules apply to the carriage of inflammable liquids. These liquids are the chemical substances listed in the Petroleum (Inflammable Liquids) Order 1971 [1061/71/2(1)].

Persons engaged in carrying, loading, or unloading inflammable liquid must take care not to spill any [3] and must not make or carry any naked flame [4]; a portable light, explosive or other article capable of causing fire by spontaneous decomposition must not be carried on a vehicle carrying inflammable liquid [5]; and a suitable fire-extinguisher

The prescribed 'inflammable' notice. On a vehicle it must be 7·9 in square and on a container 3·9 in square. The flame symbol and letters must be black and the background bright red [1062/71/Sched. 1]

must be accessible on the vehicle [6]. These requirements do not apply to the carriage of any inflammable liquid (except acetaldehyde) if the liquid is contained in receptacles of prescribed construction holding not more than 1 kg or the total quantity of inflammable liquid on the vehicle (except a tanker) does not exceed 500 kg [9].

Unless exempt, the owner of a vehicle used to carry inflammable substances or liquids must provide a copy of the Regulations for his employees to read [1061/71/7, 1062/71/6].

PETROLEUM

Comprehensive constructional and operational requirements are laid down in relation to the conveyance of petroleum spirit by road [191/57 and 1190/66].

Vehicles other than tank wagons or tank trailers used for the 'conveyance' of petroleum spirit must not carry petroleum spirit except in metal containers of not more than 50 gal capacity (if a mixture containing not more than 75% of petroleum is carried, the container can be up to 90 gal capacity [962/58]), or in glass or earthenware containers of not more than 1 pt capacity. These small containers must be packed in sawdust or other suitable material in an outer container to a maximum of 3 gal of spirit [191/57/23].

Ordinary vehicles (not tank wagons or tank trailers) are exempt from the provisions of the Petroleum-Spirit (Conveyance by Road) Regulations and may carry, in addition to any spirit in the fuel tank necessary for the vehicle's propulsion, up to 50 gal of petroleum spirit in a single steel barrel or up to 32 gal in metal containers of up to 10 gal capacity or other containers of up to 2 gal capacity [191/57/1].

No petroleum-spirit tank wagon may have a capacity of more than 6600 gal and every tanker of more than 1100 gal capacity must be divided into self-contained compartments none of which must exceed 1100 gal capacity [1190/66]. For any capacity over 1500 gal the vehicle design must be approved by a Government inspector. For a tank trailer the limit is 1000 gal [191/57/1st Sched.]. A petroleum-spirit tank wagon of more than 1500 gal capacity may not draw a trailer of any kind [191/57/18].

No trailer except one used solely for carrying petroleum must be drawn by a petroleum-carrying vehicle [191/57/25]; no trailer conveying petroleum spirit may be attached to any vehicle other than a motor tractor or vehicle used to convey petroleum [191/57/8]; and no trailer other than a tank trailer may be drawn by a tank wagon [191/57/18].

When a vehicle carrying petroleum other than petroleum spirit is used to draw a trailer carrying petroleum spirit, the aggregate load must not exceed 2500 gal [8(3)(b)].

Within the Greater London area, in the territory formerly occupied by the County of London and in that part of the London Borough of Newham formerly occupied by the County Borough of West Ham, the hauling of trailers by tank wagons is forbidden as also is the use of composite vehicles for conveying petroleum spirit unless they are approved by a Government inspector [191/57/18, 20].

Every vehicle while carrying petroleum spirit by road must (except while halted at a place approved by a local authority empowered to grant petroleum-spirit licences) be constantly attended by the driver or 'some other competent person of not less than 18 years of age' [191/57/7].

During the filling or emptying of a tank wagon the vehicle must be similarly attended [191/57/15].

When petroleum spirit is being delivered from a tank wagon to a storage tank the person in charge of the latter must enter details of the delivery on two identical certificates [191/57/2nd Sched.]. These certificates must be retained for 6 months—one being retained by the owner of the storage tank and the other by the employer of the driver who made the delivery [191/57/16].

Somewhat similar but separate regulations are laid down governing the constructional and operational requirements relating to the conveyance of carbon disulphide [257/57, 313/58, 2527/62 and 571/68].

POISONOUS WASTE

It is an offence for a person to deposit, or cause or permit to be deposited, on land, any poisonous, noxious or polluting waste which is liable to give rise to an environmental hazard [Act 1972/1(1)]. The fact that waste is deposited in containers does not in itself exclude risk [1(3)]. It is a defence to a person charged with contravening these restrictions to prove that he acted under his employer's instructions or he relied on information supplied by someone else and in either case did not know or suspect the waste was poisonous, noxious or polluting [1(6)].

No person may remove or deposit waste, or cause or permit it to be removed or deposited, unless specified authorities have been notified [3(1)]. Waste for these purposes includes waste of any description other than any specified by the Secretary of State as not being poisonous, noxious or polluting [3(4)]. Most domestic and industrial wastes are specified as being excluded provided they do not contain any hazardous quantity of poisonous, noxious or polluting substance [1017/72/3 and Schedule]. Also excluded are certain farm chemicals, radioactive waste, waste deposited in case of emergency or under certain statutory authorities [1017/72/4]. The notice must contain details of the premises from which the waste is removed, the name of the remover, the chemical composition and quantity of the waste and details of the land on which it is to be put [Act 1972/3(2)]. If a person who notifies a removal of waste is not to remove it himself he must give a copy of the notice to the remover before the waste is removed [3(3)]. The authorities to be notified are the local authority and river authority (or river purification board in Scotland) of the area from which the waste is to be removed and the area in which it is to be deposited [3(5)]. The notice must be given at least 3 days before the removal or deposit. Saturday, Sunday and bank holidays are disregarded in counting the 3 days [3(6)]. It is a defence for a person charged with contravening Section 3(1) to prove that while he had not himself given notice he had relied on information that notices had been given by others and he neither knew nor suspected that the information was wrong [3(8)].

POISONS

Poisons must be packed by consignors sufficiently stoutly to avoid leakage arising from the ordinary risks of handling and transport [726/71/27].

Specified poisons [726/71/8th Sched.] must have their contents conspicuously labelled on their package with an indication that the package must be kept separate from food and empty food containers. Protection for food against contamination must be afforded by the carrier. Medicines are exempt [28].

RADIOACTIVE SUBSTANCES

Restrictions are placed on the carriage by a road vehicle of any radioactive substance whose specific gravity exceeds 0·002 of a microcurie per gramme of substance. Among general prohibitions are that a radioactive substance must not be carried on a public service vehicle or any vehicle carrying explosives. Packages containing radioactive material and vehicles carrying them must be labelled in a prescribed manner. It is an offence to remove or damage such labels. Only the carrier or his employees may travel in a vehicle carrying radioactive material and they must be in a compartment separate from the material. Restrictions are placed on the amount of radioactive material which can be carried on a vehicle; the action to be taken when a package is lost or damaged is prescribed and particular obligations affecting vehicle drivers are laid down [1735/74].

When certain radioactive substances are carried and the radiation dose rate in the personnel compartment of a vehicle exceeds or is likely to exceed 2 millirem per hour during the journey specified action has to be taken in connection with the welfare of workers engaged in such transport. The operator must notify the Licensing Authority at least 1 month before starting to carry radioactive substances and give the Licensing Authority particulars of the vehicles, depots and scheme for limiting the workers' exposure to radiation. Such a scheme must be approved by the Licensing Authority and records must be kept of its operation. There are requirements regarding medical examination of workers, the keeping of a health register and other records [1827/70].

DRIVER LICENSING

Road Traffic Act 1960
Road Traffic Act 1972 *as amended by Road Traffic Act* 1974
Road Traffic (Drivers' Ages and Hours of Work) Act 1976
P.S.V. (Drivers' and Conductors' Licences) Regulations, **No. 1321/34**
P.S.V. (Drivers' and Conductors' Licences) (Amendment) Regulations, **No. 1061/72**
Motor Vehicles (International Circulation) Order, **No. 1208/75**
Motor Vehicles (Minimum Age for Driving) (Community Rules) Regulations, **No. 2036/75**
Goods Vehicles (Ascertainment of Maximum Gross Weights) Regulations, **No. 555/76**
Motor Vehicles (Driving Licences) Regulations, **No. 1076/76**
Motor Vehicles (Driving Licences) (Amendment) Regulations, **No. 1764/76**
Motor Vehicles (Driving Licences) (Amendment) Regulations, **No. 871/77**
Heavy Goods Vehicles (Drivers' Licences) Regulations, **No. 1309/77**
Heavy Goods Vehicles (Drivers' Licences) (Amendment) Regulations, **No. 2174/77**
Heavy Goods Vehicles (Drivers' Licences) (Amendment) Regulations, **No. 669/78**
Motor Vehicles (Driving Licences) (Amendment) Regulations, **No. 697/78**
Motor Vehicles (Driving Licences) (Amendment) (No. 2) Regulations, **No. 1109/78**

No one may drive a motor vehicle on a road unless he is the holder of a driving licence granted under Part III of the Road Traffic Act 1972 [Act 1972/84(1)]. No one may cause or permit an unlicensed driver to drive a motor vehicle on a road [84(2)]. A steersman of a vehicle limited to 5 m.p.h. does not require a licence when he acts under the orders of the driver who is the holder of a Part III licence and a heavy goods vehicle driver's licence and a person may cause or permit such an unlicensed person to act as steersman [84(3)].

A person cannot be granted a licence unless at some time during the 10 years preceding the commencing date of the licence applied for he has passed a driving test or has held a licence for the class of vehicle concerned or has held an external licence for that class. An external licence means one granted in Northern Ireland, the Isle of Man or the Channel Islands [85(1)].

A full driving licence issued on or after January 1, 1976 will last till the holder's 70th birthday or for 3 years, whichever is the longer, and a provisional licence may last for one year. A full licence issued to a person suffering from a prescribed or prospective disability will last for not more than 3 years [89(1) as amended by 1974 Act and 1076/76/7]. The fee for a full licence is £5; a provisional licence, £2; and a full licence granted before May 1, 1979 to a person over 65, £1. Exchange licences cost £2 [1076/76/6, 1764/76 and 1109/78].

An applicant for a licence must declare whether he suffers or has suffered from a prescribed disability or any other disability likely to cause his driving to be a source of danger. He must also declare any other disability which at the time of the application is not a prescribed disability but due to its intermittent or progressive nature or otherwise may become a prescribed disability (referred to as a prospective disability) [87(1)]. The prescribed disabilities are epilepsy, specified mental disorders, deficiencies or subnormality, liability to sudden giddy or fainting attacks (including such attacks caused by a heart defect for which a cardiac pacemaker is fitted), and inability to read a number plate at the specified distance [1076/76/22(1)]. If the Secretary of State is satisfied that a person suffers from a disability he must generally refuse to grant a licence [87(2)]. But a licence will not be refused (a) if the applicant has passed a test and a prescribed disability has not become more acute since then; (b) in the case of a person suffering from epilepsy, if he has had no attacks while awake during the preceding 3 years and his driving is not likely to cause danger; (c) in the case of a person who has sudden attacks of fainting or giddiness due to a heart defect for which he has a cardiac pacemaker if his driving will not cause danger and he has medical supervision by a cardiologist; or, (d) in the case of an applicant for a provisional licence, if his disability is not a prescribed disability [87 (3) and 1076/76/22(2)(3)(4)]. The disability prescribed for (a) and (d) above is one which is not progressive in nature and consists solely of (i) the absence of one or more limbs, (ii) deformity of one or more limbs and/or (iii) loss of use of one or more limbs. A reference to a limb includes part of a limb [22(4)]. If the Secretary of State finds that a licence holder suffers from a prescribed or prospective disability he can revoke that licence [87(5)(5A)].

If a licence holder finds that he is suffering from a prescribed or prospective disability not previously disclosed or that a disclosed disability has become worse he must notify the Secretary of State unless he believes the condition will not last for more than 3 months [Act 1972/87A(1)]. If the Secretary of State believes that an applicant for, or the holder of, a licence suffers from a relevant disability he may (a) require that person to supply him with an authorisation enabling him to obtain medical information from that person's doctor, or (b) require him to submit to a medical examination or (c) in the case of a full licence, require that person to take a test. If a person does not comply with these requirements the Secretary of State may refuse or revoke the licence [87A (2)–(7)].

If in court proceedings for a motoring offence it appears to the court that the accused may be suffering from a prescribed or prospective disability it must notify the Secretary of State [92(1)]. If an insurer refuses to issue a third-party insurance policy on health grounds it must give details to the Secretary of State [92(2)].

MINIMUM AGE

Minimum ages for driving different classes of motor vehicles are now contained in section 96 of the Road Traffic Act 1972 as replaced by the Road Traffic (Drivers' Ages and Hours of Work) Act 1976 and modified by Regulations [1076/76 and 1764/76]. The revised age limits are as follows:

Class of Vehicle	Age
1. Invalid carriage	16
2. Motor cycle	16
(other than mopeds, mowing machines and pedestrian controlled vehicles for which the age is 16)	
3. Small passenger vehicle or small goods vehicle	17
4. Agricultural tractor	17
5. Medium-sized goods vehicle	18
6. Other motor vehicles	21

The age for driving an agricultural tractor is reduced to 16 years where the vehicle is not over 8 ft wide, draws no trailer other than a two-wheeled or close-coupled four-wheeled trailer not over 8 ft wide and is taxed as an agricultural machine [1076/76/4(1)(b)]. A road roller not over $11\frac{1}{2}$ tons unladen, not steam driven and not fitted with soft tyres can be driven at 17 years [4(1)(c)]. The age for driving heavy goods vehicles is reduced from 21 years to 18 years in the case of a driver registered under a training scheme if the vehicle is owned by his registered employer or by a registered training establishment [4(1)(d)]. 'Close-coupled' for this purpose means that the centres of two wheels on the same side of the trailer are not more than 33 inches apart [4(2)].

For the purposes of the above Table, an agricultural tractor is a tractor used primarily for work on land in connection with agriculture. A small passenger vehicle is a motor vehicle constructed solely to carry passengers and their effects and is adapted to carry not more than

9 persons inclusive of the driver. A small goods vehicle is a motor vehicle constructed or adapted to carry or haul goods, is not adapted to carry more than 9 persons (including the driver) and its permissible maximum weight does not exceed 3·5 tonnes. A medium-sized goods vehicle is a like-constructed vehicle which exceeds 3·5 tonnes but does not exceed 7·5 tonnes permissible maximum weight [1972 Act/110 and 1976 Act/Sched. 1]. Motor vehicles for more than 9 passengers and goods vehicles over 7·5 tonnes permissible maximum weight are 'other motor vehicles' for which the minimum age is 21 years.

The permissible maximum weight of a goods vehicle is obtained by reference to a number of involved definitions. They are given below (page 45) in the section on heavy goods vehicle drivers' licences where they have more relevance.

Schedule 2 of the 1976 Act provides savings for persons affected by the change in the minimum age criteria. They apply to a person who, immediately before January 1, 1976, held a licence (whether full or provisional) to drive a motor car, or would have held or been entitled to hold a full licence or another provisional licence but for a court disqualification, or a person who is a resident from abroad treated as holding such a licence. Such a person is not, by reason of his age, disqualified from driving the classes of vehicles in entries 5 or 6 of the Table above. This saving, however, does not entitle such a person to the grant of a licence to drive goods vehicles with a maximum permissible weight over 10 tonnes or passenger vehicles adapted to carry more than 15 passengers inclusive of the driver [Sched. 2/2(3)].

The provisions of Article 5 of E.E.C. Regulation 543/1969 (given below) relating to minimum ages of goods vehicle drivers and minimum ages and other qualifications of passenger vehicle drivers have been suspended in specified cases. They are suspended in the case of carriage in Great Britain by a driver resident in the United Kingdom and who, immediately before January 1, 1976, held a licence or but for a court disqualification would be entitled to hold a licence or another provisional licence or who is a resident from abroad treated as the holder of such a licence [2036/75].

MINIMUM AGE—E.E.C. RULES

Article 5 of E.E.C. Regulation 543/1969 states that the minimum age for a goods vehicle driver is 18 years if the vehicle (including any trailer) has a permitted maximum weight not over 7·5 metric tons (7·38 imperial tons). For heavier vehicles the minimum age is 21 years but this may be reduced to 18 years where the driver holds a recognised certificate of professional competence which confirms his completion of a goods vehicle driver's training course. On occasions when two drivers have to be carried one of them must be 21 years of age.

A passenger vehicle driver must be 21 years of age and he must (a) have been employed for at least one year as the driver of a goods vehicle having a permitted weight over 3·5 metric tons, or (b) must have been employed for at least one year as a driver on a regular passenger service on routes of not more than 50 km, or (c) hold a recognised certificate of professional competence that he has completed a training course for passenger vehicle drivers. When a driver has reached the age of 21 years he is exempted from conditions (a), (b) and (c) if he was employed as a driver for at least one year before October, 1970.

The minimum age for drivers' mates and conductors is 18 years. A person who is carried on a vehicle to be available for driving is not classed as a driver's mate but is classed as a driver even though he may not do any driving.

The minimum age for a driver's mate may be reduced to 16 years by a Member State in respect of domestic transport within a radius of 50 km of the vehicle's base and provided the reduction is for training purposes.

PROVISIONAL LICENCES

With a view to passing a driving test a person can apply for a provisional driving licence [Act 1972/88(2)]. Conditions attached to a provisional licence are that the driver must not drive otherwise than under the supervision of a qualified driver, 'L' plates are displayed so as to be clearly visible within a reasonable distance from the front and rear of the vehicle and a trailer is not drawn [1076/76/8]. However, the licence holder may drive without supervision (a) on an ordinary or h.g.v. driving test, (b) if the vehicle (not being a motor car) is not constructed to carry another person, (c) an electrically propelled goods vehicle not over 16 cwt unladen and constructed to carry only one person, (d) a goods-carrying road roller not over 3 tons unladen, or (e) on a road in an exempted island [8(2) and 697/78]. The definition of exempted island excludes the main off-shore islands of Great Britain [697/78]. The ban on drawing a trailer does not apply to the driving of an agricultural tractor or in the case of an articulated vehicle [8(3)]. A provisional licence holder driving a motor cycle is subject to additional restrictions and exemptions [Act 1972/88(2)(c) and 1076/76/8].

A qualified driver for these purposes is the holder of a full licence authorising him to drive the class of vehicle driven by the provisional licence holder including a person whose full licence is restricted due to a leg disability [1076/76/8(5) and 697/78]. If an applicant for a provisional licence cannot perform the driving test eyesight requirements (reading a number plate at prescribed distances) he can be granted a licence for group K only (pedestrian-controlled vehicles) [8]. A full licence granted on or after June 1, 1970, can serve as a provisional licence to enable the holder to drive vehicles of a different class but if he does so he is subject to the same conditions as a provisional licence holder [Act 1972/88(4)]. However, this provision does not entitle a person to drive a vehicle of another class if he is not old enough to drive that class [88(4)(a)] or the full licence relates to specially adapted vehicles or to vehicles in group K [1076/76/10].

TESTS

Driving tests may be conducted by (a) examiners appointed by the Licensing Authority, (b) the Secretary of State for Defence as respects service personnel, (c) a fire chief as respects employees of the fire service, (d) a police chief as respects policemen and employees of the police authority, (e) the Metropolitan Police Commissioner as respects taxi drivers or p.s.v. drivers (who reside in the Metropolitan Traffic Area), and (f) operators of large vehicle fleets, if appointed to do so by the Licensing Authority, as respects their own staff [1076/76/13]. A fleet operator may apply to be appointed to conduct tests of his employees if he ordinarily employs over 250 drivers, proper arrangements are made for the conduct of tests and records are made [14]. A person referred to in (b) to (f) above can delegate the function to a suitable person [15].

Driving tests of members of the public are normally carried out by an examiner appointed under Regulation 13(a) and an applicant for such a test should apply to the clerk of the traffic commissioners of the area in which he wishes to take the test [16(1)]. The test fee is £6·75, except for an invalid carriage driver's test which is free [16]. The fee can be refunded only if no appointment is made or it is cancelled by the Secretary of State; if the applicant gives 3 clear days' notice cancelling the appointment; if the test does not take place due to some fault other than his or his vehicle's; or a court orders it to be repaid because the test was not properly conducted [Act 1972/86].

A person taking a test must satisfy the examiner that he is fully conversant with the Highway Code, that he is competent to drive the vehicle without danger to others and that he can perform specified movements with the vehicle [1076/76/18]. The person taking a test must provide a vehicle which is suitable and on which only the driver can operate the accelerator. He must also sign the examiner's record sheet. On failure to do either of these things the examiner can refuse to conduct the test [19 and 871/77]. A person who passes the test is given a certificate and a person who fails is given a statement of failure [20]. If a person fails the test he cannot submit himself for another test on the same group of vehicles for at least one month [21 and Act 1972/85(2)(c)].

A person who considers that his test was not properly conducted can appeal to a magistrates' court or sheriff who, if satisfied that the test was not properly conducted, can order that the applicant may take another test without waiting the statutory one month and that the test shall be free [Act 1972/85(3)].

A person from abroad who becomes resident in Great Britain may drive without holding a British Part III licence for a period of 3 months following his taking up residence provided he holds an international driving permit, a domestic driving permit of his own country or a British Forces driving licence which, in each case, authorises the driving of the class of vehicle being driven [1076/76/23].

ENDORSEMENT AND DISQUALIFICATION

Schedule 4 of the Road Traffic Act 1972 sets out clearly the offences against that Act, and other Acts, which involve obligatory or discretionary licence endorsement and disqualification.

If disqualification is obligatory the court must order the offender to be disqualified for at least 12 months unless there are special reasons for not doing so [Act 1972/93(1)]. This minimum period is 3 years for a second drink/driving offence in 10 years [93(4)]. On a person's third conviction in 3 years for an offence involving obligatory or discretionary disqualification, details of which have been endorsed on his licence, the court must disqualify him for at least 6 months unless, having regard to all the circumstances, it decides otherwise [93(3)]. This disqualification is in addition to any other which may be imposed [93(5)]. Except for the 'totting-up' provisions, a disqualification takes effect as soon as it is ordered and a court has no power to make a disqualification period consecutive to one imposed by the same or a different court—*R.* v. *Meese*, [1973] 2 All E.R. 1103; [1973] 1 W.L.R. 675.

When a person is convicted of an offence involving obligatory or discretionary disqualification the court may order that he be disqualified until he passes a driving test [93(7)]. This action should not be taken unless the competence of the driver is in question—*R.* v.

Donnelly, [1975] 1 All E.R. 785; [1975] 1 W.L.R. 390. A person disqualified under Section 93(7) can hold a provisional licence and drive in accordance with conditions attached to the licence [98(3)].

A disqualified person can apply to the court which imposed the disqualification to have it removed. An application cannot be made before 2 years have passed in the case of a disqualification of less than 4 years; one half of the period in the case of a disqualification of 4 to 10 years; or 5 years in any other case [95].

When a person is disqualified particulars of the conviction must be endorsed on his licence [101(1)]. If the person is not disqualified the court need not endorse the licence if there are special reasons for not doing so [101(2)]. If a person is convicted of an endorsable offence the court may take into account any conviction recorded on the licence [101(4)A]. Particulars of an endorsement must be entered on any new licence obtained [101(5)] but after 4 years of the conviction (11 years in specified drink/driving offences) the offender is entitled to obtain a licence free from that endorsement [101(7)].

Disqualification and endorsement will not be ordered in the case of a person convicted of a Construction and Use offence relating to dangerous condition, tyres, steering or brakes if he proves that he did not know and had no reasonable cause to suspect that the facts were such that an offence would be committed [Act 1972/Sched. 4].

When a disqualified driver appeals against conviction or sentence

GROUPS OF MOTOR VEHICLES FOR DRIVING TEST PURPOSES

Group	Class of vehicle included in the group	Additional groups covered
A	A vehicle without automatic transmission, of any class not included in any other group.	B, C, E, F, K, and L
B	A vehicle with automatic transmission, of any class not included in any other group.	E, F, K and L
C	Motor tricycle weighing not more than 410 kg unladen, but excluding any vehicle included in group E, J, K or L	E, K and L
D	Motor bicycle (with or without sidecar), but excluding any vehicle included in group E, K or L	C, E and motor cycles in group L
E	Moped	—

Group	Class of vehicle included in the group	Additional groups covered
F	Agricultural tractor, but excluding any vehicle included in group H	K
G	Road roller	—
H	Track-laying vehicle steered by its tracks	—
J	Invalid carriage	—
K	Mowing machine or vehicle controlled by a pedestrian	—
L	Vehicle propelled by electrical power, but excluding any vehicle included in group E, J or K	K
M	Trolley vehicle	—
N	Vehicle exempted from duty under section 7(1) of the Vehicles (Excise) Act 1971	—

(1076/76/Sched. 3 and 1764/76)

to the Crown Court or Court of Appeal that court may suspend the disqualification order. Also, if a disqualified driver appeals to the House of Lords, appeals by case stated to the Divisional Court or applies to that court for an order of certiorari the High Court may suspend the disqualification. The court may suspend a disqualification on its own terms. Similar provision is made for appeals to the High Court of Justiciary in Scotland [Act 1972/94A, 94B].

HEAVY GOODS VEHICLES

A person must not drive, or cause or permit another person to drive, a heavy goods vehicle of any class on a road unless he holds an h.g.v. licence authorising him to drive a vehicle of that class [Act 1972/112(1), (2)]. Neither must he cause or permit a person under 21 years of age to drive a heavy goods vehicle in contravention of conditions attached to the driver's licence [114(4)]. An h.g.v. licence is not required by a steersman on a vehicle limited to 5 m.p.h. who is supervised by a licensed driver [112(3)]. Neither is an h.g.v. licence required to drive a vehicle taxed as an agricultural machine when used for specified purposes [112(4)].

'Heavy goods vehicle' means any of the following vehicles—(a) an articulated goods vehicle; (b) a large goods vehicle, that is to say, a motor vehicle (not being an articulated goods vehicle) which is constructed or adapted to carry or to haul goods and the permissible maximum weight of which exceeds 7·5 tonnes [Act 1972/124 and Act 1976/Sched. 1/11].

'Articulated goods vehicle', for these purposes, means a motor vehicle so designed that a trailer may be partially superimposed on it and 'articulated goods vehicle combination' means such a motor vehicle which has a trailer so attached to it [Act 1972/110,124 and Act 1976/Sched. 1].

'Permissible maximum weight' for these purposes means:

(a) in the case of a motor vehicle which neither is an articulated goods vehicle nor is drawing a trailer, the relevant maximum weight of the vehicle;
(b) in the case of an articulated goods vehicle—
  (i) when drawing only a semi-trailer, the relevant maximum train weight of the combination;
  (ii) when drawing a trailer as well as a semi-trailer, the total of the relevant maximum train weight of the articulated combination and the relevant maximum weight of the trailer;
  (iii) when drawing a trailer but not a semi-trailer, the total of the relevant maximum weight of the articulated goods vehicle and the relevant maximum weight of the trailer;
  (iv) when drawing no trailer, the relevant maximum weight of the vehicle;
(c) in the case of a motor vehicle (not being an articulated goods vehicle) which is drawing a trailer, the total of the relevant maximum weights of the motor vehicle and trailer.

'Relevant maximum weight' in relation to a motor vehicle or trailer means—
(a) if the vehicle is fitted with a Department of the Environment plate, the maximum gross weight marked on that plate;
(b) if the vehicle does not have a D.o.E. plate but is required to be fitted with a manufacturer's plate, the maximum gross weight on that plate;
(c) if the vehicle has a manufacturer's plate though not required to be fitted with one, the maximum gross weight on that plate;
(d) if the vehicle does not have a plated gross weight, the notional maximum gross weight produced by multiplying the vehicle's unladen weight by a prescribed figure.

MULTIPLIERS FOR MOTOR VEHICLES AND TRAILERS

(1) *Class of vehicle*	(2) *Number*
Part A—Motor Vehicles	
1. Dual purpose vehicles not constructed or adapted to form part of an articulated goods vehicle combination	1·5
2. Break-down vehicles	2
3. Works trucks and straddle carriers used solely as works trucks	2
4. Electrically propelled motor vehicles	2
5. Vehicles constructed or adapted for, and used solely for, spreading material on roads to deal with frost, ice or snow	2
6. Motor vehicles used for no other purpose than the haulage of lifeboats and the conveyance of the necessary gear of the lifeboats which are being hauled	2
7. Living vans	1·5
8. Vehicles constructed or adapted for, and used primarily for the purpose of, carrying equipment permanently fixed to the vehicle, in a case where the equipment is used for medical, dental, veterinary, health educational, display or clerical purposes and such use does not directly involve the sale, hire or loan of goods from the vehicle	1·5
9. Three wheeled motor vehicles designed for the purpose of street cleansing, the collection or disposal of refuse or the collection or disposal of the contents of gullies	2
10. Steam propelled vehicles	2
11. Vehicles designed and used for the purpose of servicing, controlling, loading or unloading aircraft on an aerodrome	2
12. Motor vehicles of a class not mentioned above where equipment, apparatus or other burden is permanently attached to and forms part of the vehicle and where the vehicle is only used on a road for carrying, or in connection with the use of, such equipment, apparatus or other burden	1
13. Motor vehicles of a class not mentioned above which are either— (a) heavy motor cars or motor cars first used before 1st January 1968, or (b) locomotives or motor tractors first used before 1st April 1973.	2
14. Any motor vehicles not mentioned above	4
PART B—Trailers	
1. Engineering plant	1
2. Trailers which consist of drying or mixing plant designed for the production of asphalt or of bituminous or tar macadam	1
3. Agricultural trailers	1
4. Works trailers	1
5. Living vans	1·5
6. Any trailers not mentioned above	3

MULTIPLIERS FOR ARTICULATED GOODS VEHICLE COMBINATIONS

(1) *Class of Combination*	(2) *Number*
1. Articulated goods vehicle combinations where the semi-trailer is a trailer of a kind mentioned in paragraph 1, 2, 3, 4 or 5 of Part B above	1·5
2. Any other articulated goods vehicle combination	2·5

'Relevant maximum train weight' in relation to an articulated combination means—

(a) if the motor vehicle is fitted with a D.o.E. plate, the maximum train weight marked on that plate;

(b) if the motor vehicle does not have a D.o.E. plate but is required to be fitted with a manufacturer's plate, the maximum train weight marked on that plate;

(c) if the motor vehicle has a manufacturer's plate though not required to be fitted with one, the maximum train weight marked on that plate;

(d) if the motor vehicle does not have a plated train weight, the notional maximum gross weight of the combination obtained by multiplying the sum of the unladen weights of the motor vehicle and semi-trailer by a prescribed figure.

Act 1972/110, 124 and Act 1976/Sched. 1

The table opposite contains the multipliers prescribed for obtaining a notional gross or train weight from a vehicle's unladen weight. The notional weight figure is obtained by multiplying the unladen weight of a vehicle in a specified class by the corresponding number in the right hand column [555/76]. It must be noted that the notional gross weights are of relevance only to driving licence provisions and are to be used only where a vehicle had no plated gross or train weight.

Except where Regulations so provide, an h.g.v. licence cannot be granted to a person unless at some time during the preceding 5 years he has passed a test or held a full licence for the class of vehicle concerned (114(1)). A full licence lasts for 3 years and a provisional 6 months (115). If the holder of a full h.g.v. licence applies for a new licence his existing licence will continue in force till the application is disposed of even though it lasts for over 3 years (115(4)). A full licence costs £3 and a provisional £1.50 [1309/77/8].

RESTRICTED H.G.V. LICENCES

Paragraph 3 of Schedule 2 of the 1976 Act provides savings to benefit drivers affected by the change in definition of a heavy goods vehicle. The paragraph applies to a goods vehicle (not forming part of an artic) not over 3 tons unladen weight which became classified as a heavy goods vehicle by the 1976 Act. It applies also to a person who immediately before the passing of the Act (March 25, 1976) held a licence (whether full or provisional) or would have been entitled to hold a full licence or another provisional licence but for a court disqualification. A vehicle to which the paragraph applies could be driven by a person to whom the paragraph applies during 1976 without the need for an h.g.v. driving licence. Also, if such a person applied in 1976 he could obtain an h.g.v. licence without passing a test if he could satisfy the Licensing Authority that in any 12-month period between January 1, 1975, and April 15, 1976, he had been in the habit for 6 months of driving vehicles to which the paragraph applies.

The licence granted under Schedule 2 of the 1976 Act is known as a restricted standard licence. It authorises the driving of heavy goods vehicles of Class 3 or 3A which have a permissible maximum weight not exceeding 10 tonnes [1309/77/2]. When the holder of such a licence renews it it will, unless he has passed a test, be subject to the same restriction [31(2)]. The restricted licence can be used as a provisional licence for vehicles of Class 3 or 3A over 10 tonnes permissible maximum weight if the holder is 21 years of age [31(3)]. But the holder of a restricted licence is not to be regarded as the holder of a full standard licence of Class 3 or 3A for the purpose of accompanying a trainee driver or provisional licence holder if the vehicle being driven has a permissible maximum weight over 10 tonnes [31(4)].

EXEMPTIONS

An h.g.v. driver's licence is not required for the driving of any of the following classes of vehicle:

    (a) track-laying vehicles;
    (b) vehicles propelled by steam;
    (c) road rollers;
    (d) road construction vehicles used or kept on the road solely for the conveyance of built-in road construction machinery (with or without articles or materials used for the purpose of that machinery);
    (e) engineering plant;

(f) works trucks;

(g) an industrial tractor (i.e. a works tractor not over 3·5 tons unladen weight and incapable of exceeding 20 m.p.h.);

(h) land locomotives and land tractors;

(i) digging machines;

(j) vehicles exempted from excise duty because used less than 6 miles a week on public roads;

(k) an artic drawing unit not over 3 tons unladen and without a trailer attached;

(l) public service vehicles;

(m) vehicles used for the haulage of lifeboats and necessary gear;

(n) vehicles manufactured before January 1, 1940, used unladen and not drawing a laden trailer;

(o) vehicles of a visiting force or headquarters;

(p) wheeled armoured vehicles owned or controlled by the Secretary of State for Defence;

(q) a vehicle driven by a police constable for the purpose of removing or avoiding obstruction to other road users or danger to other road users or members of the public, for the purpose of safeguarding property, including the heavy goods vehicle and its load, or for other similar purposes;

(r) any articulated vehicle which has a permissible maximum weight not over 7·5 tonnes or the tractive unit of which does not exceed 15 cwt unladen weight;

(s) any rigid vehicle with a relevant maximum weight not over 3·5 tonnes which is drawing a trailer;

(t) rigid vehicles not over 10 tons unladen, owned or hired by the holder of a p.s.v. licence and driven for him by the holder of a p.s.v. driver's licence for

    (i) going to or from a place to assist or having assisted a disabled p.s.v., or

    (ii) moving a disabled p.s.v. to prevent it causing obstruction or towing it from where it has become disabled to a place for repair, storage or breaking up;

(u) vehicles fitted with apparatus for lifting a disabled vehicle partly from the ground and for drawing it when so raised and which are

    (i) used solely for dealing with disabled vehicles,

    (ii) not used to carry any load other than a disabled vehicle and articles required for the operation of the vehicle or for dealing with disabled vehicles, and

    (iii) not over 3 tons unladen weight;

(v) play buses.

(w) fire fighting or fire salvage vehicles used by Ministry of Defence when driven by a member of the armed forces.

[1309/77/29 and 2174/77]

APPLICATION

H.g.v. licences are granted by the goods vehicle Licensing Authorities and a person who wants such a licence should apply to the Licensing Authority of the traffic area in which he resides or, in the case of armed services' personnel, to the South Eastern Licensing Authority [Act 1972/113 and 1309/77/26]. An application should be made to the Licensing Authority not more than 2 months before the commencing date of the licence and it should be accompanied by a medical certificate (on first application and by applicants over 60 years of age only); the licence fee; the applicant's ordinary licence; and either his full h.g.v. licence or a pass certificate [1309/77/3(1)]. An application for an h.g.v. trainee driver's licence must be accompanied by the Training Committee's certificate as to registration and an application by the holder of such a licence must be accompanied by that licence [3(1) (v), (vi)]. A person must not apply for a licence if he holds an h.g.v. licence which has been suspended; if he is disqualified from holding an h.g.v. licence or an ordinary licence; or he already holds an h.g.v. licence [3(3)]. An applicant must hold an ordinary licence authorising the class of vehicle concerned; he must not have had an epileptic attack since the age of 3 or suffer from any disease or disability likely to cause his driving to be dangerous. An applicant for an h.g.v. trainee driver's licence must have an ordinary licence free from endorsements; he must be the registered employee of a registered employer; and where the application is for a Class 1 or 2 licence 12 months must have elapsed since he passed the test respectively on a Class 2 or 3 vehicle [4].

A learner may take out a provisional h.g.v. licence and the holder of a full licence may use that as a provisional licence for other classes of vehicles provided he is old enough to drive those vehicles [Act 1972/113(2) and 1309/77/9(1)]. The holder of a provisional licence, including a full licence used as a provisional, must, when driving a heavy goods vehicle, be under the supervision of the holder of a full standard licence for that class of vehicle; must display h.g.v. 'L' plates on the front and rear of the vehicle and, except in the case of an artic or a rigid vehicle with a relevant maximum weight not over 7·5 tonnes, a trailer must not be drawn [9(3)].

A supervisor is not required during a test and the above conditions do not apply to a provisional licence holder who has passed a test on the class of vehicle being driven [9(4)].

If a licence is lost or damaged a duplicate can be obtained for 75p [14]. If the original licence is found the holder must inform the Licensing Authority and, if he has possession of it, return it to the Authority [14(2)].

H.G.V. TRAINEE DRIVERS' LICENCES

Employers' associations and trade unions in the road goods transport industry have established a National Joint Training Committee for Young H.G.V. Drivers in the Road Transport Goods Industry which has a constitution approved by the Secretary of State. The Training Committee has established a scheme for training young drivers and provides for (a) registration of employers willing to provide h.g.v. training for their employees; (b) registration of h.g.v. driver training schools; (c) a syllabus for h.g.v. driver training; and (d) registration of employees who receive training in the service of a registered employer under an approved training agreement [1309/77/2].

An h.g.v. trainee driver's licence is a licence to drive heavy goods vehicles of Class 1, 1A, 2, 2A, 3 or 3A; is applied for by a person under 21 years; and has effect while the holder is under 21 years [1309/77/2]. Such a licence is issued subject to the conditions that the holder does not drive a heavy goods vehicle of the class for which it is issued unless (a) he is the registered employee of the registered employer named in the licence; (b) the vehicle is of a class to which his training agreement applies; and (c) the vehicle is owned by that employer or by a registered h.g.v. training establishment named in the licence [10(1)].

An h.g.v. trainee driver's full licence which does not cover Classes 4 or 4A shall be treated as a provisional licence for those classes [10(2)]. The holder of a h.g.v. trainee driver's full licence to drive vehicles of a class shown in column 1 of the Table below may, after one year from the date of passing the test for that class of vehicle and on surrendering his licence, be granted a h.g.v. trainee driver's licence which will be a full licence for the class to which the surrendered licence relates and a trainee's provisional licence for the class corresponding to it in column 2—

Class of licence held	Class for which treated as a provisional
Class 3	Class 2 and 2A
Class 3A	Class 2A
Class 2	Class 1 and 1A
Class 2A	Class 1A

[10(3)]

A trainee's provisional h.g.v. licence and a full licence which is treated as a provisional is subject to the conditions that the holder must not drive a heavy goods vehicle (a) unless under the supervision of the holder of a standard full licence for that class of vehicle (except when taking a test); (b) unless h.g.v. 'L' plates are displayed at the front and back of the vehicle; and (c) if the vehicle is drawing a drawbar trailer [10(4)(5)].

When a trainee has passed a test for the class of vehicle for which his licence is or acts as a provisional he need not be under the supervision of a standard licence holder—

 (a) when driving a Class 4 or 4A vehicle if the test he has passed covers such class;
 (b) when driving a Class 2, 2A, 3, or 3A vehicle if his test covers such vehicle and a drawbar trailer is not drawn if the licence holder is under 21 years of age;
 (c) when driving a Class 1 or 1A vehicle if his test covers such class and he is not under 21 years of age.

[10(6)]

A trainee driver's full h.g.v. licence is also subject to the condition that he does not drive unless under the supervision of a holder of a standard licence for that class of vehicle (a) a vehicle of Class 1 or 1A when under the age of 21 years or (b) a vehicle of Class 2, 2A, 3 or 3A when under 21 years and a drawbar trailer is drawn [10(7)].

TESTS (H.G.V.)

Tests may be conducted by (a) examiners appointed by the Secretary of State, (b) examiners appointed to test armed forces personnel only, (c) a fire brigade chief, in respect of fire brigade employees, or (d) a police chief, in respect of police officers or civilian employees. In (c) and (d) the function may be delegated to a suitable person [1309/77/18].

An applicant for a test conducted by a D.o.E. examiner should send his application to the clerk of the Licensing Authority of the area in which he wishes to take the test [15] and send with it the test fee of £30 [23 and 669/78]. An applicant must (1) hold an ordinary driving licence for the class of vehicle concerned and (2) an applicant (who is under 21 years) for a test on a Class 3 or 3A vehicle must also (a) have held a h.g.v. trainee driver's provisional licence for, and been regularly driving, that class of vehicle for 3 months immediately before the test or (b) have held an ordinary licence for, and been regularly driving, motor cars for one year immediately before the test [17].

A person taking a test must supply a suitable, unladen vehicle of the appropriate class, and which for classes 2, 2A, 3 or 3A must not be an artic or artic drawing unit. The vehicle must be fitted with a seat for the examiner which is protected against bad weather; the vehicle must be one which does not require a statutory attendant; and must be such that the accelerator can be operated by the driver only. The driver must sign the examiner's attendance record [22].

A candidate for a test must satisfy the examiner that he is fully conversant with the Highway Code, that he has sufficient mechanical knowledge of the vehicle and the effects of load distribution, that he is competent to drive without danger to others and that he can safely and competently carry out specified manœuvres [19]. A person who passes a test must be supplied with a certificate of competence and a person who fails, a statement of failure [21]. Test fees are repayable in the same circumstances as for ordinary driving licences, explained above (page 41) [24].

A person who passes an h.g.v. test is treated as also having passed an ordinary driving test for the appropriate class of vehicle in relation to his age [25].

A person who takes a test which he believes was not properly conducted can complain to a magistrates' court or sheriff who can, if it appears that the test was not properly conducted, order another test which is free [Act 1972/117].

REVOCATION

A Licensing Authority may suspend or revoke a driver's h.g.v. licence on the grounds that due to his conduct as a driver or due to a disability he is not a fit person to hold a licence [Act 1972/115(1)]. When this action is taken the Licensing Authority can also disqualify the driver from holding an h.g.v. licence or can require him to take an h.g.v. driving test [116]. A person disqualified may apply for its removal after the same periods of time, as explained above (page 43), for an ordinary licence disqualification [1039/77/12]. When an h.g.v. licence is suspended or revoked the holder must return it to the Licensing Authority when required [11].

If an h.g.v. licence holder under 21 years contravenes prescribed circumstances the Licensing Authority must revoke his licence [115(1A)]. If the licence is revoked the holder must also be disqualified from holding one until he is 21 years of age [116(1A)] but if the contravention ceases the disqualification must be removed [116(4)]. The prescribed circumstances are that the holder's ordinary driving licence bears more than one endorsement [1309/77/11(4)].

CLASSES OF H.G.V. DRIVERS' LICENCES

Class	Definition	Additional classes covered
I	An articulated vehicle not with automatic transmission, other than a vehicle coming within class 4	1A, 2, 2A, 3, 3A, 4 and 4A
1A	An articulated vehicle with automatic transmission, other than a vehicle coming within class 4A	2A, 3A and 4A
2	A heavy goods vehicle not with automatic transmission, other than an articulated vehicle, designed and constructed to have more than 4 wheels in contact with the road surface	2A, 3 and 3A
2A	A heavy goods vehicle with automatic transmission, other than an articulated vehicle, designed and constructed to have more than 4 wheels in contact with the road surface	3A
3	A heavy goods vehicle not with automatic transmission, other than an articulated vehicle, designed and constructed to have not more than 4 wheels in contact with the road surface	3A
3A	A heavy goods vehicle with automatic transmission, other than an articulated vehicle, designed and constructed to have not more than 4 wheels in contact with the road surface	—
4	An articulated vehicle not with automatic transmission, the tractive unit of which does not exceed 2 tons unladen weight	4A
4A	An articulated vehicle with automatic transmission. the tractive unit of which does not exceed 2 tons unladen weight	—

For the purposes of the above definitions where a vehicle is fitted with 2 wheels in line transversely and the distance between the centres of their respective areas of contact with the road is less than 18 in they shall be regarded as only one wheel.

[1039/77/Sched. 2]

If the holder of an h.g.v. licence is disqualified from holding, or is refused the grant of, an ordinary licence he must give details of the event and send his h.g.v. licence to the Licensing Authority. The licence will be returned when the driver produces an ordinary current licence [13].

A person who is refused an h.g.v. licence; whose licence is revoked or suspended; or who has been disqualified can require the Licensing Authority to reconsider the matter and is entitled to be heard personally or be represented [Act 1972/118(1)]. If he is dissatisfied with the Licensing Authority's reconsidered decision the applicant can appeal to a magistrates' court or sheriff [118(2)]. The court cannot order the Licensing Authority to do something which he has otherwise no power to do—*R.* v. *Ipswich Justices*, [1971] 2 Q.B. 340; [1971] 2 All E.R. 1395. The existing licence of a full licence holder who appeals against refusal or failure to grant a renewal of a licence shall continue in force until the appeal is disposed of even though it may have expired [118(4)].

NORTHERN IRELAND LICENCES

Most of the references above to an ordinary licence and an h.g.v. licence include references to Northern Ireland licences of the same description.

PUBLIC SERVICE VEHICLES

Both the driver and conductor of a public service vehicle must hold the appropriate licence [Act 1960/144(1)]. A p.s.v. driver must be 21 years of age and a conductor 18 years [144(3)]. Licences are granted by the traffic commissioners for traffic areas, except in the Metropolitan area where licences are issued by the Commissioner of Police, Public Carriage Office, 14, Penton Street, London, N.1. [144(2)].

A licence will not be issued unless the commissioners are satisfied that the applicant is a fit person and they may require him to produce (a) evidence as to his age, (b) evidence that he can read and write, (c) a certificate from his employer or sufficient reason for not supplying one, (d) a certificate of character from 2 householders who have known the applicant for 3 years, (e) in the case of a driver, evidence that he knows the Highway Code, a medical certificate of his fitness to drive a p.s.v., a vehicle for test purposes, and evidence that since the age of 3 years he has not had an epileptic attack [1321/34/5 and 1061/72].

A licence lasts for 3 years [Act 1960/144(6)] and costs 15p [1321/34/7]. If a licence is lost or damaged a duplicate can be obtained for 5p [12]. If a licence holder changes his address he must notify the commissioners who granted the licence within 7 days [10].

A licence may be suspended or revoked at any time by the issuing authority on the grounds that the holder, by his conduct or physical disability, is not a fit person [Act 1960/144(5)]. When this action is taken the licence holder must return it to the issuing authority within 5 days of being requested to do so [1321/34/13].

A person refused a licence, or whose licence is suspended or revoked, can ask the commissioners to reconsider the matter and, if then still dissatisfied, can appeal to a magistrates' court or sheriff (as described above in respect of h.g.v. licences) [Act 1960/145].

A licensed driver or conductor, after depositing 12½p, is issued with a badge which must be worn in a conspicuous place when on duty on a p.s.v. [1321/34/14]. If a p.s.v. licence is suspended or revoked the badge must be returned to the issuing authority [15]. A lost or damaged badge can be replaced for 12½p [17].

INTERNATIONAL PERMITS

A person over 18 years of age can obtain an international driving permit for use outside the United Kingdom if he is a competent driver and a resident of the U.K. [1208/75/1]. Permits are issued on behalf of the Secretary of State by the Royal Automobile Club, the Royal Scottish Automobile Club and the Automobile Association [1(8)]. The fee for a permit is £1·50 [Schedule 2].

A person who resides outside the United Kingdom, is temporarily in Great Britain and who holds an international driving permit, a domestic driving permit of a foreign country or a British Forces driving licence does not require a British driving licence during the 12-month period following his last entry into the U.K. provided his permit or licence authorises the driving of the class of vehicle being driven [1074/57/2(1)]. In the same period, such a person (except the holder of a British Forces licence) does not require a p.s.v. licence or an h.g.v. licence to drive such a vehicle brought temporarily into Great Britain as long as his permit authorises the driving of the vehicle [2(2)].

DRIVING INSTRUCTION

No instruction in the driving of a motor car for which payment of money or money's worth is, or is to be, made by, or in respect of, the person instructed may be given unless the instructor is registered as an approved driving instructor in a register maintained by the Secretary of State [Act 1972/126]. The only exceptions, apart from persons in Crown services, are police instructors [127].

DRIVERS' HOURS

The law regulating the driving hours, working hours and rest periods of goods and passenger vehicle drivers has become very involved in the last few years. A driver may be subject to the British hours' law, the E.E.C. hours' law, to a combination of both or to no control at all depending on what vehicle he drives, where he drives it or for what purpose. Exemptions and modifications to both the British and the E.E.C. law add to the basic complications.

THE E.E.C. HOURS' LAW

Since April 1, 1973, the drivers' hours law in E.E.C. Regulation 543/1969 has applied to goods and passenger vehicle drivers on international journeys. On that date the application of the British hours' law, in Section 96 of the Transport Act 1968, was removed from drivers who performed international work only [379/73/2] and continues not to apply [1157/78/2].

The E.E.C. law applies to 'carriage by road in respect of any journey or part of a journey made within the Community by vehicles registered in a Member State or in a third country' [543/69/2]. Carriage by road is defined as any journey by road of a vehicle, whether laden or not, used for the carriage of passengers or goods. No distinction is made between carriage for hire or reward, for own account purposes or for pleasure purposes so it appears that all such journeys are subject to the E.E.C. law.

The E.E.C. law does not apply to:

1. Passenger vehicles constructed to carry not more than nine passengers inclusive of the driver;
2. Goods vehicles with a permissible maximum weight (including any trailer) not over 3·5 metric tonnes. Permissible maximum weight means the maximum authorised operating weight of the vehicle fully laden;
3. Vehicles used for carrying passengers on regular services where the route covered does not exceed 50 km;
4. Vehicles used by police; gendarmerie; armed forces; fire brigades; civil defence; drainage or flood prevention authorities; water, gas or electricity services; highway authorities; refuse collection, telegraph or telephone services; by postal authorities for the carriage of mail; by radio or television services or for the detection of radio or television transmitters or receivers; or by other public authorities for public services and which are not in competition with professional road hauliers;
5. Vehicles used for the carriage of sick or injured persons and for carrying rescue material and any other specialised vehicles used for medical purposes;
6. Tractors with a maximum authorised speed not over 30 k.p.h.;
7. Tractors and other machines used exclusively for local agricultural and forestry work;
8. Vehicles used to transport circus and fun fair equipment; and
9. Specialised breakdown vehicles. [543/69/4 and 2827/77/1]

Where a vehicle is drawing
   (a) more than one trailer,
   (b) a passenger trailer with a permissible maximum weight over 5 tonnes, or

(c) a goods trailer and the outfit has a permissible maximum
weight over 20 tonnes

and, in each case, the distance to be covered between two consecutive daily rest periods exceeds 450 km the driver must be accompanied by another driver from the start of the journey or, at the
end of that distance, be relieved by another driver [543/69/6].
This requirement does not apply where there is used in a vehicle
a tachograph complying with E.E.C. Regulation 1463/1970
[2827/77/1].

A continuous period of driving must not exceed 4 hours and
a period of driving is deemed continuous unless it is broken by
specified rest periods [543/69/7(1)].

The total period of driving time between two consecutive daily
rest periods must not exceed 8 hours [7(2)]. Except for the drivers
referred to in Article 6, above, the total driving period may be
extended on two occasions a week to 9 hours [7(3)].

The total driving time in a week must not exceed 48 hours and
in any two consecutive weeks must not exceed 92 hours [7(4)].

A week, for the purposes of the E.E.C. Regulation, means any
period of 7 consecutive days [543/69/1(4)].

The breaks which a driver must take during a day's driving are
specified in Article 8. The driver of a vehicle to which Article 6
applies must have a break from driving of at least one hour at the
end of the first 4 hour period of continuous driving. However, this
break may be replaced by two breaks of at least 30 minutes each
spaced out over the whole daily driving period as long as 4 hours
driving is not exceeded between each break [8(1)]. Drivers of other
vehicles must have a break from driving of at least 30 minutes at
the end of 4 hours' driving. But this break may be replaced by
two 20-minute breaks or three 15-minute breaks spread over the
4-hour period or partly in it and partly following it [8(2)]. During
these breaks a driver must not perform any driving or be in attendance at work [8(3)] but if a vehicle has two drivers it is sufficient
if the one having his break does not do any physical work during
that break [8(4)].

A goods vehicle driver must have had a rest period of 11 consecutive hours during the 24 hours preceding any moment when he
is driving or working. This may be reduced to 9 hours twice a
week if it is taken at the place where the driver is based or to 8
hours twice a week if taken away from base [11(1)].

A passenger vehicle driver must have had in the 24-hour period
preceding any moment he is driving or working either (a) a rest
period of 10 consecutive hours which may not be reduced or (b)
a rest period of 11 consecutive hours which may be reduced twice

a week to 10 hours and twice a week to 9 hours provided that the transport operation includes a scheduled, uninterrupted break of at least 4 hours or two such breaks of 2 hours and during the breaks the driver does not drive or do any other work in a professional capacity. A driver must show in his record book which system he is following [11(2)].

If a vehicle is manned by two drivers and does not have a bunk enabling the non-active member to lie down comfortably each crew member must have had a rest period of 10 consecutive hours during the 27-hour period preceding any moment he is driving or working [11(3)].

Where a vehicle is manned by two drivers and it does have a bunk enabling a crew member to lie down comfortably each crew member must have had a rest period of at least 8 consecutive hours during the 30-hour period preceding any moment he is driving or working [11(4)].

Any daily rest period must be taken outside the vehicle. But if the vehicle has a bunk the rest period may be taken on that bunk provided the vehicle is stationary [11(5)].

Any reductions in rest periods taken under Article 11(1) or 11(2) have to be compensated [11(6)].

If a goods or passenger vehicle driver accompanies a vehicle carried by ferry boat or train the daily rest period may be interrupted once provided the following conditions are met:

(a) the part of the daily rest period taken on land may be taken before or after that part taken on the ferry or train;

(b) the period between the two parts of the rest period must not exceed one hour before embarkation or after disembarkation, customs formalities being included in the embarkation or disembarkation operations;

(c) during both parts of the rest period the driver must have access to a bunk or couchette;

(d) a daily rest period interrupted in this way must be increased by 2 hours; and

(e) any time spent on the boat or train which is not counted as part of a daily rest period shall be regarded as a rest break under Article 8.

[543/69/11a and 2827/77/1]

A driver must have a weekly rest period of a least 29 consecutive hours which must be immediately preceded or followed by a daily rest period. This weekly rest period may be reduced to not less than 24 hours provided a rest period equivalent to the reduction is granted to the driver in the same week [543/69/12 and 2827/77/1].

Drivers on international road passenger transport (except regular services) may, between April 1 and September 30, instead of taking the above weekly rest period, take a rest period of at least 60 consecutive hours within a 14-day period. This rest must also be immediately preceded or followed by a daily rest period [12(3)].

Payment to drivers, even in the form of a bonus or wage supplement, related to distance travelled or the amount of goods carried are prohibited unless they are of a kind which do not endanger road safety [543/69/12a and 2827/77/1].

In a case of danger, in circumstances outside his control, to render assistance or as a result of a breakdown and to the extent necessary to ensure the safety of persons, the vehicle or load and to enable him to reach a suitable stopping place, or according to circumstances, the end of his journey, a driver may (so long as road safety is not jeopardised) depart from the requirements of Article 6, 7(2) & (4) and 11. The driver must show the reasons for the departure in his record book or on his tachograph disc [543/69/13a and 514/72/3].

THE BRITISH HOURS' LAW

The hours of work of goods and passenger vehicle drivers on journeys within Britain may, depending on the type of vehicle and operation, be governed by British or E.E.C. law or a modified combination of both.

In this section the British hours' law contained in Part VI of the Transport Act 1968, as amended by the European Communities Act 1972 and the Road Traffic (Drivers' Ages and Hours of Work) Act 1976, will be explained.

It applies in full, subject to the exemptions and modifications given in this section, to drivers of goods and passenger vehicles who are not subject to E.E.C. Regulation 543/1969. The E.E.C. rules do not apply to drivers of vehicles listed in the preceding section or to drivers on the national transport operations listed in the following section (pages 69 to 71).

The hours' restrictions of the Transport Act do not apply to a goods vehicle driver engaged solely on international work or to a passenger vehicle driver engaged solely on international or national work to which the E.E.C. rules apply [1157/78/2]. They do apply but in modified circumstances to goods vehicle drivers who perform both international and national work to which the E.E.C. rules apply and to both goods and passenger vehicle drivers who perform both international work and national work to which the E.E.C. rules do not apply [1157/78/3, 4 and 5]. The modifications will be given in a following section (page 71).

The reason for the control of drivers' hours under the Transport Act is given in Section 95(1). It states 'This Part of this Act shall have effect with a view to securing the observance of proper hours of work by persons engaged in the carriage of passengers or goods by road and thereby protecting the public against the risks which arise in cases where the drivers of motor vehicles are suffering from fatigue ...'. A question often arises as to whether the hours' law applies to drivers who drive goods or passenger vehicles but do not drive them on roads. On this sub-section it can be argued that where a person does not drive on a road there is no need for the public to be protected against his fatigue by the hours' law. Special provision is made for cases where a person drives both on land and on a road.

The hours' law applies to passenger vehicles which, for these purposes, are either

(a) public service vehicles, or
(b) other motor vehicles constructed or adapted to carry more than 12 passengers

and to goods vehicles which, for these purposes, are

(a) locomotives, motor tractors or articulated drawing units, or
(b) motor vehicles constructed or adapted to carry goods other than the effects of passengers.

[Act 1968/95(2)].

In this chapter these vehicles will be referred to as Part VI vehicles.

A driver is either an employee-driver or an owner-driver. An employee-driver is a person who drives a Part VI vehicle in the course of his employment and an owner-driver is a person who drives such a vehicle for the purpose of a trade or business carried on by him. Driving means driving for these purposes (therefore excluding pleasure driving) [Act/95(3)] and means being at the driving controls of the vehicle for the purpose of controlling its movement, whether it is moving or is stationary with the engine running [103(3)].

The basic hours law is contained in Section 96 of the Act and this will be dealt with first before going into the many exemptions which exist.

A driver must not drive a Part VI vehicle for more than 10 hours on a working day [96(1)]. A working day is the aggregate period of time a driver is on duty, together with breaks between on-duty periods, until he takes an 11-hour or, where permitted, a $9\frac{1}{2}$-hour rest period [103(1)].

When a driver has been on duty for $5\frac{1}{2}$ hours and during that time has not had a 30-minute break for rest and refreshment he must then have such a break unless the end of the $5\frac{1}{2}$ hours also marks the end of that working day [96(2)]. 'On duty' in the case of an employee-driver means being on duty for driving, or other purposes or in any other employment of the person by whom he is employed as a driver [103(4)(a)] and in the case of an owner-driver means driving a Part VI vehicle in connection with his trade or business or doing other work in connection with the vehicle or its load [103(4)(b)].

The working day of a driver must not exceed 11 hours [96(3)(a)] but it may be up to $12\frac{1}{2}$ hours if the driver is off duty during the day for an amount of time at least equal to the time by which 11 hours is exceeded [96(3)(b)] or, in the case of an express or contract carriage driver, it may be up to 14 hours if he is able to obtain rest and refreshment for a period of 4 hours during that day [96(3)(c)].

Between two successive working days a driver must take an 11-hour rest period [96(4)(a)] but, in the case of a passenger vehicle driver, it may be reduced to $9\frac{1}{2}$ hours once in a working week [96(4)(b)]. A working week begins at midnight between Saturday and Sunday, unless a Licensing Authority permits otherwise [103(1)].

A driver must not be on duty for a total of more than 60 hours in a working week [96(5)]. During each working week a driver must be off duty for a period of at least 24 hours [96(6)]. This 24-hour period can begin in the week to which it relates and end in the following week [96(6)(a)] and, in the case of a stage carriage driver, it need not be taken if, in the preceding week, he had a 24-hour off-duty period or was not on duty at all [96(6)(b)].

Total exemption from the hours law in a working week is given to a driver who does not drive Part VI vehicles for more than 4 hours in each day (midnight to midnight) of that week [96(7)].

If a driver does not drive a Part VI vehicle on a working day subsections 96(2) and 96(3) do not apply to that day and, if he is on duty for more than 11 hours, only 11 hours count towards the 60-hour limit in sub-section 96(5) [96(8)].

In counting the 10 hours in sub-section 96(1) and the 4 hours in sub-section 96(7) no account is to be taken of time spent driving a vehicle in the course of agriculture of forestry operations when it is not on the road [96(9)]. Other driving work of which no account is to be taken for these purposes is given below.

Goods vehicle exemptions from British law

Light goods vehicles

Most of the hours law does not apply to the driver of a light goods vehicle engaged on specified classes of work. A light goods vehicle for this purpose is either a goods vehicle with a plated gross weight not over $3\frac{1}{2}$ tons (if not plated, not over 30 cwt unladen) or a dual-purpose vehicle. Where during a working week a driver does not drive a Part VI vehicle, other than a light goods vehicle, and apart from social, domestic or pleasure purposes, drives the light goods vehicle

    (a) solely in connection with specified medical professions,
    (b) mainly in connection with carrying out any service of inspection, cleaning, maintenance, repair, installation, or fitting,
    (c) solely while acting as a commercial traveller and the only goods carried are those for soliciting orders,
    (d) solely in employment of the R.A.C., A.A. or R.S.A.C., or
    (e) solely in connection with cinematography, radio or television broadcasting

he is exempt from all the hours law except for the limit of 10 hours driving per day and for this purpose a day is to be taken as midnight to midnight [257/70/3 and 818/71/5].

Site work

In addition to the exemption given to agriculture and forestry vehicles in sub-section 96(9) the driving of a vehicle when off the road does not count towards the 10-hour limit or the 4-hour exemption if it is done in quarrying, construction, reconstruction, alteration, extension or maintenance of a building or other fixed works of construction or civil engineering, including the construction, maintenance or improvement of roads. Time spent driving in connection with the improvement or maintenance of a road shall be regarded as if it was spent off the road [257/70/4 and 818/71/5].

Emergency work

A driver who spends time on duty to deal with an emergency is given various exemptions. An emergency is defined as 'events which (a) cause or are likely to cause such (i) danger to the life or health of one or more individuals or animals or (ii) a serious interruption in the maintenance of public services for the supply of water, gas, electricity or drainage or of telecommunications or postal services, or (iii) a serious interruption in the use of roads or airports, or (b) are likely to cause such serious damage to property' in any of these cases 'as to necessitate the taking of immediate action to prevent the occurrence or continuance of such danger or interruption or the occurrence of such damage'. The exemptions he is given, on a working day on which he does emergency work, are from sub-sections 96(1), 96(2), 96(3) as long as any time over 11 hours is spent on emergency work, 96(4) as long as he has 10 hours for rest between working days, 96(5) as long as time on duty (excluding emergency work) does not exceed 66 hours and 96(6) as long as he takes the 24-hour rest period in the next following 3 weeks [1364/78/3].

Special needs

Drivers who work wholly or mainly in connection with the handling of mail at Christmas time; the carriage of food, drink or bread at specified times; the carriage of liquid egg in bulk; the carriage of fish, agricultural produce, parts for farm machines, trees, animal fodder, lime, seeds and fertiliser; the carriage of building or civil engineering materials to and from sites are allowed to be on duty for 14 hours a day, 66 hours a week and are exempt from taking a 24-hour off-duty period so long as it is taken in the next three following weeks. In addition to the above exemptions, a driver engaged in the carriage of animals is allowed to take only 10 hours for rest between working days. Drivers engaged in the carriage of milk can be on duty 14 hours a day, 66 hours a week and are exempt from taking a 24-hour off-duty period in a working week if in the 14-day period comprising that week and the following week an off-duty period of 48 hours is taken. Drivers working in the carriage of animal waste not intended for human consumption can be on duty for 14 hours a day, 66 hours a week and can take 10 hours for rest between working days. Drivers engaged in the distribution of newspapers and magazines can be on duty for 14 hours a day and have a daily rest period of 10 hours. Drivers working in connection with household furniture removals, the carriage of explosives, radioactive substances and ships' stores can be on duty for 14 hours a day. A driver moving an exceptional load, which is at some time escorted by the police, can be on duty for 14 hours a day provided that he is off duty for periods which are at least equal to the time by which his day exceeds 11 hours, he can be on duty for 66 hours a week and take his 24-hour off-duty period in the next following three weeks. Twice a week a driver engaged in carrying blood for transfusions can be on duty for 14 hours a day provided that during that day he is able to obtain rest and refreshment for periods which are at least equal to the time by which his day exceeds 10 hours. A driver whose journey involves a ferry crossing to and from a place in Great Britain can be on duty for 14 hours a day provided he is off duty during that day for periods which are at least equal to the time by which his day exceeds 11 hours [1364/78/3 and Schedule].

Passenger vehicle exemptions from British law

Emergency work

The driver of any passenger vehicle who spends time on duty to deal with an emergency is given liberal exemptions from the hours law. An emergency here means 'an event which (a) causes or is likely to cause such (i) danger to the life or health of one or more individuals, or (ii) a serious interruption in the maintenance of public services for the supply of water, gas, electricity or drainage or of telecommunications or postal services, or (iii) a serious interruption in the use of roads, or (iv) a serious interruption in private transport or public transport (not being an interruption caused by a trade dispute ... involving persons who carry passengers for hire or reward), or (b) is likely to cause such serious damage to property' in any of these cases 'as to necessitate the taking of immediate action to prevent the occurrence or continuance of such danger or interruption or the occurrence of such damage'. Time spent by a driver on emergency work is deemed not to be driving time for the purposes of sub-section 96(1) and for sub-sections 96(1) to 96(6) be deemed to be time spent off duty [145/70/3].

Special needs

Twice a week a driver who works solely in connection with the carriage of blood for transfusions or the carriage of physically or mentally disabled people can be on duty for 14 hours a day provided that he is able to obtain rest and refreshment for periods which are at least equal to the time by which his day exceeds 10 hours [145/70/4 and 649/70/2].

General variations

When in a working week or working day all or the greater part of time spent by a driver in driving Part VI vehicles is spent in driving passenger vehicles the requirements of Section 96(2) to (7) are modified. The need to take a break after $5\frac{1}{2}$ hours relates to driving time and not on-duty time and it is provided that the break need not be taken if, in any continuous period of 8½ hours, a driver does not drive for more than a total of 7¾ hours and the last of his driving periods marks either the end of the working day or the start of a 30-minute break [818/71/4(2)]. He can be on duty for 16 hours a day and the limit of 60 hours on-duty time in a working week does not apply [4(3), (5)]. Section 96(4) is varied so that only 10 hours' rest is required between working days and, on three occasions in a working week, it can be reduced still further to 8½ hours [4(4)].

The requirement to take a 24-hour off-duty period is modified so that a driver need take only one such period in any period of two successive weeks [818/71/4(6)]. The 4-hour exemption in Section 96(7) is replaced to allow a driver to drive for more than 4 hours on two occasions a week, which are subject to the hours law, and yet benefit by exemptions on the remaining days of that week [4(7)].

THE E.E.C. LAW AND NATIONAL TRANSPORT MODIFICATIONS AND EXEMPTIONS

The Treaty of Accession to the Community provided that E.E.C. Regulation 543/1969 should have applied to national transport operations within Britain on January 1, 1976. However, Britain was not ready to implement the hours, rest and records requirements of the Regulation on that date and obtained a number of deferments from the Commission. The last deferment [312/77] expired on December 31, 1977. Meanwhile Britain sought permission to phase-in the Regulation over a 3-year period. Authorisation to take this action was given by the E.E.C. Commission on December 21, 1977.

Till December 31, 1980, therefore, the hours' law of E.E.C. Regulation 543/1969 (explained in the first section in this chapter) applies, subject to the below listed modifications, to drivers of goods and passenger vehicles on national transport operations [7/78/3 and Schedule].

The temporary modifications:

Goods vehicles

1. *Article 7(1) (continuous driving period):*
   from January 1, 1978 to June 30, 1979 the continuous driving period shall not exceed five hours;
   from July 1, 1979 to December 31, 1980 the continuous driving period shall not exceed four and a half hours.

2. *Article* 7(2) (*daily driving period*):
from January 1, 1978 to November 30, 1978 the daily driving period shall not exceed ten hours;
from December 1, 1978 to June 30, 1979 the daily driving period shall not exceed nine and a half hours;
from July 1, 1979 to December 31, 1980 the daily driving period shall not exceed nine hours.

3. *Article* 7(4) (*weekly and fortnightly driving periods*):
from Januray 1, 1978 to June 30, 1979 the driving period shall not exceed 57 hours in any one week or 112 hours in any two consecutive weeks;
from July 1, 1979 to December 31, 1980 the driving period shall not exceed 54 hours in any one week or 106 hours in any two consecutive weeks;

4. *Article* 12 (*weekly rest period*):
from January 1, 1978 to December 31, 1978 the weekly rest period may be taken at any time between 0000 hours on a Sunday and 2400 hours on a Saturday;
from January 1, 1979 any period of seven consecutive days must include a weekly rest period;
from January 1, 1978 to June 30, 1979 the weekly rest period may be reduced to at least 24 consecutive hours, immediately preceded or followed by a daily rest period;
Article 12 shall apply in full from July 1, 1979.

Passenger vehicles

1. *Article* 7(1) (*continuous driving period*):
from January 1, 1978 to November 30, 1978 the continuous driving period shall not exceed five and a half hours;
from December 1, 1978 to September 30, 1979 the continuous driving period shall not exceed five hours;
from October 1, 1979 to December 31, 1980 the continuous driving period shall not exceed four and a half hours.

2. *Article* 7(2) (*daily driving period*):
from January 1, 1978 to November 30, 1978 the daily driving period shall not exceed ten hours;
from December 1, 1978 to September 30, 1979 the daily driving period shall not exceed nine and a half hours;
from October 1, 1979 to December 31, 1980 the daily driving period shall not exceed nine hours.

3. *Article* 7(4) (*weekly and fortnightly driving periods*):
from January 1, 1978 to November 30, 1978 the driving period shall not exceed 60 hours in any one week or 118 hours in any two consecutive weeks;

from December 1, 1978 to September 30, 1979 the driving period shall not exceed 57 hours in any one week or 112 hours in any two consecutive weeks;

from October 1, 1979 to December 31, 1980 the driving period shall not exceed 54 hours in any one week or 106 hours in any two consecutive weeks.

4. *Article* 11(2) (*daily rest period*):

from January 1, 1978 to September 30, 1978 every crew member shall have had a daily rest period of ten consecutive hours during the twenty-four hour period preceding any time when he is performing any activity covered by Article 14(2)(*c*) or (*d*) of the Community Drivers' Hours Regulation, which may be reduced to eight and a half hours three times a week;

from October 1, 1978, September 30, 1979 the daily rest period of ten hours may be reduced to eight and a half hours twice a week;

from October 1, 1979 to December 31, 1980 the daily rest period of ten hours may be reduced once a week to eight and a half hours for the drivers of vehicles on regular routes;

from October 1, 1979 Article 11(2) shall apply in full for passenger services on non-scheduled routes.

5. *Article* 12 (*weekly rest period*):

from January 1, 1978 to September 30, 1979 the weekly rest period may be taken at any time between 0000 hours on a Sunday and 2400 hours on a Saturday;

from October 1, 1979 any period of seven consecutive days must include a weekly rest period;

from January 1, 1978 to September 30, 1979 the weekly rest period may be reduced to at least 24 consecutive hours, not necessarily preceded or followed immediately by a daily rest period; however, from January 1, 1978 to September 30, 1978 the weekly rest period may be replaced by a periodical rest period of 24 hours to be taken before the end of any fortnight;

from October 1, 1979 to December 31, 1980 the weekly rest period may be reduced to at least 24 consecutive hours, immediately preceded or followed by a daily rest period.

Exemptions from some or all of the E.E.C. hours' rules can be granted by Member States in respect of certain vehicles engaged on specified national transport operations [543/69/14a]. Regulations have been made under these enabling powers and the following exemptions are given.

Exemption is given in the case of internal goods transport

operations carried out within a radius of 50 kilometres of the vehicle's base

(a) from Articles 7(1) and 8—continuous driving periods and rest breaks—provided the daily driving period includes sufficient breaks to ensure that the periods laid down in Article 8(1) and (2) are observed and that in each case there is a break of at least 30 minutes or two breaks of 15 minutes;

(b) from Article 11(1)—daily rest period—for the transport of harvest produce on not more than 30 days a year provided a daily rest period of 10 hours is taken and the reduction made good by a corresponding addition to the weekly rest period;

(c) from Article 14—drivers' control books—provided daily driving does not exceed four hours and only till the compulsory installation of tachographs.

[1158/78/2].

Exemption from the whole of E.E.C. Regulation 543/69 is given to the following national transport operations:

(i) the use of vehicle constructed or equipped to carry not more than 15 passengers, including the driver;

(ii) the use of vehicles on local road rests for purposes of repair or maintenance;

(iii) the transport of live animals from farms to local markets or vice versa, or for the transport of animal carcases or waste not intended for human consumption.

Vehicles in (i) and (ii) above are also exempt from the need to be fitted with a tachograph under the E.E.C. Regulation 1463/70.

[1158/78/3].

Exemption from the whole of E.E.C. Regulation 543/69 is given to the following national transport operations involving the use of specialised vehicles:

(a) at local markets

(b) for door-to-door selling,

(c) for mobile banking, exchange or savings transactions,

(d) for purposes of worship,

(e) for the lending of books, records or cassettes, or

(f) for cultural events or mobile exhibitions.

The above vehicles and uses are also exempt from the need to be fitted with a tachograph under E.E.C. Regulation 1463/70.

[1158/78/4].

Exemption from the whole of E.E.C. Regulation 543/1969 is given, till December 31, 1980, for national transport of milk from farm to dairy or vice versa provided:

(i) no period of continuous driving exceeds 5 hours,
(ii) the total driving in two consecutive weeks does not exceed 108 hours, and
(iii) in any week a continuous rest period of 24 hours or, in any two weeks, a continuous rest period of 48 hours is taken.

[1158/78/5].

MODIFICATIONS TO BRITISH LAW FOR GOODS VEHICLE DRIVERS TO WHOM E.E.C. LAW APPLIES

Specified provisions of the British hours' law continue to apply to goods vehicle drivers who perform, within Great Britain, transport operations which are subject to the E.E.C. law. Which provisions apply and what modifications are made to them depend on whether or not the driver also performs international work.

British but no international work

The following requirements and modifications relate to a goods vehicle driver who does national transport work subject to the E.E.C. law (whether or not he also does work subject to the British but not the E.E.C. law) but they do not apply to such a driver in any 7-day period at the beginning of which he performs international work [1157/78/4(1)].

The provisions which continue to apply to his E.E.C. controlled work, subject to the modifications given below, are those in sub-sections (2), (3), (5), (7), (8) and (9) of Section 96 of the Transport Act 1968 [4(2)].

(a) For the purposes of sub-sections (2), (3), (7) and (8) of Section 96 in relation to the driver's E.E.C.-controlled work and sub-sections (1) to (9) in relation to his non-E.E.C.-controlled work the definition of a working day in Section 103 of the Transport Act is amended to take into account the shorter daily rest periods allowed under the E.E.C. law [4(3)].

(b) Sub-section (2) (30-minute rest breaks) is amended in relation to a driver's work (whether E.E.C. controlled or not) with a vehicle other than one to which Article 6 of E.E.C. Regulation 543/69 applies (i.e. over 20 tonnes with a trailer). Where such a driver has been on duty for $5\frac{1}{2}$ hours and he has not had one 30-minute break, two 20-minute breaks or three 15-minute breaks and the end of the $5\frac{1}{2}$

hours does not mark the end of the working day the driver must have a break of 30 minutes or one of 20 minutes if he has already had a break of 20 minutes or one of 15 minutes if he has already had two breaks of 15 minutes [4(4)].

(c) Sub-section (3) (limit on working day) is amended in relation to a driver on E.E.C.-controlled or other work. The amendment preserves the basic 11-hour working-day and 12½-hours spreadover limits and makes new provision for double-manned vehicles. This new provision states that where a vehicle is manned by two drivers a crew member's working day shall (i) where the vehicle has no bunk, not exceed 17 hours as long as for at least 6 hours he is not required to perform any work in connection with the operation of the vehicle and (ii) where a vehicle has a bunk, not exceed 22 hours as long as for at least 11 hours he is not required to perform any such work [4(5)].

(d) Sub-section (4) (daily rest period) as far as it relates to the driver's work which is not subject to the E.E.C. law is amended so that its effect is just the same as the E.E.C. law in Article 11(1), (3) and (4) of Regulation 543/69 [4(6)]. Article 11 allows for shorter rest periods and makes provision for double-manned vehicles—see pages 59 and 60.

(e) Sub-section (6) (weekly rest period) as far as it relates to the driver's work which is not subject to the E.E.C. law is amended to require the drivers to take a daily rest period immediately before or after the 24-hour weekly rest period [4(7)].

(f) From January 1, 1979 the definition of a working week in Section 103 is changed from 'Sunday to Saturday' to 'any period of seven consecutive days' in relation to (i) sub-sections (1) to (9) of Section 96 as they apply to a driver's non-E.E.C.-controlled work and (ii) sub-sections (2), (3), (5), (7) and (8) as they apply to his E.E.C. controlled work [4(8)].

If a person drives both goods and passenger vehicles he is not to be regarded in a working day or working week, as the case may be, as a goods vehicle driver for the above purposes unless in that period at least half his driving or working time is spent with goods vehicles [4(9)].

British and international work

The following requirements and modifications relate to a goods vehicle driver who does British work not subject to the E.E.C. law (whether or not he also does E.E.C.-controlled work) in a seven day period at the beginning of which he also performs international work [1157/78/5(1)].

In relation to the work not controlled by the E.E.C. law and which is performed in the 7-day period:

(i) Sections 103 and 96(2), (4) and (6) are amended as described in paragraphs (a), (b), (d) and (e) above [5(3)];

(ii) Sub-section (2) is further amended so that in the above amendment the requirement to take a break comes after $5\frac{1}{2}$ driving and not $5\frac{1}{2}$ hours on-duty time [5(4)];

(iii) Sub-sections (3) and (5)—limits on the working day and working week—do not apply [5(5)];

(iv) The definition of a working week in Section 103 is changed to any period of seven consecutive days' [5(6)].

If a person drives both goods and passenger vehicles in the 7-day period concerned he is not to be regarded as a goods vehicle driver for these purposes unless at least half of his driving and working time is spent with goods vehicles [5(7)].

N.B. The British hours' law does not apply to the international or national work of a passenger vehicle driver which is subject to the E.E.C. law [1157/78/2]. Any British work he performs which is not subject to the E.E.C. law is subject to the British law as modified some years ago. These modifications are given on page 66.

PROSECUTIONS

It is an offence for the British hours law to be contravened by (a) a driver and (b) any other person, being the driver's employer or a person to whose orders he was subject, who caused or permitted the contravention. But a person will not be liable to be convicted 'if he proves to the court that the contravention was due to unavoidable delay in the completion of a journey arising out of circumstances which he could not reasonably have foreseen'. It is also a defence for a person, described at (b), to prove that the contravention was due to the driver being on duty otherwise than in his employment and that he was not and could not reasonably have become aware of that fact [Act 1968/96(11) and Act 1976].

If there is a contravention in Great Britain of E.E.C. Regulation 543/69 regarding periods of driving, distance driven or periods on or off duty then the driver or crew member, his employer and any other person to whose orders he was subject commits an offence [Act 1968/96(11A) and Acts 1972 and 1976]. The maximum penalty is a fine of £200. The statutory defences to contraventions of the British law (described in the preceding paragraph) are also available to a person contravening the E.E.C. law in Britain [Act 1968/96(11B) and Act 1978/10].

Vehicles used for police or fire brigade purposes are exempt from the British hours' law [Act 1968/102(4)].

Except for naval, military and air force purposes, the British hours' law applies to Crown vehicles [102(1), (2)].

A court has jurisdiction to deal with an hours' or records offence under Part VI of the Transport Act 1968 as if the offence had been committed at the place

   (a) where the defendant was driving when evidence of the offence first came to the attention of a policeman or vehicle examiner;

   (b) where the defendant lives or is believed to live at the time when proceedings are commenced; or

   (c) where the defendant, his employer or, in the case of an owner-driver, the person for whom he was driving, has his principal place of business or his operating centre for the vehicle in question [Act 1968/103(7) and Act 1976].

DRIVERS' RECORDS

Transport Act 1968
Drivers' Hours (Keeping of Records) Regulations, **No. 1447/76**
Transit of Animals (Road and Rail) Order, **No. 1024/75**
E.E.C. Regulations **543/69,** as amended by Regulations **514** and **515/72** and
2827/77
E.E.C. Regulations **1463/70,** as amended by Regulations **1787/73** and **2828/77**
Passenger and Goods Vehicles (Recording Equipment) Regulations, **No. 777/77**
Community Road Transport Rules (Exemptions) Regulations, **No. 1158/78**

A driver's record book for the purposes of the following requirements must comprise of a front sheet; instructions for use of
the book; daily sheets; an example of a completed daily sheet;
weekly reports and must conform to a prescribed model (see pages
87 to 92) [1447/76/3(1)]. The book is the same as that prescribed
in the Annex to E.E.C. Regulation 543/69 and no requirement is
made as to the number of daily or weekly sheets to be contained
in it.

NATIONAL AND INTERNATIONAL TRANSPORT
OPERATIONS TO WHICH THE E.E.C. LAW APPLIES

Article 14 of E.E.C. Regulation 543/69 requires crew members of
vehicles not assigned to regular services to carry an individual control book complying with the Annex to the Regulation. Crew
members must enter the information required on the sheets and
produce the book whenever required by an inspecting officer. The
transport undertaking must keep a register of control books and
produce it when required by an inspecting officer. Completed control books must be kept by the undertaking for at least one year
[E.E.C. 543/69/14].

British law places an additional duty on the employer of an

employee-driver of a British goods or British passenger vehicle to cause the driver (a) to enter in the record book the information required under the E.E.C. rules and to comply with those rules and (b) to comply with the following described requirements of the British records regulations [1447/76/14].

All the following requirements apply to goods vehicles registered in Great Britain. Of these requirements only those contained in Regulations 6 and 11 apply to passenger vehicles registered in Great Britain [15 and 16].

If a person is employed by more than one employer as an employee-driver the employer who is to issue him with a record book is the one for whom he first works after October 30, 1976 (6(1)). Where, during the currency of a record book such a driver leaves the employ of the employer who issued it he must return the book, with all duplicate and unused daily and weekly sheets, to the employer who issued it. If at that time he is employed by another person as a vehicle driver that other person must issue him with a new record book or, if there is more than one other employer, the one for whom he first works after ceasing the first employment [6(2)].

Each record book used by an owner-driver or issued by an employer must bear a different serial number [7(2)]. If a book has more than 15 daily sheets it must contain a duplicate of each sheet together with carbon paper or other material for producing duplicate entries [7(3)]. A book with 15 or less daily sheets may be kept in duplicate [7(4)].

An owner-driver or an employer must, before a book is used, cause to be entered on the front sheet and on each daily sheet the number of his operator's licence and, on the front sheet, the book serial number and the number of daily sheets in the book [8(2)]. When a book has duplicate sheets the driver must ensure that the entries he makes, including his signature, are reproduced on the duplicate [8(3)].

Where a record sheet which has a duplicate has been completed the driver must detach, and his employer cause him to detach, the duplicate of the sheet from the book and (a) in the case of an employee-driver, he must deliver it within 7 days of completion to the employer who issued or should have issued it, and such employer shall cause the driver so to deliver the sheet, and, within 7 days of receiving the sheet, the employer must examine and sign it; or (b) in the case of an owner-driver, he must deliver the sheet within 7 days of its completion to the address required to be given on the book's front sheet [8(4)]. A person is not to be treated as having failed to comply with any of these requirements if he can show that it was not reasonably practicable to comply and that it was complied with as soon as reasonably practicable to do so [8(4) Proviso].

If an employee-driver uses a record book which does not have duplicate sheets his employer must, within 7 days of the completed book being returned to him, examine and sign each daily sheet unless he had already done so [8(5)]. A record book is to be regarded as completed (a) in the case of a book with 15 or less single pages, when all those pages have been used or at the end of 28 days from when it was first used, whichever is the earlier and (b) in the case of any other book, when all the sheets have been used [8(6)]. A driver must not make entries in a driver's record book if (i) he is an employee-driver and the book was not supplied by his employer, unless a record book supplied by his employer is not available or (ii) he is in possession of another book which he has used but not completed [8(7)].

Where a driver works for more than one person as an employee-driver the employer who did not issue the driver's record book must require the driver to produce it and must enter his (the employer's) name and address on the front sheet. An employer must also supply any other employer of an employee-driver with specified information when asked to do so [9(1)]. That specified information must also be given by an employer to an employee-driver when he ceases to be employed by him and to any new employer [9(2)]. The information, which must be in writing if required [9(3)], relates to any 24-hour rest period taken by the driver in a seven-day period and any daily rest period taken immediately before or after if [9(4)]. A driver must produce his record book for inspection when required by an employer for whom he is an employee-driver [9(5)] and, if required, must return it at the end of each week to the employee-driver who issued it [(6)].

An owner-driver and an employer must preserve completed record books and any detached sheets for a period of one year from, in the case of an owner-driver, the date the book was completed and, in the case of an employer, from the date it was returned to him. A driver who keeps a copy of a weekly report must preserve it for as long as the record book to which it relates remains in his possession. An employer must preserve weekly reports handed to him for signature for 12 months from the week concerned [10].

In *Blakey Transport Ltd* v. *Casebourne*, [1975] R.T.R. 221 an employer who re-issued a record book within the prescribed period was held not to have preserved the book. In *Cassady* v. *Ward and Smith Ltd* [1975] R.T.R. 353 a book issued to a driver after use by a succession of temporary drivers was held not to be a new book.

An owner-driver and an employer must maintain a register of drivers' record books he uses or issues and must record in it the required information [11(1)]. The register should comply with a prescribed form (see page 93) but it may differ as to size, layout, sequence, numbering, content or otherwise as long as the wording is not changed and all the required information can be entered [11(4)]. If an employer operates vehicles from different places he may keep a register for each place but such a register may relate only to books used by drivers of vehicles operated from that place [11(2)]. A register must be preserved for 12 months from the last date required to be entered in it [11(3)]. If a record book is not returned an entry must be made in the register, in place of the date of return, giving the reason and the date of such entry [11(1) Proviso].

In these Regulations references to 'employee-driver', 'owner-driver', 'goods vehicle', 'passenger vehicle', 'working day' and 'working week' have to be interpreted as in Part V and VI of the Transport Act 1968 [3(1)]. They are explained on pages 62 and 63.

Exemptions

Till the compulsory installation of tachographs, exemption from keeping a record book under E.E.C. rules is given to a driver engaged on national transport operations within a radius of 50 km of the vehicle's base provided daily driving does not exceed 4 hours (1158/78/2].

Also exempt from the E.E.C. law while on national transport operations are 15-seat minibuses, vehicles on local tests, vehicles carrying live animals or animal waste and certain specialised vehicles used for prescribed purposes [1158/78/3 and 4]. They are fully listed on page 69 in the E.E.C. hours' exemptions for national transport operations.

Being exempt from keeping records under the E.E.C. law does not necessarily mean that a goods vehicle driver is totally exempt from keeping records. He may have to keep them under the provisions described in the next following section. Exemptions from those requirements are given at the end of that section.

GOODS TRANSPORT OPERATIONS TO WHICH THE E.E.C. LAW DOES NOT APPLY

The driver of a goods vehicle must enter in a driver's record book information required to be entered in it and the employer of an employee-driver must cause such information to be entered [1447/ 76/5(1)(a)]. No requirement is made as to the number of daily sheets and weekly reports to be contained in a book. An owner-driver and the employer of an employee-driver must make entries in the book which are required to be made by the undertaking [5(1)(b)]. A driver and employer must comply, and an employer must cause his employee-driver to comply, with the instructions in the record book relating to the issue, use, preservation and return of the book [5(1)].

If in any working week a person drives both goods and passenger vehicles the information to be entered in his record book is that relating to both activities [5(2)]. When such a person drives passenger vehicles for a person different from the one for whom he drives goods vehicles the duties placed on an employer by Regulation 5(1) are to be construed as placed on the goods-vehicle employer [5(2)].

All the requirements described in the preceding section (apart from those in the first three paragraphs) also apply.

In addition a record book must bear a stamped or perforated serial number and be a minimum of A6 format (105 × 148 mm) [7(1)]. The information to be given by an employer to an employee under Regulation 9(4) is different in that it is to relate to any 24-hour off-duty period taken by the driver and the number of hours he has been on duty in the current working week.

Exemptions

A driver who on any day, midnight to midnight, does not drive a goods vehicle other than goods vehicles exempted from operators' licensing is exempt from keeping a record sheet for that day [1447/76/12(1)].

Or, where a driver on any day, from midnight to midnight, does not drive a goods vehicle for more than 4 hours and does not drive it outside of a radius of 25 miles of its operating centre he is exempt from keeping a record sheet for that day [12(2)]. The 4 hours does not include driving, when not on the road, for the purposes of agriculture, forestry or quarrying or in connection with construction, reconstruction, alteration, extension of maintenance of a building or other fixed works of construction or civil engineering. Driving on a road in the course of carrying out roadworks shall be deemed not to be on a road [12(2)].

Where a driver keeps a record sheet on a day following a day when he was exempted from keeping a record sheet he must enter in the record book the time and date his last working day ended if it ended during the exempted period [12(2) Proviso]. Such an entry could be made on the next record sheet to be used.

For exemption when a tachograph is fitted and used see page 86.

PROSECUTIONS

Any person who contravenes the records regulations or any requirement as to books or records under the Community rules is liable to a fine of £200 on summary conviction. But the employer of an employee-driver will not be convicted of failing to cause records to be kept if he proves to the court that he has given proper instructions to his employees regarding the keeping of records and has from time to time taken reasonable steps to secure that those instructions are being carried out [Act 1968/98(4)].

The place where a records' offence can be brought before a court is the same as that for an hours' offence and is given on page 74.

PRODUCTION OF RECORDS, ETC.

Record books and registers must be produced when required by traffic examiners or police [Act 1968/99(1)]. The owner of a vehicle can also be required to produce any other document for use in checking that the hours and records law is complied with [99(1)(c)]. Records and documents can also be required to be produced at the office of the Licensing Authority [99(1)].

Examiners and police have power to enter premises, at any reasonable time, and inspect any records, books, registers, documents or Part VI vehicles found there [99(2)].

It is an indictable offence for a person to make, or cause to be made, an entry in a record book or register which he knows to be false or which, with intent to deceive, he alters or causes to be altered [99(5)].

TACHOGRAPHS—E.E.C. RULES

The installation of tachographs in goods and passenger vehicles registered in a Member State is dealt with in E.E.C. Regulation 1463/1970.

From January 1, 1976, it has required a tachograph to be fitted in British registered vehicles first registered on or after that date and in vehicles used to carry dangerous goods irrespective of their date of registration.

Vehicles registered before 1976 were required to be fitted with a tachograph on January 1, 1978 but, in the case of specified vehicles, this date has been deferred till July 1, 1979. The vehicles which are given till this later date are those used exclusively for the carriage of goods (other than dangerous goods) and which (a) are engaged in transport operations within a 50 km radius of the vehicle's depot or (b) which have a maximum authorised weight (including any trailer) not over 6 tonnes or a payload of not more than 3·5 tonnes.

In Britain there is no legislation to enforce E.E.C. Regulation 1463/70 in the courts so a person does not commit an offence by not complying with it. Regulations have been made, however, which provide for the voluntary use of E.E.C. tachographs and which give exemption to their users from keeping records. They are described in the following section.

Exempt from the E.E.C. tachograph requirements are:

(a) vehicles listed in Article 4 of E.E.C. Regulation 543/1969 as being exempt from the E.E.C. hours and records law (page 58) [1463/70/3(1)];
(b) passenger vehicles used on regular services where the route covered exceeds 50 km [1463/70/3(1)];
(c) vehicles on national transport operations constructed to carry not more than 15 passengers including the driver [1158/78/3];
(d) vehicles used within Great Britain on local road tests for purposes of repair or maintenance [1158/78/3];
(e) specialised vehicles used within Great Britain
  (i) at local markets;
  (ii) for door-to-door selling;
  (iii) for mobile banking, exchange or savings transactions;
  (iv) for purposes of worship;
  (v) for the lending of books, records or cassettes;
  (vi) for cultural events or mobile exhibitions.

[1158/78/4].

A tachograph may be installed in a vehicle or repaired only by fitters or workshops approved by a Member State. The fitter or workshop must place a special mark on the seals which it uses and lists of the fitters, workshops and marks have to be circulated between Member States. An installation plaque certifying that it has been properly installed must be fixed on or beside the tachograph [E.E.C. 1463/70/14].

The employer and crew member are responsible for seeing that the tachograph functions correctly and that seals remain intact. Seals may be broken only in cases of absolute necessity which will have to be proved. Any operation or interference with the tachograph which results in false recordings is prohibited [15].

The employer must issue crew members with enough tachograph sheets to cover their period of work and having regard to the possibility of sheets being damaged or taken by an inspecting officer. The employer must keep completed sheets for a year and produce them to an authorised inspector [16].

Crew members must not use dirty or damaged sheets. If a sheet is damaged it must be attached to the spare sheet used to replace it [17(1)]. A crew member must see that the tachograph is kept running continuously while he is responsible for the vehicle and that the time recorded on the sheet is the official time of the vehicle's country or origin. He must operate the controls enabling driving time, other working time and breaks to be recorded and, where a vehicle has more than one crew member, make changes to the record sheets so that distance, speed and driving time is recorded in relation to the person who is driving. When a crew member is away from the vehicle and unable to operate the tachograph the various periods of time must be entered on the sheet in a legible manner [17(2)].

A crew member must enter on the tachograph sheet:

(a) his full name;
(b) the date and place where use of the sheet starts and ends;
(c) the registration number of the vehicle and any other vehicle to which he changes;
(d) the odometer reading at the start of the first and end of the last journey recorded on the sheet and, if there is a change of vehicle, the same readings for the other vehicle or vehicles;
(e) the time any change of vehicle takes place. [17(3)].

The tachograph must be designed so that an inspecting officer can read the recordings (if necessary by opening the instrument) relating to the preceding nine hours without damaging the sheet. It must also be designed that it is possible, without opening the instrument, to verify that recordings are being made [17(4)].

Crew members must be able to produce to an authorised inspector tachograph sheets for the preceding seven days [17(5)]. A Member State may reduce this period to two days in the case of vehicles registered in its own territory which are engaged on national transport operations [17(6)].

An employer must have a defective tachograph repaired by approved fitters or workshops which must be, at the latest, as soon as the vehicle has returned to the operator's premises. If the vehicle is not able to return to its premises within one week of the defect it must be repaired en route [18(1)].

While the tachograph is defective crew members must mark on the record sheet, or on a temporary sheet attached to the record sheet, the information which is not being correctly recorded by the instrument [18(2)].

The construction of tachographs, their installation, use and testing are prescribed in Annex 1 to Regulation 1463/70. The following is a summary of the more day-to-day requirements.

The tachograph must be capable of recording, automatically or semi-automatically, the distance travelled and speed of the vehicle, driving time, other periods of work, breaks from work and daily rest periods, and the opening of the part of the equipment which contains the record sheet. If a vehicle has more than one crew member the instrument must be capable of recording simultaneously, but distinctly and on separate sheets, the driving, work and breaks of two crew members. If more than two persons are crew members preference must be given to those who are drivers. The tachograph must include a distance recorder, speedometer and clock which can all be seen by the driver. The distance recorder can measure either forward or reverse movements or forward movements only, but if reverse movements are shown they must not interfere with the clarity of other recordings.

The control for re-setting or winding the clock must be inside that part of the tachograph which contains the record cards, so that each time the instrument is opened a mark is made on the card. Where the clock controls the forward movement of the record sheet it must be capable of running 10% longer than the time value of the record sheets in use at the time. All internal parts of the tachograph must be protected against damp and dust, and the casing must be capable of being sealed to prevent tampering. The speedometer, odometer and clock must be provided with lighting. The odometer has to be able to record 99,999·9 kilometres in units of 0·1 km. The speedometer must be calibrated in units of 1, 2, 5 or 10 kilometers per hour.

Whether the tachograph records on either a strip or disc record sheet, there must be provision on the sheet to ensure that times on the sheet and tachograph correspond. A record sheet must cover a period of at least 24 hours. The part of the tachograph containing the record sheet and clock winder must be provided with a lock. The equipment must be fitted so that the driver has a clear view of it and, in the case of a vehicle with a two-speed rear axle, the tachograph must have an adaptation which operates automatically with selection of the different axle ratio.

Seals must be fitted to both ends of the speedometer drive cable, the adaptor and compensator for the two-speed axle, and the casing of the tachograph. If seals are broken a written statement of the reason must be available to the authorities. The tachograph must be checked on installation, after each repair and every two years.

TACHOGRAPHS—BRITISH RULES

The Passenger and Goods Vehicles (Recording Equipment) Regulations 1977 provide for the enforcement of E.E.C. Regulation 1463/70 on vehicles from other Member States and on British-based vehicles which are fitted voluntarily with tachographs. They provide exemption from the keeping of drivers' record sheets in prescribed circumstances. They do not make the use of tachographs compulsory on either British or foreign vehicles.

The Regulations apply to passenger vehicles and goods vehicles which are registered in any of the Member States and in which tachographs are installed for the purposes of E.E.C. Regulation 1463/70 [777/77/2].

Where a tachograph conforms to the construction requirements of the E.E.C. Regulation and is used in accordance with Articles 15 and 17 of that Regulation any record produced by the equipment shall, in proceedings under the hours and records law, be evidence of the matters appearing from the record [3(1)]. For these purposes the tachograph is presumed to comply with the construction requirements if it carries a prescribed installation plaque and its seals are unbroken [3(2)].

The requirements of Articles 15 and 17 are described in the preceding section.

Any entry made by a crew member on a sheet under Article 17 or 18(2)—which deals with temporary sheets while the tachograph is defective—is admissible, in proceedings under the hours and records law, as evidence of the matters appearing from the sheet in question [3(3)].

Where a tachograph is used in accordance with Articles 15 and 17 it is an offence.

(a) for an owner-driver or employer before using a record sheet to fail to number it with a number different from any other used by him in the preceding 12 months, or

(b) for an employer to fail
    (i) to supply record sheets to crew members, or
    (ii) without reasonable excuse to secure that completed record
        sheets are returned to him, or
    (iii) to examine and sign a record sheet within 7 days of its
         return, or
    (iv) to retain tachograph and temporary sheets for at least 12
        months, or
(c) for a crew member to fail—
    (i)   to be able to produce to an authorised officer record sheets
        for a prescribed period, or
    (ii) to return to his employer each tachograph sheet or tem-
        porary sheet within 21 days of its completion, or
    (iii) to return damaged or unusable, dirty record sheets to his
        employer, or
    (iv) on leaving his employment to return any unused record
        sheets in his possession to his employer, or
    (v) if an owner-driver, to retain sheets for 12 months.

[777/77/4(1)]

The period prescribed for a crew member to keep records, referred
to in (c) (i) above, is, in the case of a British-registered vehicle, two
days [5].

Where a tachograph is used in accordance with Articles 15 and 17
an employer and an owner-driver must keep a register of the record
sheets he supplies to crew members or takes into use, as the case may
be [6(1)]. An owner driver's register can also be used for record sheets
issued to any of his employees [6(2)].

The register must be numbered and the pages consecutively numbered
and bear the number of the register. Each page must contain—

(a) the name and address of the employer or owner-driver,
(b) the operator's licence number (goods vehicles only),
(c) the address of the place where record sheets are supplied,
(d) on each occasion when record sheets are
    supplied—
    (i)   the serial numbers of the sheets,
    (ii) the date they are supplied,
    (iii) the name of the crew member to whom supplied,
    (iv) the employer's signature,
    (v) the crew member's signature,
    (vi) the date of their return or their removal from the vehicle
        by the owner-driver.

[6(3)].

The register must be kept for at least 12 months after the last entry in it [6(4)].

Powers to inspect tachographs, records and vehicles are given in Regulation 7 to traffic examiners, certifying officers and police. Such a person may—

(1) require any person to produce and permit him to inspect and copy any record sheet produced by a tachograph or kept as a temporary sheet which that person has to retain or be able to produce,

(2) at any time enter a vehicle and inspect the recording equipment and any record sheet on the vehicle,

(3) at any reasonable time, enter premises where he has reason to believe such a vehicle is kept or such records or registers, are to be found and inspect any vehicle, records or register he finds there.

He may also, by written notice, require a person to produce records at the office of the traffic commissioners or licensing authority not less than 10 days after service of the notice [7(2)]. References to inspection and copying a record include applying the record to any process for eliciting information from it [7(9)].

The making of false entries or altering entries, with intent to deceive, in records or registers is an offence and such documents can be seized [7(5)(6)].

Tachographs cannot be used in accordance with the E.E.C. Regulation unless they are installed by approved fitters and workshops. Regulation 8 of the 1977 Regulations enables the Secretary of State to approve fitters and workshops for the installation and repair of recording equipment. His approval must be in writing and it may contain conditions as to fees, the work premises, procedure, training, inspection of premises and the display of an approval sign [8(2) (3)]. A list of approved fitters and workshops has to be published from time to time by the Secretary of State [8(4)].

The exemption from keeping ordinary record sheets is given to a driver and his employer by Regulation 9. It states that where recording equipment in a vehicle to which the Regulations apply conforms to the construction requirements of E.E.C. Regulations 1463/70, is used in accordance with Articles 15 and 17 and the requirements relating to manual entries and temporary sheets are complied with they are exempt from the Drivers' Hours (Keeping of Records) Regulations 1976.

MODEL FOR DRIVER'S RECORD BOOK

(Note: The model set out below is that prescribed by Council Regulation (EEC) No. 543/69 of March 25, 1959 as amended by Council Regulation (EEC) No. 514/72 on February 28, 1972, and described by those Regulations as an 'individual control book'. The book must be of standard A6 format (105 mm × 148 mm) or a larger format.)

(*a*) FRONT SHEET

| I | INDIVIDUAL CONTROL BOOK |
| | FOR CREW MEMBERS IN ROAD TRANSPORT |

II Country ....

III Date book first used: ....19.........

IV Date book last used:...19.........

V Surname, first name(s), date of birth and address of holder of book:
....
....

VI Name, address, telephone number and stamp (if any) of the undertaking:
....
....
....
....
....
....

VII Operator's Licence No. (goods vehicles only). ....

Book No...

                (to be stamped or perforated)

INSTRUCTIONS
FOR THE USE OF THE INDIVIDUAL CONTROL BOOK

1.   This individual control book is issued in conformity with (specify relevant laws and regulations) ....

To the Undertaking

2.   After completing items V, VI and VII on the front sheet, issue a book to each crew member employed by you, in conformity with the laws and regulations referred to in paragraph 1 above.

3.   Keep a register showing the names of the persons to whom books have been issued, the serial number of each book issued, and the dates of issue. Require the holder to sign in the margin of the register.

4.   Give the holder the necessary instructions for correct use of the book.

5.   Examine the daily sheets and the weekly report every week or, if prevented from doing so, as soon thereafter as possible. Sign the weekly report.

6.   Withdraw the used books, observing the time-limit specified in paragraph 9 below, and hold them at the disposal of the authorized inspecting officers for not less than one year. Enter the date of the last daily sheet in the register referred to in paragraph 3 above.

To Crew Members

7.   This control book is personal. Carry it with you when on duty and produce it to any authorized inspecting officer on request. Hand it over to your employer when you leave the undertaking.

8.   Produce this control book to your employer every week or, if prevented from doing so, as soon thereafter as possible, so that he can check your entries and sign the weekly report.

9.   When the book is completed, keep it for two weeks so that you can produce it at any time to an authorized inspecting officer, and then hand it as soon as possible to your employer. Keep a copy of the weekly reports.

Front sheet

10. Make sure that your surname, first name(s), date of birth and address are filled in correctly (item V).

11. Enter the date on which you first use the book (item III).

12. After use, enter the date when you last used the book (item IV).

Daily sheet

13. Fill in a daily sheet for every day on which you have been employed as a crew member.

14. Enter in box 2 the registration number of any vehicle used during the day.

15. The symbols used have the following meaning:

total period of uninterrupted rest before going on duty

daily rest period

breaks

driving periods

periods of attendance at work

16. Enter your period of daily rest (symbol), breaks (symbol) and the time during which you were engaged in activities represented by symbols 6 and 7 by drawing a horizontal line across the hours concerned opposite the appropriate symbol, and connect the horizontal lines by vertical lines. There will thus be a continuous line over the full length of each strip (see example in the book).

17. Entries must be made at the beginning and end of each period to which they relate.

18. In box 16 ("Remarks") enter the name of the second driver, if any. This box may also be used to explain any breach of the requirements or to correct particulars given elsewhere (see paragraph 24). The employer or an inspecting officer may also insert his remarks in this box.

19. Opposite box 12, enter the number of hours of uninterrupted rest (daily rest) taken immediately before coming on duty. If this period begins in one day and ends in the following day the figure will be the total achieved by adding together the rest period taken at the end of the previous day and the rest period taken at the beginning of the day to which the sheet relates.

20. Before departure, enter opposite "Beginning of duty" in box 11 the number of kilometres/miles shown on the recorder; at the end of duty, enter opposite "End of duty" in box 11 the new number of kilometres/miles shown on the recorder and note the total distance covered.

21. Sign the daily sheet.

Weekly report

22. This report should be made out at the end of every period of one week in which one or more daily sheets have been made out. For days on which you were on duty without being a crew member, ie for which there was no need to make out a daily sheet, enter the figure "0" opposite box G and the duration of duty periods opposite box H; if you did not engage in a particular activity, enter the figure "0" opposite boxes G and H and add an explanation, such as "on leave", "day off".

23. Enter opposite boxes F and G the figures shown opposite boxes 12 and 13 of the relevant daily sheets.

General note

24. No erasures, corrections or additions may be made in the book. Any mistakes, even of form only, must be corrected under "Remarks" (box 16).

25. No sheets may be destroyed.

26. All entries must be made in ink or with a ball-point pen.

(c) **DAILY SHEET**

2. Registration No. of vehicle(s)		1. DAILY SHEET No		3. Day of week and date

Operators Licence Nos

(Time grid chart from 1–12 and 13–24 hours with rows 4, 5, 6, 7 repeated twice)

8. Place of coming on duty: 9. Place of going off duty:

10. Transport of goods.
Permissible maximum weight of the combination of vehicles – Lorry with trailer or articulated vehicles (where applicable) :

10a. Passenger transport.
System of daily rest selected:

		Number of hours
11. Distance recorder:	End of duty	km/miles	12.
	Beginning of duty:	km/miles	13.
	Total distance covered .... km/miles		14.
16. Remarks and signature:			15. Total 13 + 14 If applicable.

Book No

(d) Example of Completed Daily Sheet

| 2. Registration No. of vehicle(s) ABC 123 L Operators Licence Nos D . 123456 | 1. DAILY SHEET No 11 | 2. Day of week and date Tuesday 7 September 1972 |

(Time chart columns: 13, 14, 15, 16, 17, 18, 19, 20, 21, 22, 23, 24 / 1, 2, 3, 4, 5, 6, 7, 8, 9, 10, 11, 12)

Book No 21

8. Place of coming on duty: Bristol

9. Place of going off duty: Nottingham

10. Transport of goods.
Permissible maximum weight of the combination of vehicles – Lorry with trailer or articulated vehicles (where applicable) 19 Tons

10a. Passenger transport.
System of daily rest selected:

		Number of hours
12.		12
13.		6¾
14.		3
15. Total 13 + 14		9¾
	If applicable	

11. Distance recorder: End of duty 21230 miles
Beginning of duty 21090 miles
Total distance covered ......140.... miles

16. Remarks and signature: J. Smith

Note 1.   In practice, boxes 10 and 10a will both be completed on the same daily sheet only where a crew member has carried out a passenger transport operation and a goods transport operation on the same day. In box 10a (completed only by crew members of passenger vehicles) the entry should be either "10 h" or "11 h", according to the system of daily rest periods applying to the crew member.

Note 2.   Opposite box 12, if 12 hours is entered as the total period of uninterrupted rest taken prior to going on duty, this means that the driver went off duty at 7 pm on the previous day, because adding the 5 hours from 7 pm to midnight on the previous day to the 7 hours entered in box 4 gives a total of 12 hours.

(e) WEEKLY REPORT

A.   Surname and first name(s) of crew member

....

B.   WEEKLY REPORT

C.   From .... to .... 19 ..... inclusive

D. Days of the weekly period								J. Weekly total:
E. Daily sheet no								
F.								

Hours of occupational activities	G.								
	H.								
	I G+H								

K.   Remarks: ....

....

....

L.   Date of preceding weekly rest period: ....

M.   Signature of crew member: ....

N.   Signature of employer: ....

     Book No ....

FORM OF REGISTER OF DRIVERS' RECORD BOOKS

Transport Act 1968/Council Regulation (EEC) No. 543/69: Register of Record Books

REGISTER NO. ....

PAGE NO. ....

Name of Employer or Owner-Driver..................................

Operator's Licence Number (Goods Vehicles)..................................

Place at which Books Issued..................................

1. Record Book Serial No.	2. Issued to: (Driver's full name and address)	3. Date of Issue	4. Signature of employer issuing book	5. Name and address of any other known employer of driver	6. Date of return of book	7. Date of last daily sheet in book	8. Driver's signature

CARRIAGE OF ANIMALS

The operator of a road vehicle used for carrying animals must keep or cause to be kept a record in a prescribed form (shown on page 95) in respect of the vehicle and animals [1024/75/17]. Animals are cattle, sheep, swine, goats and horses [2(1)].

Entries in the record sheet relating to loading, unloading, watering and feeding must be made immediately the event has taken place. All other entries must be made within 18 hours of the movement. The record must be available at all reasonable times at the operator's usual place of business [17(2)]. If an animal is transferred from one vehicle to another on a journey the first carrier must supply the second carrier with information to enable him to complete his record [17(3)].

Exemptions from record keeping are given to a vehicle (a) used by a circus owner for carrying circus animals; (b) used to carry a horse on a journey completed within 3 hours; (c) used by its owner for the carriage of his own horse and used by him or his agent for recreational purposes only; and (d) used by the owner of stables licensed by the Jockey Club to take horses to or from races or places for training. The last two exemptions do not apply where the journey is not completed within 12 hours [17(4), (5)].

The records requirements do not apply to a vehicle having an internal length not over 3·1 metres owned by the owner or occupier of an agricultural unit (other than a dealer) and which is used by him, his family or employees for carrying animals to or from the unit as long as the journey is within a 40 kilometre radius of the point of loading or unloading [19(1)]. Neither are records required in respect of a vehicle registered outside Great Britain, or normally kept outside Great Britain, and which is used to carry a horse brought temporarily into Great Britain for racing, breeding or other temporary purpose [19(2)].

It is the duty of a local authority to enforce these requirements [21].

Form of record in respect of the carriage of animals by road

Name and full address of owner or other
person having the management of vehicle ....

....

....

Description of vehicle ....

Registration number ....

Name of driver	Date and time of loading animals	Number and description of animals carried	(i) Premises from which moved person from whom delivery was taken (if known)	Time(s) and place(s) of feeding and watering (see Note 4)	Time of unloading animals	(i) Premises to which moved (ii) person taking delivery (if known)	Date when and premises where vehicle was cleansed and disinfected in accordance with the order
(1)	(2)	(3)	(4)	(5)	(6)	(7)	(8)

NOTES
1. Entries relating to times of loading, feeding and watering, and unloading, to be made when loading, feeding and watering, and unloading, take place, and other entries as soon as possible after completion of the journey; and in any case within 18 hours.
2. Entries to be made in a permanent and legible form.
3. Record to be available at the office or usual place of business of the person having the management of the vehicle to which it relates; to be retained there for a period of 6 months from date of latest entry; and to be produced on demand.
4. Column (5) to be completed where a journey exceeds 12 hours.

[1024/75/Sched. 4]

LIGHTING

Road Traffic Act 1972
Road Vehicles (Registration and Licensing) Regulations, No. 450/71
Road Vehicles Lighting Regulations, No. 694/71
Motor Vehicles (Rear Markings) Regulations, No. 1700/70
Motor Vehicles (Rear Markings) (Amendment) Regulations, No. 842/72
Road Vehicles Lighting (Amendment) Regulations, No. 1006/73
Road Vehicles (Use of Lights during Daytime) Regulations, No. 245/75
Road Vehicles Lighting (Standing Vehicles) (Exemption) (General) Regulations, No. 1494/75
International Carriage of Dangerous Goods (Rear Markings on Motor Vehicles) Regulations, No. 2111/75
Road Vehicles Lighting (Amendment of Enactments) Regulations, No. 1559/77
Road Vehicles Lighting (Amendment) Regulations, No. 1560/77
Road Vehicles (Rear Fog Lamps) Regulations, No. 1260/78

FRONT LAMPS

During the hours of darkness vehicles, other than invalid carriages and solo motor cycles, must carry two lamps each showing a white light to the front [Act 1927/68]. Yellow lights may be shown if they are incorporated in headlamps which show only a yellow light [1559/77]. The hours of darkness are those between half-an-hour after sunset and half-an-hour before sunrise [Act 1972/82]. If these lamps are not fitted with frosted glass or other diffusing material and their total power exceeds 7 W they must be capable of being dipped in the same way as headlights [694/71/9].

These lamps, known as obligatory front lamps, must be fixed at the same height above the ground [694/71/5] except in the case of an asymmetric vehicle where the requirement shall be complied with as far as reasonably possible having regard to the shape of the vehicle [3(6A)]. The highest part of the illuminating surface of a front obligatory lamp above the ground should not be more than 1900 mm in the case of a horse-drawn vehicle and 2100 mm in the case of a land tractor, agricultural tractor, industrial tractor, agricultural implement

96

or engineering plant [4(1)(a)]. In the case of any other vehicle the height should not exceed 1700 mm but if, due to the shape of the vehicle's body, this limit cannot be met the height may be up to 2100 mm [4(1)(b)]. These height limits do not apply to passenger vehicles with eight or more seats or to vehicles propelling a snow plough [4(2)].

Except in the case of a tower wagon, the distance between the outer edge of the illuminating surface of an obligatory front lamp and the outer edge of the vehicle must not exceed 400 mm [4(3)].

A vehicle drawn by another vehicle need not carry obligatory front lamps if the distance between the two vehicles does not exceed 5 ft [Act 1972/77(1)]. A drawn vehicle which is more than 5 ft behind the towing vehicle need not carry obligatory front lamps if its width does not exceed 1600 mm [77(2A) and 1559/77] but it must, instead, be equipped with white forward facing reflectors [694/71/35A]. These reflectors, which cannot be triangular, must be fitted vertically so that their outer edge is not more than 400 mm from the outer edge of the vehicle; not closer together than 600 mm or, if the vehicle is less than 1300 mm wide, 400 mm; not less than 350 mm nor more than 900 mm above ground; and be kept clean and marked with a specified approval mark [35A(2)].

If the trailer or any part of its load projects laterally more than 1 ft beyond the drawing vehicle's obligatory front lamp on that side the trailer must carry a white light within 1 ft of the outer edge of the trailer or its load [Act 1972/77(3)].

An additional white lamp, of not more than 7 W and with frosted glass, must be used to show the position of every jack when in use on a vehicle with a movable platform [694/71/67].

The centre of a front lamp which exceeds 7 W must not be more than 1200 mm above ground level, except in the case of a vehicle fitted with a snow-plough, certain aerodrome vehicles, land tractors, agricultural tractors, industrial tractors, land implements or engineering plant, and it must not be less than 500 mm from the ground, except in the case of a lamp used only in fog or falling snow [694/71/8]. These restrictions do not apply to a vehicle first used before January 1, 1952, or to specified Crown vehicles [8(2)].

A front lamp which exceeds 7 W must be fitted so that the light (a) is at all times a dipped beam, (b) can be deflected by the driver to become a dipped beam, or (c) can be switched off by a device which at the same time either causes that lamp or another lamp to emit a dipped beam. A lamp (unless used only in fog or falling snow) will not comply with (a) above unless it is also fixed so that the lower edge of its illuminating surface is at least 500 mm above the ground [694/71/9]. A dipped beam is defined as a beam of light emitted by a headlamp which is deflected downwards or both downwards and to the left so that it is at all times incapable of dazzling a person more than 7·7 metres from the lamp and whose eye level is at least 1·1 m above ground level [3].

No more than two front lamps, other than obligatory lamps, may be deflected sideways by the movement of the front wheels when steered provided a dipped or dippable headlamp is not more than 1200 mm above the ground [10]. Bulbs and sealed beam lamps must be marked with their wattage [11] and obligatory front lamps on vehicles first used on or after January 1, 1972, must have an approval mark [12].

Lamps which exceed 7 W must not be kept lit while the vehicle is stationary on a road but this does not apply during an enforced stoppage of the vehicle; to a large passenger vehicle setting down or picking up passengers; to interior lighting; a lamp on a breakdown vehicle lighting the scene of an accident or breakdown; a tower wagon in operation; direction indicators; authorised blue and amber beacons; searchlights on military, police or fire brigade vehicles; or searchlights on specified repair vehicles [13].

No vehicle must show a red light to the front [Act 1972/70].

OBLIGATORY HEADLAMPS

Wheeled motor vehicles which have electrically operated obligatory front lamps must be equipped with headlamps when used on a road [694/71/14].

Exceptions are: vehicles first used before 1931; pedestrian-controlled vehicles; agricultural implements, land locomotives, land tractors, works trucks or road rollers; vehicles incapable of exceeding 6 m.p.h. on the level; certain vehicles brought temporarily into Great Britain; vehicles purchased in Great Britain free from purchase tax and which are to leave Britain within 12 months; military vehicles; vehicles of a visiting force; electrically propelled goods vehicles incapable of exceeding 15 m.p.h. on the level [14(2)]; and vehicles made in Great Britain and supplied at zero rate of value added tax for export [1006/73].

Special provisions are made for vehicles with two wheels, for vehicles with three wheels first used before 1972 and for vehicles with three wheels first used on or after January 1, 1972, which do not exceed 400 kg unladen or 1·3 m wide [15].

A vehicle which has (a) three wheels (other than a motor cycle combination), was first used on or after January 1, 1972, and has an unladen weight over 400 kg or is over 1·3 m wide, or (b) has four or more wheels, must be fitted with either (1) a matched pair of headlamps which can emit main and dipped beams or, in the case of a vehicle which cannot exceed 25 m.p.h., only dipped beams, or (2) two or more matched pairs of headlamps so arranged that the outermost pair of headlamps is capable of emitting dipped beams without at the same time emitting main beams and a switch enables all main beams to be extinguished and at the same time leaving a dipped beam or causing a dipped beam to be emitted (except for a p.s.v. first used before October, 1969 which can emit one dipped beam) [694/71/16(1), (2)]. The rated wattage of each lamp must be at least 30 W [16(3)]. Except for engineering plant and industrial tractors, the headlamp which emits a dipped beam must be positioned on one side of a vehicle so that (a) in the case of a vehicle used before October 1, 1969, it is at least 350 mm away from the other such lamp or, in the case of a vehicle first used on or after that date, is at least 600 mm away from the other such lamp, and (b) in the case of a vehicle first used on or after January 1, 1972, the lamp is not more than 400 mm from the outermost part of the vehicle on that side [16(4)].

Headlamps and side lamps may be combined in one unit [17]. Except for public service vehicles first used before October, 1969, the lamps forming a pair of headlamps must have the same area and shape when lit and both main or dipped beams must be capable of being switched on or off together [19]. Both lamps in a pair must emit the same colour light which must be either white or yellow [19(3), 20].

Subject to specified exceptions, when a vehicle with at least four wheels, and which is required to have obligatory headlamps, is in motion during the hours of darkness on a road which is not equipped with lighted street lamps placed not more than 200 yards apart a pair of its obligatory headlamps must be lit. The exceptions are (1) in fog or falling snow if two 'permitted' lamps are kept lit; (2) to a p.s.v. used before October, 1969, if one obligatory headlamp is kept lit or, in fog or falling snow and the vehicle has a fog lamp, if that lamp is kept lit; (3) to a vehicle being drawn by another vehicle; or (4) to a vehicle with a snow-plough in front. Two 'permitted' lamps here means two front fog lamps or one front fog lamp and one headlamp (other than an obligatory headlamp) and which are (a) one on each side of the vehicle, (b) the same height above the ground, (c) the same distance from the centre of the vehicle, and (d) in the case of a vehicle first used before January 1, 1971, the lamps are at least 350 mm apart and, on a vehicle first used on or after this date, the lamps are not more than 400 mm from the side of the vehicle [21]. Similar requirements but different exceptions are made for two- and three-wheeled vehicles [22].

A requirement that lamps forming a pair be fitted at the same height or the same distance from the centre of the vehicle shall, in the case of an asymmetric vehicle, be complied with as far as reasonably possible having regard to the shape of the vehicle [694/71/3(6A)].

When a vehicle fitted with obligatory side and headlamps is moving on a road in daytime hours those lamps must be lit if conditions of poor visibility prevail on that road [245/75/2(1)]. Poor visibility conditions are defined as such conditions affecting visibility (whether consisting of, or including, fog, smoke, heavy rain or spray, snow, dense cloud or similar conditions) which seriously reduce the ability of the driver, after cleaning the windscreen, to see others on the road or of others to see the vehicle [1(2)]. Front fog lamps and single headlamps can be used if they can legally be used instead of headlamps at night on unlit roads [2(3)].

DUAL-PURPOSE LAMPS

Where a dual-purpose lamp (a combined obligatory front lamp and obligatory rear lamp) is carried on a sidecar, land tractor, agricultural tractor or a hand-propelled vehicle, the illuminated area must be within 410 mm of the side of the vehicle or its equipment [694/71/7].

REAR LAMPS

Two obligatory rear lamps are required on all vehicles and trailers (unless the distance between any two is not more than 5 ft, in which case only the rearmost one needs rear lamps [Act 1972/77]. Existing passenger vehicles with 8 or more seats may have only one obligatory rear lamp [694/71/1st Sched.(5)]. There are special provisions for vehicles in the service of Home and Visiting Forces [57, 58].

The prescribed position of the two rear lamps varies between different types of vehicle, but on all motor vehicles requiring two rear lamps, the lamps must be at least 21 in apart with one on each side of the centre line. In the case of passenger-carrying vehicles and trailers (other than goods-carrying and special trailers, agricultural implements or engineering plant) the rear lamps must be not more than 30 in from the rear of the vehicle. For locomotives, heavy tractors (not defined), goods vehicles and trailers, including special trailers, the distance must not exceed 3 ft 6 in and, for agricultural implements and engineering plant, 4 ft 6 in.

Prescribed maximum distances from the edge of the vehicle or its equipment to each rear lamp on its respective side are: motor cycles and sidecars, 1 ft 4 in; new 8- or more seat passenger vehicles, 2 ft; locomotives, heavy tractors, goods vehicles and all trailers, 2 ft 6 in; agricultural implements and engineering plant, 1 ft 4 in.

The maximum height from ground is 3 ft 6 in but for special trailers, engineering plant and agricultural implements, 6 ft 3 in. There is no maximum height for existing passenger vehicles with 8 or more seats.

Minimum heights are 1 ft 3 in except for special trailers, engineering plant and agricultural implements for which there is no limit.

All the foregoing measurements are subject to exceptions which are specified [694/71/23 and Sched. 1].

None of the positioning requirements of Regulation 23 and Schedule 1 applies to a vehicle which carries two obligatory rear lamps which comply with Schedule 1A [23A and 1560/77]. This Schedule states that both lamps should be the same distance from the centre line of the vehicle and the same height above the ground; the outer edge of the lamp should not be more than 400 mm from the outer edge of the vehicle; the lamps should not be closer together than 600 mm or, if the vehicle is less than 1300 mm wide, 400 mm; not less than 350 mm nor more than 1500 mm above the ground (but if the shape of the body prevents them being fitted under 1500 mm they may be up to 2100 mm high); the minimum horizontal angles of visibility of each lamp should be 45° outboard and 80° inboard or vice versa; and the minimum vertical angles of visibility of each lamp should be 15° above and below the horizontal or, in the case of a lamp less than 750 mm above ground level, 15° above and 5° below the horizontal.

Except for existing large passenger vehicles and lamps bearing specified approval marks, the illuminated area of a rear lamp must be at least equal to the area of a 2 in diameter circle [694/71/24(2)]. When lit both lamps must have the same appearance and be so wired that failure of one does not affect the other [24(6)]. Existing large passenger vehicles are those first used before October 1, 1954 [3(1)].

Any requirement that lamps forming a pair be fitted at the same height or the same distance from the centre of the vehicle shall, in the case of an asymmetric vehicle, be complied with as far as reasonably possible having regard to the shape of the vehicle [694/71/3(6A)].

Different specification numbers or approval marks are required on various classes of vehicle of varying ages [694/71/25]. Except for lamps with certain approval marks, the rated wattage of a bulb must not be less than 5 W and it must be marked on it [24(5)].

An additional red lamp not over 7 W and with frosted glass must be used to show the position of jacks in use on a vehicle with a movable platform [694/71/67].

Except for lights needed to illuminate a vehicle interior, a number plate, a taximeter or 'any device for giving signals to overtaking traffic' or, in a p.s.v., lights needed to illuminate route or destination indicators, no light must be shown to the rear of a vehicle other than a red light or a white light for the purpose of reversing [Act 1972/70].

Special provisions, however, apply to ambulance and vehicles used for police, fire-brigade or fire salvage purposes, blood transfusion or coastguard services which can carry a blue light, and to road clearance vehicles, breakdown vehicles, road cleansing or maintenance vehicles and mains servicing vehicles which can carry an amber light.

PARKED VEHICLES

Motor cars for not more than 7 passengers, goods vehicles not over 30 cwt unladen and invalid carriages may be parked in a recognised parking place or on a road during the hours of darkness without displaying front and rear lights so long as the vehicle does not carry a load which has a side or rear projection which requires lighting and the vehicle is not drawing a trailer. If parked on a road the road must be subject to a 30 m.p.h. speed limit; except in a one-way street, the near-side of the vehicle must be close to the kerb; and no part of the vehicle may be within 15 yd of any road junction [1494/75]. A recognised street parking place is defined as a place (a) set apart by the local authority under specified statutory provisions, (b) marked out with broken white lines, (c) which has a different surface or texture from the main carriageway, or (d) the limits of which are indicated by a continuous strip of surface different from the main carriageway.

REAR REFLECTORS

Generally all vehicles when on a road during the hours of darkness must carry two red reflectors facing to the rear [Act 1972/69] but, in the case of a vehicle drawing another vehicle, the leading vehicle does not require reflectors unless the drawn vehicle is more than 5 ft behind it [77(1)].

The positioning of reflectors varies from one vehicle to another but no part of a reflector should be more than 3 ft 6 in above ground level except for locomotives, heavy tractors, goods vehicles or goods trailers which are permitted 4 ft 6 in and special trailers, engineering plant and agricultural implements which are permitted 5 ft. No part of a reflector should be below 15 in above ground level except for special trailers, engineering plant and agricultural implements for which no minimum height is specified. Generally reflectors should be 21 in apart and not more than 30 in from the rear of the vehicle but there are specified exceptions, just as there are with any of the above positioning figures [694/71/30 and Sched. 2].

None of the positioning requirements of Regulation 30 and Schedule 2 applies to a vehicle which carries two obligatory reflectors which comply with Schedule 2A [30A and 1560/77]. This Schedule states that both reflectors should be the same distance from the centre line of the vehicle and the same height above the ground; the outer edge of the reflector should not be more than 400 mm from the outer edge of the vehicle; the reflectors should not be closer together than 600 mm or, if the vehicle is less than 1300 mm wide, 400 mm; not less than 350 mm nor more than 900 mm above the ground; the minimum horizontal angles of visibility of each reflector should be 30° inboard and 30° outboard; the minimum vertical angles of visibility of each reflector should be 15° above and below the horizontal or, in the case of a reflector less than 750 mm above ground level, 15° above and 5° below the horizontal; and triangular reflectors must not be fitted to motor vehicles but must be fitted to trailers.

Any requirement that reflectors forming a pair be fitted at the same height or the same distance from the centre of the vehicle shall, in the case of an asymmetric vehicle, be complied with as far as reasonably possible having regard to the shape of the vehicle [694/71/3(6A)].

A reflector must be fitted in a vertical position, face squarely to the rear and be kept clean and plainly visible [694/71/31(2)]. Except for reflectors bearing specified approval marks, the reflecting area must be at least equal to the area of a 1½ in diameter circle [31(2), (3)].

Reflectors on motor vehicles first registered or supplied before July 1, 1970, must be marked with a specification number B.S. 2515 or AU40 or with an international approval mark containing the roman numeral I or II (certain vehicles imported from Italy are exempt) [694/71/32]. Reflectors on motor vehicles first registered or supplied on or after this date cannot be marked with B.S. 2515 or with an international mark containing the roman numeral II [33]. Reflectors fitted to trailers must be the triangular type and marked with either the specification number AU40, followed by LIII or LIIIA, or with an international approval mark containing the roman numeral III [34, 35].

REVERSING LIGHTS

One or two reversing lights may be fitted at the rear of a vehicle. They must be white lights, of a total of not more than 24 W each, and fitted so that they cannot dazzle anyone standing more than 25 ft away with an eye level at or above 3 ft 6 in [694/71/26, 27].

Reversing lights must be switched on either by the selection of the vehicle's reverse gear or by a separate switch which, except on vehicles first registered before July 1, 1954, is used for no other purpose. Vehicles first registered on or after July 1, 1954, and fitted with reversing lights which are operated by a driver's switch must be equipped with a tell-tale device to indicate to the driver, while in his seat, when the reversing lights are in operation [28].

No reversing lamp shall be lit except so far as is necessary for the purpose of reversing [29].

REARWARD PROJECTING LOADS

When, during the hours of darkness, a vehicle carries a load projecting more than 3 ft 6 in behind its tail-lights, it must carry a rear lamp within 3 ft 6 in of the rear end of the load. This must be in addition to the obligatory rear lamps [Act 1972/76(2)].

For a vehicle carrying a fire-escape, and a land tractor or an agricultural tractor carrying an agricultural implement, whether the implement is a vehicle or not, the additional rear lamp must be within 6 ft of the rear of the load [694/71/36].

When a goods vehicle carries a projecting load which would obscure the rear lamps and reflectors if carried in the normal position, the rear lamps and reflectors must be attached to the load, instead of the vehicle, in corresponding positions except that the permitted distance from the rear must be measured from the rear of the load instead of from the rear of the vehicle [694/71/62].

SIDE PROJECTING LOADS

Except for a tower wagon, no part of a vehicle may extend laterally more than 400 mm beyond the outer edge of the illuminating surface of an obligatory front lamp [694/71/4(3)]. Any vehicle carrying a load which projects beyond the side of a vehicle must have a sidelight within 12 in of the extremity of the load. This can be an additional sidelight or the normal one in an altered position [Act 1972/76/(1)].

When a wide load is carried, an additional rear lamp must be fitted within 12 in of the outer edge of the load on the same side of the vehicle. If the vehicle is drawing one or more trailers, the extra rear lamp or lamps necessary to indicate the overhang of the load on the vehicle or trailers must be fitted on the rearmost trailer. Vehicles carrying loose agricultural produce which is not baled or crated are exempt [694/71/37].

Special equipment on a vehicle with a movable platform is not, for the above purposes, regarded as a load [36(1), 37(4)].

SIDE MARKER LAMPS

These are lamps showing a white light to the side of some trailers and some vehicle and trailer combinations through an arc of 70 degrees forward from a line at right angles to the vehicle length, and a red light to the side through a 70-degree arc rearward from that line [694/71/3]. Lamps must not exceed 7 W each, and, except for vehicles carrying abnormal indivisible loads, on which lamps can be up to 2300 mm from the ground, must be not more than 1530 mm from the ground (or 2100 mm if the bodywork does not allow fitting below 1530 mm) [48].

Side marker lamps must be fitted where the overall length of a vehicle or vehicles, inclusive of any load, is more than 60 ft and be so placed on each side that (a) one lamp is not more than 30 ft from the front of the outfit or load and (b) one lamp is within 10 ft of the rear of the outfit or load. Additional lamps must be fitted between (a) and (b) so that there is no space of more than 10 ft without a lamp [694/71/ 40, 41]. Side marker lamps are not needed: when a vehicle being drawn is broken down; when the vehicle is a single vehicle, fitted with a special appliance or carrying a projecting load marked with projection marker boards and which are illuminated by indirect light [42].

Where a combination of two or more vehicles (not including an articulated vehicle) carries a supported load (a load supported by any two of the vehicles forming part of such a combination) and the overall length of the outfit or load is over 40 ft but not more than 60 ft, side marker lamps must be fitted to each side so that one lamp is not forward of, or more than 5 ft to the rear of, the rearmost part of the motor vehicle. Also, if the supported load extends more than 30 ft behind the rear of the motor vehicle, a lamp must be fitted in a position not in front of, and not more than 5 ft to the rear of, the centre point of the length of the load [43, 44].

If a trailer exceeds 9·15 metres in length (excluding its drawbar), a side marker lamp must be fitted on each side, so that they are not forward of, or more than 1530 mm behind, the trailer's centre point [45].

FRONT CORNER MARKER LAMPS

Trailers and semi-trailers must, in general, be fitted with front corner marker lamps [694/71/45]. Exceptions are: a trailer not exceeding 2300 mm long (excluding its drawbar); a trailer drawn by a passenger vehicle (not more than 7 passengers) or dual-purpose vehicle provided that the overall length of the combination does not exceed 12·2 metres; a broken-down vehicle when drawn by another vehicle; a trailer which in any case is required to have its own lights to the front because it is more than 5 ft from the drawing vehicle; and a trailer not over 1600 mm wide [47(1)]. Nor are front corner marker lamps needed on a trailer if it or its load projects more than 12 in sideways beyond the lamps on the drawing vehicle and the trailer is already fitted, as required by Section 77(3) of the 1972 Act, with front lights within 1 ft of the extreme width of the trailer or its load [47(2)].

One front corner marker lamp must be fitted on each side of the trailer so that no part of the illuminated area is more than 1530 mm from the front of the trailer. This distance may go up to 3660 mm provided no part of the width of the trailer in front of the lamps exceeds one half of the overall width of the trailer [694/71/46]. No part of the trailer must project outwards more than 310 mm beyond the nearest illuminated part of the lamp, or any point in a vertical line above or below. If the lamps are fitted over 910 mm but not more than 1530 mm from the trailer front, and within 1530 mm from the ground, within which height limit they are within 310 mm of the trailer sides, it is permissible for some higher part of the trailer (e.g. an elliptical shaped tank) as well as any part of the trailer behind the lamps to protrude up to 510 mm beyond the vertical line of the lamps. The foremost part of a trailer does not include the drawbar or any part of the trailer or body which protrudes forward if it is more than 1520 mm from the ground [46(3)].

A front corner marker lamp is defined as a lamp showing a white light to the side and front of the trailer through an arc of 90 degrees [694/71/3]. The highest part of each lamp must not be more than 1530 mm (or 2100 mm if the bodywork does not allow fitting below 1530 mm) from the ground or, when an indivisible load is carried, 2300 mm. Each lamp must be connected to the electric lighting system of the outfit (trailers built and used for carrying round timber may use a battery of at least 3 V) and fitted with a bulb or bulbs with a rated wattage not exceeding 7 W. The light must be diffused and each lamp must have an illuminated area equivalent to a circle of 25 mm diameter or carry a specified approval mark [48, 49].

SIDE-FACING REFLECTORS

Motor vehicles over 8 m (26 ft 3 in) long and trailers over 5 m (16 ft 4¾ in) long, must when on a road during the hours of darkness, carry side-facing amber-coloured reflectors marked with an international approval mark [694/71/50–52]. Exempt are certain temporarily imported vehicles; public service vehicles; a trailer which is a broken-down motor vehicle not over 8 m; an unfinished vehicle going for completion; a vehicle going to a port for export; a mobile crane; engineering plant; or a dump truck authorised under the Special Types Order [50].

On each side of the vehicle there must be two reflectors one of which must be within 500 mm (19·7 in) of the rear of the vehicle and the other must be in the centre third portion of the vehicle [52–55]. No part of a reflector must be within 400 mm (15¾ in) of the ground; on motor vehicles first used on or after October 1, 1970, and trailers made on or after this date reflectors must be within 1200 mm (47¼ in) of the ground; on older vehicles the maximum height is 1500 mm (59 in); the reflecting area must be vertical, and kept clean and plainly visible [56]. Drawbars and towing brackets are excluded from the length of a trailer [54(3)].

None of the positioning requirements of Regulations 52 to 56 apply to a vehicle which is fitted with side-facing reflectors in accordance with Schedule 2B [56A and 1560/77]. This Schedule requires that side-facing reflectors be carried not lower than 350 mm nor higher than 900 mm above ground level (or up to 1500 mm if the bodywork prevents them being carried below 900 mm); the foremost reflector must not be more than 3 m from the front of the vehicle and at least one reflector must be fitted in the middle third of the vehicle (in the case of a drawbar outfit the drawbar is included in determining these distances); the rearmost reflector must not be more than 1 m from the rear of the vehicle; the distance between two reflectors must not be more than 3 m; reflectors must be kept clean and plainly visible; and they cannot be triangular.

BLUE AND AMBER BEACONS

A rotating blue light may be carried on motor vehicles used for police, fire brigade or ambulance purposes; fire salvage purposes; Forestry Commission or local authority fire-fighting vehicles; vehicles used for disposal of bombs or explosives; vehicles used for nuclear accidents or incidents involving radioactivity; blood transfusion service vehicles; N.C.B. vehicles used for mine rescue operations; coastguard vehicles; R.A.F. mountain rescue vehicles and R.N.L.I. vehicles used for launching lifeboats [694/71/64(1)(a) and 1006/73]. An amber rotating light may be carried on road-clearance vehicles; breakdown vehicles; vehicles used for inspecting, cleansing, maintaining, adjusting, renewing or installing any apparatus in, on, under or over a road; and on vehicles authorised under the Special Types Order [64(1)(b)]. The centre of the lamp must be at least 5 ft above the ground [64(2)], the light must be visible from a point round it not less than 60 nor more than 150 equal times a minute [64(5)], the total wattage of a blue lamp must not exceed 55 W, that of an amber lamp 36 W [64(7)].

The amber light on a breakdown vehicle may be used only in connection with and in the immediate vicinity of an accident or breakdown, or while a broken-down vehicle is being drawn. Other amber lamps and blue lamps can be used only for the relevant purposes given in Regulation 64(1)(a) & (b) [64(8)].

A breakdown vehicle may carry a lamp which shows a white light to the rear for the purpose of illuminating the scene of an accident or breakdown and an amber rotating lamp must be lit at the same time. The lamp must not be within 5 ft of the ground, it must not be used so as to dazzle drivers but it may be moved by swivelling or deflecting when in immediate vicinity of an accident or breakdown [694/71/65].

STOP LAMPS

Apart from specified exceptions, every motor vehicle first used before January 1, 1971, and every trailer manufactured before that date must be fitted with a stop lamp [694/71/73]. The lamp must be red, be fitted between the centre and off-side of the vehicle at the rear and a duplicate may be fitted on the near-side [72]. Apart from the same exceptions, every motor vehicle first used on or after January 1, 1971, and every trailer manufactured on or after that date must be fitted with two stop lamps which comply with prescribed conditions [74]. The excepted vehicles are:

1. Agricultural trailers, land implements, land locomotives, land tractors, pedestrian-controlled vehicles, works trailers and works trucks.

2. Certain mopeds.

3. Motor vehicles first used before January 1, 1936.

4. Motor vehicles which cannot exceed 15 m.p.h.

5. Motor vehicles and trailers which do not have electrically operated obligatory side lamps or which have no such lamps.

6. Trailers whilst drawn by any motor vehicle not required to be fitted with stop lamps.

7. Trailers drawn by motor vehicles fitted with two stop lamps, the dimensions of the trailer being such that when the trailer is squarely behind the drawing vehicle both stop lamps are visible from a point 6 m behind the rear of the trailer whether it is loaded or not.

8. Every trailer which is a broken-down motor vehicle or which forms part of a broken-down articulated vehicle.

9. In the case of a combination of two or more vehicles, being a motor vehicle drawing a trailer or trailers, the vehicles in that combination other than the rearmost.

[694/71/Sched. 6, Pt. 1]

The conditions which post-1970 vehicle stop lamps have to comply with are that they must show a steady red light visible through an angle 15 degrees above and below the horizontal throughout an angle of 45 degrees to each side of the centre of each lamp; the wattage of a lamp must be 15–36 W; a lamp must not be within 400 mm (15¾ in) of the ground nor higher than 1500 mm (59 in) but may be up to 2100 mm (82·7 in) if the vehicle structure does not allow fitting below 1500 mm; lamps on a motor vehicle or trailer must be operated by application of the driver's foot brake; lamps must be at the same height, the same distance from the centre of the vehicle and not within 600 mm (23·6 in) of each other [Sched. 6, Pt. II].

Stop lamps fitted to motor vehicles first used on or after January 1, 1974, and on trailers manufactured on or after that date, must comply with additional conditions [75] but they do not apply to a motor vehicle manufactured before August 1, 1973 [75(2)]. The additional conditions are that the stop lamps are marked with an approval mark and if they are capable of being operated at two levels of illumination they must be so wired that when the vehicle's obligatory lights are off the higher level of light is emitted by the stop lamps and when the obligatory lights are on the lower level of light is emitted. If a fog lamp is in use at the same time as obligatory lights the stop lamps *may* emit the higher level of light [Sched. 6, Pt. III].

DIRECTION INDICATORS

Apart from excepted vehicles, every motor vehicle first used before September 1, 1965, must be fitted with direction indicators which comply with Part I, II or III of Schedule 5 to the Road Vehicles Lighting Regulation 1971; a motor vehicle used on or after September 1, 1965, and which was made before August 1, 1973 or first used before January 1, 1974, must be fitted with indicators which comply with Part III; and every trailer made after July 1, 1955, and before January 1, 1974, must be fitted with indicators which comply with Part III or VI, but Part III must be complied with if the drawing vehicle complies with Part III [694/71/70(1)].

The excepted vehicles are:—

(a) a motor vehicle—
  (i) which is a two-wheeled motor cycle with or without a side-car attached;
  (ii) which is an industrial tractor, a land locomotive, a land tractor, a works truck or a pedestrian-controlled vehicle;
  (iii) which carries obligatory lamps which are not electrically operated or which carries no such lamps;
  (iv) first used before January 1, 1936;
  (v) which cannot exceed 15 m.p.h.

(b) to a trailer—
  (i)   which is a land implement, a works trailer or an agricultural trailer;
  (ii) which carries obligatory lamps which are not electrically operated or which carries no such lamps;
  (iii) which is drawn by a motor vehicle not fitted with direction indicators;
  (iv) which forms part of an articulated vehicle and was manufactured before September 1, 1965;
  (v)   the dimensions of which are such that when the trailer is squarely behind the drawing vehicle both rear or both side direction indicators on that vehicle are visible from a point 6 m behind the rear of the trailer whether it is loaded or not; or
  (vi) which is a broken-down motor vehicle or forms part of a broken-down articulated vehicle or which draws another trailer behind it.   [70(2)]

Regulations 69(1), (3) & (4) and 70 do not apply to a motor vehicle or trailer fitted with direction indicators in accordance with Schedule 5A [70A and 1560/77].

Parts I and II of Schedule 5 deal with electrically operated indicator arms (known as the semaphore type) and flashing lights.

Fitted on the sides of a vehicle, indicator arms must have an illuminated length of at least 6 in and a breadth of not more than a quarter of the length. When in use, they must remain steady and show a steady or flashing amber light to the front and to the rear. The arms, which must be fitted not more than 6 ft behind the base of the windscreen, must protrude horizontally to the side at least 6 in behind the driver's cab or the body side immediately behind the driver's seat. An additional indicator may be fitted on either side at the front or at the rear. An additional indicator, if fitted, must be operated by the same switch as for the other indicator on the same side of the vehicle. Except for additional indicators fitted before April 1, 1955, any indicator intended to indicate a right-hand turn must be fitted to the right of the centre line and one intended to indicate a left-hand turn must be on the left of the centre line.

A single flashing-light indicator on each side of the vehicle is permissible provided it is not more than 6 ft behind the base of the windscreen and that it shows a flashing light 'visible at a reasonable distance from both the front and the rear of the vehicle'.

When two flashing-light indicators are fitted on each side of a vehicle those at the front and the rear on the same side must be operated by the same switch.

The area of illumination, both to the front and to the rear, must not be less than 12 sq in except in the following cases when it must be at least 3½ sq in; any vehicle of not more than 2 tons unladen or a vehicle with seats for not more than 12 passengers (excluding the driver); provided that in neither case a trailer with four or more wheels is drawn. For this purpose, four-wheeled trailers with two close-coupled wheels on either side are excepted.

No direction indicator must be less than 1 ft 5 in nor more than 7 ft 6 in from the ground except for a public service vehicle which can have a flashing indicator up to 8 ft 6 in on either side if an additional indicator is fitted on the same side within 6 ft 6 in of the ground.

A trailer hauled by a vehicle fitted with flashing direction indicators must itself also have indicators if constructed on or after January 1, 1955. Trailers constructed before that date drawn by vehicles with indicators do not have to carry indicators themselves.

All trailers which are broken-down vehicles are completely exempted.

It is not necessary for the indicators on a trailer to match the type fitted on the hauling vehicle. Thus, when a hauling vehicle has flashing indicators, the indicators on the trailer may be of the flashing or semaphore types.

When trailer indicators are fitted they must be visible at a reasonable distance from any point to the rear of the trailer and they must be operated by the same switch as for those on the drawing vehicle.

Every direction indicator which shows to the front and rear must be amber coloured; those showing only to the front, amber or white; and those showing only to the rear, amber or red. In all cases the light must be diffused by frosted glass or other means. The total power of the bulb or bulbs in each flashing indicator must be not less than 15 W and not more than 36 W. Flashes must be at least 60, but not more than 120, per minute.

The requirements of Part III are more stringent. Only amber-coloured indicators are permitted and the indicators must be of a specified type.

On each side of a motor vehicle there must be (a) a single rear indicator and a single front indicator, or (b) a single rear indicator and at least one shoulder indicator, or (c) at least one side indicator. If the front and rear indicators are more than 19 ft 8 in apart, and always when the motor vehicle forms part of an articulated vehicle, at least one flank indicator is also required. One such flank indicator must be fitted (on each side) so that it is not farther back from the front of the vehicle than one-third of the vehicle's overall length.

Except for a trailer which is a broken-down motor vehicle or

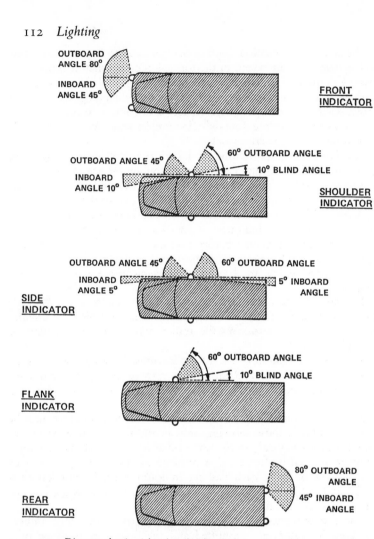

OUTBOARD
ANGLE 80°

INBOARD
ANGLE 45°

FRONT
INDICATOR

OUTBOARD ANGLE 45°

60° OUTBOARD ANGLE

INBOARD
ANGLE 10°

10° BLIND ANGLE

SHOULDER
INDICATOR

OUTBOARD ANGLE 45°

60° OUTBOARD ANGLE

INBOARD
ANGLE 5°

5° INBOARD
ANGLE

SIDE
INDICATOR

60° OUTBOARD ANGLE

10° BLIND ANGLE

FLANK
INDICATOR

80° OUTBOARD
ANGLE

45° INBOARD
ANGLE

REAR
INDICATOR

Diagrams showing inboard, outboard and blind angle requirements

semi-trailer, or a semi-trailer made before September 1, 1965, or a trailer which is wholly within 12 ft of the rear of the drawing vehicle which has appropriate indicators, every trailer must have a rear indicator provided it is drawn by a vehicle fitted with indicators.

Illuminated areas of indicators are the same as for those described for pre-September, 1965, vehicles. Indicators must be at least 12 in from the longitudinal axis of the vehicle. They must not be over 7 ft 6 in from the ground except on public service vehicles on which, if the rear indicators are within 6 ft 6 in, a shoulder or flank indicator may be fitted up to a height of 8 ft 6 in from the ground. No part of any front or rear indicators must be below 1 ft 3 in nor must any other indicator be below 1 ft 8 in from the ground, in all cases when the vehicle is unladen.

In the direction indicator diagrams on p. 101, the inboard, outboard and blind angles are illustrated.

'Inboard angle' means an angle, within which light from the indicator is visible, measured horizontally inwards from a line parallel to the longitudinal axis of the vehicle and passing through the centre of the illuminated area of the indicator; 'outboard angle' means an angle, within which light from the indicator is visible, measured horizontally outwards from a line parallel to the longitudinal axis of the vehicle and passing through the centre of the illuminated area of the indicator; and 'blind angle' means an angle, throughout which no light from the indicator need be visible, measured horizontally outwards from a line parallel to the longitudinal axis of the vehicle and passing through the centre of the illuminated area of the indicator.

Part VI deals with semaphore-type and flashing indicators and the requirements are similar to those contained in Parts I and II referred to above, except that the minimum illuminated area of a flashing indicator fitted to a trailer having two wheels or four close-coupled wheels must be $3\frac{1}{2}$ sq. in and, in any other case, 12 sq. in.

Except for motor vehicles manufactured before August 1, 1973, the direction indicators fitted to motor vehicles first used on or after January 1, 1974, and to trailers manufactured on or after that date (including excepted vehicles which are fitted with indicators) must comply with Part III and be marked with specified approval marks [694/71/71]. In addition, the same dual-intensity light provisions, given above in respect of stop lamps, also apply, except to the rear indicators of a trailer drawn by a motor vehicle (a) not required to be fitted with direction indicators or (b) equipped with rear indicators not bearing the approval mark '2b' [71(6) and 1006/73].

The requirements of Schedule 5A for the positioning of direction indicators are as follows:

1. On each side of a motor vehicle there must be fitted indicators shown as categories 1, 2 and 5 in the diagram (on page 114) and which have (a) the minimum horizontal angles of visibility shown and (b) minimum vertical angles of visibility of 15° above and below the horizontal or, in the case of a category 5 indicator fitted below 750 mm above ground level, 15° above and 5° below the horizontal; Indicators of categories 1 and 5 may be combined;

2. On each side of a trailer there must be fitted an indicator of category 2 which has (a) the minimum horizontal angles of

visibility shown in the diagram and (b) minimum vertical angles of visibility of 15° above and below the horizontal;

3. Direction indicators forming a pair should be fitted at the same distance from the centre line of the vehicle and the same height above the ground, except that in the case of an asymmetric vehicle these requirements shall be complied with as far as possible having regard to the shape of the vehicle;

4. A direction indicator must be within 400 mm of the outer edge of the vehicle;

Categories of direction indicators referred to in Schedule 5A showing their horizontal angles of visibility

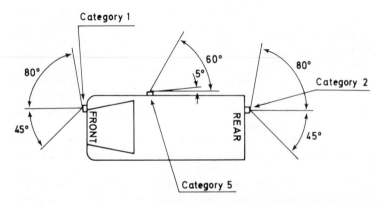

The value of 5° given for the blind angle of visibility to the rear of the category 5 flank indicator is an upper limit

5. A pair of indicators must not be less than 600 mm apart;

6. If a category 2 indicator is within 300 mm vertically of a rear obligatory lamp the indicator must not be placed more than 50 mm from the outer edge of the vehicle than is the rear obligatory lamp;

7. The minimum height above ground level for a category 1 or 2 indicator is 350 mm and for a category 5 indicator is 500 mm;

8. The maximum height above ground level for (i) a category 1 or 2 indicator is 1500 mm or, if the vehicle's structure does not enable it to be fitted below this height, 2100 mm and (ii) a category 5 indicator is 1500 mm or, if the vehicle's structure does not enable it to be fitted below this height, 2300 mm;

9. The centre of a category 5 indicator should not be more than 1800 mm from the front of the vehicle or, if the vehicle's structure does not allow that limit to be complied with, 2500 mm; and

10. The requirements of Part I of Schedule 5 relating to the rate of flashing, warning devices, not misleading other drivers, references to the side of a vehicle including the front and back and the use of a single switch for a vehicle and trailer apply.

HAZARD WARNING

When a motor vehicle is stationary on a road due to a breakdown, accident or other emergency a device may be used which operates simultaneously the vehicle's indicators for the purpose of warning other road users of a temporary obstruction of the road. The device must include a warning light to show that it is in operation and must be actuated by a switch which serves no other purpose [694/71/77].

DRIVER'S DEFENCE

If a driver is charged with an offence under any of the provisions of Sections 68 to 79 of the Road Traffic Act 1972, or regulations made under those Sections, he will not be convicted if he can prove to the satisfaction of the court that the offence arose through the negligence or default of some other person whose duty it was to provide the vehicle with any lamp or reflector. Subject to this, proceedings may be taken against any person 'causing' or 'permitting' the offence [Act 1972/81(1)]. A person cannot 'use' a vehicle in contravention of lighting regulations—*Balfour Beatty & Co., Ltd.* v. *Grindey*, [1975] R.T.R. 156.

REFLECTING MATERIAL

Material designed primarily to reflect white light as light of that or another colour, is, when reflecting light, to be treated, for the purposes of Sections 68 to 79, as showing a light [Act 1972/80].

NUMBER-PLATE LIGHTING

The standard of illumination of rear number plates has to be such that, on vehicles first registered on or after October 1, 1938, every letter and figure of the registration mark is 'easily legible' by an observer behind the vehicle, up to a distance of 60 ft, in respect of vehicles other than motor cycles, pedestrian-controlled vehicles and invalid carriages, for which the distance is 50 ft. There is no need for registration numbers on works trucks to be illuminated at all [450/71/19].

REFLECTIVE REAR MARKINGS

Motor vehicles over 3 tons unladen and trailers over 1 ton unladen must be fitted with red and yellow rear markings [1700/70/3]. The following are excepted vehicles on which the markings are not required but on which they may be fitted, provided they exceed the above weights:

(a) passenger vehicles;
(b) living van trailers not over 2 tons unladen;
(c) land tractors, land locomotives, land implements, land implement conveyors, agricultural trailers and industrial tractors;
(d) works trucks and works trailers;
(e) unfinished vehicles going for completion, storage or display;
(f) artic drawing units;
(g) a broken-down vehicle being drawn;
(h) engineering plant;
(i) a trailer drawn by a p.s.v.;
(j) fire-fighting or fire-salvage vehicles;
(k) vehicles for serving or controlling aircraft;
(l) vehicles designed to carry two or more motor vehicles, vehicle bodies or boats;
(m) vehicles going to a place for export;
(n) motor vehicles brought temporarily into Great Britain;
(nn) foreign-based trailers brought temporarily into Great Britain;
(o) vehicles of visiting forces;
(p) motor vehicles first used before January 1, 1940;
(q) armed forces vehicles;
(r) vehicles for heating and dispensing road tar;
(s) trailers being drying or mixing plant for production of asphalt, bituminous or tarmacadam.   [1700/70/2 and 842/72/3]

A motor vehicle not over 13 m (42 ft $7\frac{3}{4}$ in) long and a trailer forming part of a combination of vehicles not over 11 m (36 ft 1 in) long must be fitted with a rear marking complying with diagram 1 or 2, shown on the opposite page. If the rear of the vehicle makes it impracticable to do so a marking complying with diagram 3 may be used [1700/70/4(1)]. A trailer forming part of a combination which is over 11 m

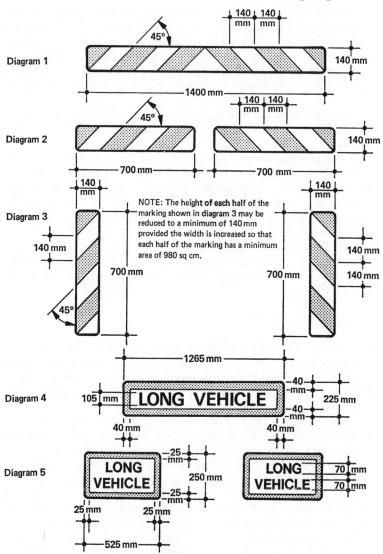

Size, colour and type of rear markings. The markings must consist of red fluorescent material in the shaded areas of the diagrams and yellow reflex reflecting material in the other areas. Letters must be black. The markings must be in the form of plates and marked with the specification number B.S. AU 152. [1700/70/Sched., Pt. II]

but not over 13 m long must be fitted with a marking complying with diagrams 1, 2, 4 or 5. Again, if it is impracticable to fit a diagram 1 or 2 marking a diagram 3 marking may be used [4(2)]. A motor vehicle which is over 13 m long or a trailer which forms part of a combination over 13 m long must be fitted with a marking complying with diagrams 4 or 5 [4(3)]. A combination of vehicles is a motor vehicle and trailer(s) [2(3)].

If a vehicle is for the time being carrying a load which so projects to the rear that a marking fitted to the vehicle would be obscured the marking may, instead, be fitted to the load [842/72/4].

A rear marking must not project beyond the side of a vehicle; the lower edge must not be higher than 1700 mm (67 in) nor lower than 400 mm ($15\frac{3}{4}$ in) above ground level; each part of the marking in diagram 2, 3 or 5 must be as near as practicable to the side of the vehicle; and every marking must be maintained in a clean and efficient condition [1700/70/Sched., Pt. III].

Vehicles carrying dangerous goods on a journey part of which has taken place or will take place outside the United Kingdom may display at the rear certain reflective plates indicating their contents and danger [2111/75].

REAR FOG LAMPS

Rear fog lamps may be used only (a) during adverse weather conditions and (b) when the vehicle is in motion, during an enforced stoppage, when a vehicle adapted for 7 or more passengers is stopped to allow them to alight or board or when a vehicle is used for ambulance, fire brigade or police purposes [1260/78/8].

From October 1, 1979 a rear fog lamp on a motor vehicle or trailer must be fitted so that it is at least 100 mm away from a stop lamp and it must not be lit by the application of the vehicle's brakes [7].

Motor vehicles and trailers made on or after October 1, 1979 and first used on or after April 1, 1980 must be fitted with one rear fog lamp or two rear fog lamps which form a pair. The lamps must bear an approval mark [5(1)]. Vehicles which are exempt are vehicles with less than four wheels and not over 1.3 m wide; agricultural vehicles; industrial tractors; pedestrian-controlled vehicles; works trucks; and works trailers [5(3)]. A motor vehicle to which Regulation 5 applies must be equipped with a device visible to the driver to show that the vehicle's or trailer's rear fog lamp is lit or that the electrical circuit is closed [5(2)]. The rear fog lamp on (a) a motor vehicle not drawing a trailer and (b) the rearmost trailer of a combination of vehicles to which Regulation 5 applies (other than a broken-down vehicle) must be capable of being lit by the driver of the vehicle [9].

MAINTENANCE

Road Traffic Act 1972
Motor Vehicles (Construction and Use) Regulations, **No. 1017/78**
Road Vehicles Lighting Regulations, **No. 694/71**

BRAKES

Every part of a braking system and its means of operation fitted to a vehicle must be maintained in good and efficient working order and properly adjusted [1017/78/101(1)(a)]. The brakes of a motor vehicle to which Schedule 4 applies must be maintained so that the required braking efficiencies (generally 50% and 25% for light vehicles) are available [101(1)(b)]. The brakes of a vehicle for which specific braking efficiencies are prescribed must be maintained so that when the vehicle is not drawing a trailer the efficiencies can be obtained [101(1)(c), (d)]. If a vehicle is required to have a parking brake capable of holding it on a 1 in 6·25 gradient the brake must be maintained so that this efficiency is obtained. In the case of a composite trailer (i.e. a semi-trailer and converter dolly) it is the brakes of the semi-trailer which must be so maintained [101(1)(e)]. The brakes of a vehicle which has a type approval certificate or certificate of conformity in respect of its conforming to E.E.C. Directive 71/320 must be maintained as required in that Directive [101(1)(f)].

If a vehicle first used on or after January 1, 1968, which is required to have 50% and 25% braking efficiencies is used to draw a trailer made on or after the same date (other than one not required to have brakes) the brakes of the vehicle and trailer must be maintained so that those efficiency figures are obtained [101(2)]. If a goods vehicle first used on or after January 1, 1968, which is required to have 50% and 25%

braking efficiencies is used to draw a trailer made before that date (other than a trailer not required to have brakes) the brakes of the vehicle and trailer must be maintained so that efficiencies of 40% and 15% can be obtained [101(3)]. If a goods vehicle which is required to have braking efficiencies of 45% and 20% or 40% and 15% is used to draw a trailer of any age (other than one not required to have brakes) the brakes of the vehicle and trailer must be maintained so that efficiencies of 40% and 15% can be obtained [101(4)]. When a motor vehicle first used on or after January 1, 1968, is attached to a trailer made on or after the same date (other than a trailer not required to have brakes) the parking brakes of the outfit must be maintained so that when it is stationary they can hold it on a gradient of at least 1 in 6·25 without the assistance of stored energy [101(5)].

For these purposes the date of manufacture of a composite trailer is deemed to be the date of manufacture of the semi-trailer forming part of it [101(6)].

TYRES

A vehicle must not be used if a pneumatic tyre fitted to a wheel

- (a) is unsuitable to the use of the vehicle or to the other types of tyres fitted;
- (b) is not correctly inflated;
- (c) has a cut deep enough to reach the body cords and the length of the cut is 1 in or 10% of the width of the tyre, whichever is the longer;
- (d) has any lump or bulge caused by separation or partial failure of its structure;
- (e) has any ply or cord structure exposed ('exposed' means exposed to view—*Renouf* v. *Franklin*, [1971] R.T.R. 469);
- (f) except in the case of a pedestrian-controlled works truck, does not have a tread depth of at least 1 mm round its outer circumference and across three-quarters of its breadth.

[1017/78/107(1)]

In *Coote* v. *Parkin* [1977] R.T.R. 61 it was held that the 'outer circumference of the tyre', in Regulation 107(1)(f), was the part of the tyre normally in contact with the road. The side walls and shoulders of the tyre were not to be included.

None of the above restrictions applies to a land locomotive, land tractor, land implement, land implement conveyor, agricultural trailer when drawn by a land tractor, or a broken-down vehicle or a vehicle going to a place for breaking up provided, in either case, it is not towed faster than 20 m.p.h. [107(3)].

A tyre which is deflated or which has a defect described in paragraph (c), (d) or (e) above can be used if the tyre and wheel to which it is fitted are constructed to make the tyre fit for use in that condition and the outside walls of the tyre are marked to that effect [107(2)].

A vehicle fitted with a recut pneumatic tyre must not be used if the tyre fabric has been cut or exposed by the recutting process [107(4)]. This does not apply to a broken-down vehicle or a vehicle going to a place for breaking up provided, in either case, it is not towed faster than 20 m.p.h. [107(3)].

Generally, all tyres must be maintained so that they are fit for the use to which the vehicle is being put, and are free from defects which might damage the road or cause danger [107(5)].

Pneumatic tyres of different types of structure must not be fitted to the same axle of a vehicle [108(1)].

A motor vehicle with two axles each of which is equipped with one or two single wheels must not be used on a road if (a) a diagonal-ply tyre or bias-belted tyre is fitted on the rear axle and a radial ply tyre is on the front axle or (b) a diagonal-ply tyre is fitted on the rear axle and a bias-belted tyre is fitted on the front axle [108(2)]. This ban does not apply if an axle of the vehicle is fitted with wide tyres other than special wide tyres for engineering plant [108(3)]. Wide tyres are at least 300 mm wide [3(1)].

A motor vehicle must not be used on a road if (a) pneumatic tyres of one type of structure are fitted on a steerable axle and tyres of a different type of structure are fitted on another steerable axle or (b) pneumatic tyres of one type of structure are fitted on a non-steerable driven axle and tyres of a different type of structure are fitted on another non-steerable axle [108(4)].

The term 'axle', for these purposes, includes a pair of stub axles on opposite sides of the vehicle and a single stub axle which is not one of a pair. A 'stub axle' is defined as an axle on which only one wheel is mounted [108(5)].

CONDITION

Every vehicle, its parts and accessories, the number of passengers carried and how they are carried, the weight, distribution, packing, and adjustment of its load must be such that no danger is caused or is likely to be caused [1017/78/97(1)]. In *Leathley* v. *Robson's Border Transport Ltd*, [1976] R.T.R. 503 it was held that this Regulation applied to a load on a vehicle and did not apply in a case when the load had fallen from the vehicle. A load on a vehicle must be secured, if necessary by physical restraint other than its own weight, and be in such a position that neither danger nor nuisance is likely to be caused to any person or property by the load falling or being blown from the vehicle or by any movement on the vehicle [97(2)]. In *Cornish* v. *Ferry Masters, Ltd.*, [1975] R.T.R. 292 using a vehicle with an insecure load contrary to this Regulation was held to be an absolute offence. Lack of knowledge that a pallet had inherent defects causing it to collapse and allow a drum to fall from the vehicle was no defence. A vehicle must not be used for a purpose for which it is so unsuitable that danger or nuisance is or is likely to be caused [97(3)]. In *B.R.S., Ltd.* v. *Owen*, [1971] 2 All E.R. 999 where a high load on a vehicle collided with a bridge, it was held that the vehicle had been used for an unsuitable purpose and the test of 'suitability' was not when it started the journey but when it approached the bridge.

A Code of Practice titled *Safety of Loads on Vehicles* has been published by the Department of the Environment and is available from H.M. Stationery Office.

SEAT BELTS

The seat belt, its anchorages, fastenings and adjusting device, required to be fitted in a vehicle, must be maintained free from obvious defects likely to adversely affect its function of restraining a body in case of accident [1017/78/102A(2)]. The fastening device must be maintained so that the belt can be readily fastened or unfastened, be kept free from obstruction and be readily accessible to the occupant of the seat [102A(3)]. Ends of a seat belt must be securely fastened to the anchorage points; anchorage points must not be used for any other purpose and load-bearing members or panelling within 30 cm of the anchorage point must be kept in sound condition, free from serious corrosion, distortion or fracture [102A(4A) (5)]. Adjusting devices and retracting mechanisms have to be maintained so that the belt can be readily adjusted [102A(6)]. Anchorages include, in the case of integral seat belts, the means of securing the seat to the vehicle [102A(7)].

SPEEDOMETER

A speedometer which is required to be fitted to a vehicle must be maintained in good working order and kept free from obstruction which might prevent it being easily read. It is a defence to proceedings taken in respect of using a defective speedometer to prove that (a) the defect occurred on that particular journey or (b) steps had already been taken to have the defect repaired [1017/78/98].

LIGHTS

When a motor vehicle is required to be fitted with lamps and reflectors during daylight hours those lamps and reflectors must be maintained so that the vehicle can be driven on a road during the hours of darkness [1017/78/105(1)]. Headlamps must be maintained to comply with anti-dazzle requirements [105(2)]. When a person is charged with contravening these provisions, during daylight hours, it is a defence to prove that the defect occurred on that particular journey or that steps had been taken to have the defect remedied before the contravention occurred [105(3)].

Direction indicators and stop lamps must be maintained in a clean condition and good and efficient working order [694/71/76].

WINDSCREENS, ETC

Glass and other transparent material fitted to motor vehicles must be maintained so that it does not obscure the driver's vision [1017/78/100].

Windscreen wipers must be maintained in good and efficient working order and be properly adjusted [103].

SILENCER

Every silencer, expansion chamber or other contrivance must be maintained in good and efficient working order and not altered to increase the noise made by the escaping exhaust gases [1017/78/106(2)]. Exhaust gases must not escape into the atmosphere without first passing through a silencer, etc. [106(1)].

SMOKE

An excess fuel device on a diesel engine must be maintained so that it does not cause excess fuel to be supplied to the engine while the vehicle is being driven on a road [1017/78/111(a)]. A person must not use the device while the vehicle is moving on a road unless it does not cause an increase in the smoke emitted from the vehicle [111(b)].

The engine of certain petrol-engined vehicles first used on or after January 1, 1972, must be maintained so that crankcase vapours do not escape into the atmosphere without first passing through the engine combustion chamber [112].

A diesel-engined vehicle which is required to have a type test certificate must not have its fuel injection equipment, governor or other engine parts altered or adjusted to increase smoke emission [110].

A motor vehicle must not be used if any smoke, visible vapour, grit, sparks, ashes, cinders, or oily substance is emitted which is likely to cause damage or danger [109].

OTHERS

All steering gear fitted to a motor vehicle must be maintained in good and efficient working order and be properly adjusted [1017/78/102].

Every motor vehicle must be so maintained that its petrol tank is reasonably secure against being damaged and leakage of liquid or vapour is adequately prevented [104].

No person must use ancillary equipment on a motor vehicle which requires a power/weight ratio of 4·4 kilowatts per 1000 kg unless with the equipment in operation the power/weight ratio is still available when the vehicle is driven at over 5 m.p.h. [99].

RECORDS

Section 59 of the Road Traffic Act 1972 enables the Secretary of State to make regulations requiring a goods vehicle operator to have his vehicles inspected and inspection records kept and preserved for up to 15 months. No regulations have yet been made. Licensing Authorities, however, are requiring such inspections to be made and records kept as a condition in granting operators' licences.

MOTORWAYS

Highways Act 1959
Road Traffic Regulation Act 1967
Motorways Traffic Regulations, **No. 1147/59**
Motorways Traffic (England and Wales) (Amendment) Regulations, **No. 1087/71**
Special Road (Classes of Traffic) Order, **No. 1156/71**
Motorways Traffic (Lengths of the M4) (Restriction on Overtaking) Regulations, **No. 1824/76**
Motorways Traffic (Lengths of the M63) (Restriction of Use of Right Hand Lane) Regulations, **No. 43/77**
Motorways Traffic (M63 Motorway Slip Road at the Princess Parkway Interchange, Manchester) (Bus Lane) Regulations, **No. 355/77**
Motorways Traffic (Length of the M5) (Restriction of Use of Right Hand Lane) Regulations, **No. 2010/77**

PERMITTED TRAFFIC

For motorway law purposes traffic is divided into 11 classes but only vehicles of classes I and II are normally allowed to use a motorway [Act 1967/13 and 1147/59]. Class I traffic is locomotives, motor tractors, heavy motor cars, motor cars, motor cycles over 50 c.c. and trailers drawn by such vehicles provided the vehicles comply with Construction and Use Regulations and the following conditions: the vehicle is entirely on wheels, the wheels have pneumatic tyres, the vehicle is not pedestrian-controlled or licensed as an agricultural machine and, in the case of a motor vehicle, is capable of 25 m.p.h. on the level under its own power when unladen and not drawing a trailer. Class II traffic is vehicles authorised under the Special Types Order including vehicles used for or in connection with the carriage of an abnormal indivisible load, vehicles constructed for defence purposes, vehicles for moving excavated material, vehicles going for export and engineering plant. The last three classes of vehicle must be capable of 25 m.p.h. on the level under their own power when unladen and not drawing a trailer [Act 1959/Schedule 4 and 1156/71/Schedule].

RESTRICTIONS

Drivers must comply with signs prohibiting entry to the carriageway (usually on slip roads), signs prohibiting left and right turns and must not make 'U' turns. The central reservation should be on the right-hand side of a driver [1147/59/6].

A vehicle must not be driven on a part of a motorway which is not a carriageway [5] except that when it is necessary for a vehicle to stop on the carriageway it must be moved on to the verge as soon as reasonably practicable [7(2)]. A vehicle may stop on a carriageway and may be driven on to and remain at rest on a verge for the following reasons only: (a) breakdown, mechanical defect, lack of fuel, oil or water, (b) accident, illness or other emergency, (c) for a person to move or recover anything which has fallen on to the motorway, or (d) to allow a person to give help in (a), (b) or (c). When a vehicle is on a verge in these circumstances it must not obstruct the carriageway and must not remain there longer than is necessary [7(2), (3) and 9]. In the 1971 High Court case of *Wallwork* v. *Rowland*, [1972] 1 All E.R. 53; [1972] R.T.R. 86 it was held that the hard shoulder is a verge and is not part of the carriageway. In the later case of *Higgins* v. *Bernard*, [1972] 1 All E.R. 1037; [1972] 1 W.L.R. 455 it was held not to be an emergency when a driver, feeling tired, stopped on the hard shoulder because there was evidence that he had felt drowsy before going on to the motorway.

A vehicle must not be reversed along a carriageway except to enable it to be driven forwards or to connect it to another vehicle [8]. A vehicle must not be driven on to the central reservation [10]. A provisional licence holder who has not passed a test must not drive a vehicle on a motorway [11]. A pedestrian must not go on any part of a motorway other than a verge except to move anything which has fallen on to the motorway or to give assistance in the circumstances described in Regulation 7(2) [12]. An animal must not leave a vehicle on a motorway unless it escapes or unless it is necessary for it to leave a vehicle in which case it may only go on to the verge and must be on a lead [13].

Motor vehicles other than those in classes I and II may use a motorway for specified maintenance purposes and, in cases of emergency, a chief officer of police may authorise the use of a motorway by excluded traffic [14]. The restrictions do not apply to emergency services working on a motorway or to specified maintenance purposes [15].

In *Trentham* v. *Rowlands*, [1974] R.T.R. 164 the High Court held that a driver who overtook another vehicle on its nearside on a three-lane motorway had been rightly convicted of dangerous driving.

USE OF OUTSIDE LANE

A locomotive, motor tractor, heavy motor car (other than one constructed solely for the carriage of passengers), and any vehicle drawing a trailer may not use the right-hand lane of a three-lane motorway except to pass a vehicle moving a load of exceptional width [1147/59/11A and 1087/71]. If a motorway has four lanes the nearside of which is a crawler lane, that lane and the one next to it are treated as a single lane for these purposes [11A(3)].

Motor vehicles other than motor cars, buses, coaches and motor cycles are banned from the right-hand lane on a two-lane uphill length of the M5 in Worcestershire [2010/77] four lengths of the M4 in Gwent [1824/76] and two lengths of the M63 in Greater Manchester [43/77].

A length of the M63 at Princess Parkway Interchange in Greater Manchester is reserved as a bus lane and, except with the permission of a uniformed policeman or traffic warden no person may cause or permit a vehicle other than a scheduled express carriage, a stage carriage, a school bus or a works bus to enter the bus lane [355/77/3]. The ban does not apply to enable a vehicle (a) to remove an obstruction (b) to be used for police, fire or ambulance purposes (c) to avoid or prevent an accident or to give help in case of accident or other emergency or (d) to be used for maintaining the road or specified public services [4] The general prohibition on heavy vehicles and vehicles drawing a trailer from the right-hand lane of a three-lane motorway does not apply to the length of road having the bus lane [5].

Speed limits on motorways are explained in the chapter on speed limits (page 223).

OPERATORS' LICENSING

Transport Act 1962
Transport Act 1968 as amended by Road Traffic Act 1974
International Road Haulage Permits Act 1975
Goods Vehicles (Operators' Licences) Regulations, **No. 1636/69**
Goods Vehicles (Operators' Licences) (Fees) Regulations, **No. 2060/74**
Transport Tribunal Rules, **No. 1687/65**
Transport Tribunal (Amendment) Rules, **Nos. 491/70 and 934/73**
Goods Vehicles (Operators' Licences) (Temporary Use in Great Britain) Regulations,
    No. 1046/75
Goods Vehicles (Operators' Licences) (Fees) (Amendment) Regulations, **No. 460/76**
Goods Vehicles Operators (Qualifications) Regulations, **No. 1462/77**
Goods Vehicles (Operators' Licences) Regulations, **No. 1737/77**
Goods Vehicles (Operators' Licences) (Temporary Use in Great Britain) (Amendment)
    Regulations, **No. 1110/78**

Any person who uses a goods vehicle on a road for the carriage of goods for hire or reward or in connection with any trade or business carried on by him must have the vehicle authorised on an operator's licence [Act 1968/60(1)].

An operator's licence granted on or after January 1, 1978 will be either a restricted operator's licence or a standard operator's licence. A restricted licence authorises the carriage of goods in connection with the holder's trade or business but not for hire or reward. A standard licence authorises the carriage of goods for hire or reward or in connection with the holder's trade or business [1462/77/3(1)]. Where a licence holder is a company any business carried on by its holding company, a subsidiary company or another subsidiary of the same holding company is, for the foregoing purposes, regarded as carried on by the licence holder [3(2)].

A standard operator's licence may authorise the carriage of goods for hire or reward on (a) national and international operations or (b) on national operations only [3(3)]. A statement must appear on a licence to show what class of licence it is [3(4)]. A person who holds a restricted licence commits an offence if he carries goods for hire or reward [3(6)]. A standard licence holder who is limited to national operations commits an offence if he carries goods for hire or reward on international operations [3(7)].

To obtain a standard licence the operator must meet prescribed qualification requirements. These are given on page 133 below.

EXEMPTIONS

An operator's licence is not required for a small goods vehicle or an exempted vehicle [Act 1968/60(2)].

A small goods vehicle is described as (a) a vehicle which has a relevant plated weight not over 3·5 tonnes or, if not plated, has an unladen weight not over 1525 kg, (b) in the case of an artic, if the sum of the relevant plated weights of both drawing unit and semi-trailer is not over 3·5 tonnes or, if either or both parts is not plated, the sum of the unladen weights is not over 1525 kg, or (c) in the case of a drawbar outfit, the relevant plated weight of the trailer together with the unladen weight of the motor vehicle is not over 3·5 tonnes or, if the trailer is not plated, the sum of the unladen weights is not over 1525 kg. Trailers not over 1 ton unladen are disregarded [60(4) and 1737/77/20]. 'Relevant plated weight' means the permitted gross weight shown on a Ministry plate or, if no Ministry plate is fitted, the maximum gross weight shown on a compulsory maker's plate [1737/77/19].

Vehicles which are exempted from operators' licensing are as follows:

1. Any vehicle licensed as an agricultural machine, including a trailer drawn thereby, being used solely for the haulage of specified objects.
2. A dual-purpose vehicle, and any trailer drawn thereby.
3. A vehicle used on a road only in passing between private premises belonging (except in the case of a vehicle used for excavation or demolition) to the same person, provided the distance travelled on a road does not exceed six miles in any week.
4. A public service vehicle, and any trailer drawn thereby.
5. A motor vehicle constructed solely for the carriage of not more than 15 passengers and their effects when adapted to draw or drawing a trailer, and any trailer drawn thereby.
6. A hackney carriage.
7. A vehicle which is being used for funerals.
8. A vehicle which is being used for police, fire brigade or ambulance purposes.

9. A vehicle which is being used for fire-fighting and rescue operations at mines.

10. A vehicle upon which no permanent body has been constructed, which is carrying burden solely for test or trial, or articles and equipment which will form part of the completed vehicle when the body is constructed.

11. A vehicle which is being used under a trade licence.

12. A vehicle in the service of a visiting force or of a headquarters.

13. A trailer not constructed primarily for the carriage of goods but which is being used incidentally for that purpose in connection with the construction, maintenance or repair of roads.

14. A road roller and any trailer drawn thereby.

15. A vehicle while being used under the direction of H.M. Coastguard or of the Royal National Lifeboat Institution for the carriage of lifeboats, life-saving appliances or crew.

16. A vehicle fitted with a machine, appliance, apparatus or other contrivance which is a permanent or essentially permanent fixture, provided that the only goods carried on the vehicle are such as are required for use in connection with the machine, appliance, apparatus or contrivance or the running of the vehicle.

17. A vehicle while being used by a local authority:
    (1) for road cleansing, road watering, snow-clearing or the collection or disposal of refuse, night-soil or the contents of cess-pools, or for the purposes of the enactments relating to weights and measures or the sale of food and drugs; or
    (2) for the distribution of grit, salt or other materials on frosted, icebound or snow-covered roads or for going to or from the place where it is to be so used or for any directly connected purpose.

18. A vehicle while being used by a local authority for civil defence.

19. A vehicle while being used by a highway authority for the purposes of weighing vehicles or maintaining weighbridges.

20. A tower wagon or trailer drawn by a tower wagon, provided the only goods carried are required for use in connection with the vehicle's ordinary work. In *Anderson and Heeley, Ltd.* v. *Paterson*, [1975] 1 All E.R. 523; [1975] 1 W.L.R. 228 a platform truck fitted with a Hiab loader and used for carrying and installing street lighting columns was held not to be a tower wagon.

21. A vehicle while being used for the carriage of goods within an aerodrome.

22. An electrically propelled vehicle.
23. A showman's vehicle and any trailer drawn thereby.
24. A vehicle first used before January 1, 1977 not over 1525 kg unladen weight and which has a maker's plated gross weight over 3·5 tonnes but not over $3\frac{1}{2}$ tons.

[1737/77/3, Sched. 1]

AUTHORISED VEHICLES

Vehicles authorised to be used under an operator's licence are (a) motor vehicles belonging to the licence holder or in his possession under an agreement for hire-purchase, hire or loan, as are specified in the licence; (b) trailers similarly owned or hired not exceeding at any time such a maximum number as is specified in the licence; and (c) a maximum number of vehicles to be acquired or taken into possession after the licence is granted. Different types of motor vehicles and trailers may be specified [Act 1968/61(1)]. An after-acquired vehicle ceases to be authorised under (c) above one month after it is acquired or taken into possession unless the operator notifies the Licensing Authority of that fact within that period [61(3)].

No operator's licence authorises the use of any vehicle unless its operating centre is in the Licensing Authority's own area or if it is outside that area and has not been the operating centre for more than 3 months [61(2)].

A Licensing Authority can remove from a licence any vehicle which, except as a result of trade fluctuation or of its undergoing repair, has ceased to be used under a licence or any vehicle which is specified in another operator's licence [61(6)]. No vehicle, specified in one operator's licence, can be specified in any other operator's licence [61(5)].

APPLICATIONS

Applications for operators' licences must be made to the Licensing Authority in the area in which the vehicle's operating centre is located. An operator can hold separate licences for different areas but not more than one in the same area [Act 1968/62(1)]. The application should reach the Licensing Authority at least 9 weeks before the date on which it is to take effect, but he can deal with applications which do not meet this requirement [1737/77/5].

The applicant must give such particulars as the Licensing Authority may require about his vehicles and state the number and type of trailers he proposes to use [62(2)].

Further information which the Licensing Authority may require
is:

(1) the use to which the vehicle will be put;

(2) arrangements for ensuring that drivers keep within the permitted hours of work and that they keep proper records;

(3) vehicle maintenance facilities;

(4) details of any past activities in operating vehicles for trade
purposes by

   (a) the applicant,

   (b) any company of which the applicant is or has been a
director,

   (c) his co-directors or partners,

   (d) any company of which his co-directors or partners are or
have been directors,

   (e) any company of which the applicant is a subsidiary;

(5) convictions during the preceding five years of the applicant or
any of his associates listed above for offences concerning

   (a) plating and testing,

   (b) maintenance,

   (c) speeding,

   (d) overloading and the loading of goods vehicles,

   (e) licensing of drivers,

   (f) forgery of, or making false statements to obtain, an
operator's licence,

   (g) operators' licensing,

   (h) drivers' hours,

   (i) underpaying drivers,

   (j) unlawfully using rebated fuel,

   (k) failing to inspect vehicles and keep maintenance records
(Section 59 of the Road Traffic Act 1972 enables the
Secretary of State to make regulations requiring that
inspections be made and records kept but he has not yet
used this power),

   (l) infringement of waiting restrictions or prescribed lorry
routes or

   (m) using a prohibited vehicle;

   (n) conviction of the operator, or his servant or agent, of
contravening Section 169 or 170 of the Road Traffic
Act 1972 in relation to an international road haulage
permit or of contravening a prohibition under the International Road Haulage Permits Act 1975;

   (o) conviction of a restricted licence holder of carrying
goods for hire or reward;

   (p) conviction of a standard licence holder limited to

na̧onal transport operations of carrying goods on
international operations;

(6) financial resources which are or are likely to become available
to the applicant; and

(7) in the case of a company the names of the directors and officers
of the applicant company and of any company of which the
applicant is a subsidiary and, in the case of a partnership, the
names of the other partners [62(4)].

A person who has applied for a licence must forthwith notify the
Licensing Authority if between making the application and it being
disposed of a conviction of the kind referred to in paragraph 5 above
occurs [62(4A)].

An applicant for a standard operator's licence must include in his
application (a) without being specifically asked, the particulars listed in
paragraphs (4), (5), (6) and (7) above (unless he was in road transport
operations before January 1, 1978); (b) where he relies on his own
professional competence, details of his professional competence qualifications; and (c) if he does not rely on his own competence, the name,
address, place or intended place of work of his transport manager
together with particulars of his professional qualifications and relevant
convictions in the preceding five years [1462/77/4(2)]. If a relevant
conviction is made against the transport manager between the application being made and being disposed of the operator must notify it
to the Licensing Authority [4(3)].

OPERATORS' QUALIFICATIONS

Since January 1, 1978 a Licensing Authority must refuse to grant a
standard operator's licence unless he is satisfied that the applicant (a) is
of good repute, (b) has appropriate financial standing and (c) is himself
professionally competent or will, throughout the currency of the
licence, employ a transport manager who is of good repute and is
professionally competent or, if the applicant has more than one operating centre, the number of such transport managers as the Licensing
Authority may require [1462/77/5(1)].

In determining whether or not a person is of good repute regard
must be had to the existence and number of relevant convictions relating to him in the previous five years [9(2)]. Relevant convictions
are those specified in Section 69(4) of the 1968 Act [2(1)]. They are
listed on page 132 opposite.

A person will be regarded as having appropriate financial standing if
he has available to him sufficient financial resources to ensure the proper
administration of his road transport undertaking, including its launch-

ing if a new undertaking [9(3)].

Only an individual can be professionally competent so that in the case of a company one or more transport managers who are of good repute and professionally competent must be employed [9(4)(5)]. In the case of a partnership it is sufficient that one of the partners is professionally competent if he is also responsible for the operation of the authorised vehicles [9(6)].

A person will be regarded as professionally competent if (a) he was engaged in road transport operations before January 1, 1975; (b) he holds a certificate issued by an approved body to the effect that he possesses specified skills of the kind appropriate to his operations; or (c) he holds any other certificate, diploma or other qualification recognised for these purposes by the Secretary of State [9(7)]. An individual will not be regarded as competent under (a) above after December 31, 1979 unless he holds a certificate issued by a Licensing Authority who is satisfied that the person was engaged in road transport operations before January 1, 1975 [9(8)]. An application for such a certificate must be made to the Licensing Authority before November 30, 1979 [1737/77/18]. A person who began road transport operations between January 1, 1975 and January 1, 1978 will be regarded as professionally competent till January 1, 1980 but after this date he must hold a certificate, diploma or other qualification [1462/77/9(9)].

A person who is an applicant for or the holder of a standard operator's licence or who is a transport manager will be regarded as being in road transport operations if the person is (a) the holder or joint holder of an operator's licence, (b) a goods vehicle operating subsidiary of the holder of an operator's licence or (c) if an individual, in responsible road transport employment [2(2)]. Responsible road transport employment means employment in road transport in a position where the individual has responsibility for the operation of goods vehicles under an operator's licence [2(1)].

The body approved by the Secretary of State for the purpose of issuing certificates of competence is the Royal Society of Acts. The Society will hold examinations for a certificate of competence in national and international transport operations. The topics covered in the examination on national transport are drivers' hours and records, driving licences, traffic regulations, accident procedure, vehicle and passenger insurance, safe vehicle loading, vehicle weights and dimensions, vehicle selection, mechanical condition of vehicles, operators' licensing, financial management, costing, commercial conduct of business, law, company law, social legislation and taxation. The additional topics for the examination in international transport are law, hours and conditions of work, tachographs, permits and tariffs, international transport documentation, fiscal charges, consignment notes and carriers liability, insurance abroad, customs practice and formalities, financial aspects of operation, route planning, vehicle construction, weights and dimensions, traffic regulations, traffic safety, accident prevention and procedure.

The other qualifications accepted by the Secretary of State as proof of professional competence are, for national and international operations, (i) Fellow or Member of the Chartered Institute of Transport (road transport sector), (ii) Member or Associate Member of the Institute of Traffic Administration (road transport sector), (iii) Member or Associate Member of the Institute of Road Transport Engineers, and (iv) Fellow or Associate of the Institute of the Furniture Warehousing and Removing Industry. For national operations only they are (a) Licentiate of the Chartered Institute of Transport (road transport sector), (b) Associate of the Institute of Road Transport Engineers and (c) General Certificate in Removals Management issued by the Institute of the Furniture Warehousing and Removal Industry.

GRANTS AND OBJECTIONS

Licensing Authorities must publish details of applications for operators' licences [Act 1968/63(1)]. They need not, however, publish such notices for any application made by an operator who holds an operator's licence issued in a different traffic area if a grant would not result in a substantial increase in the number of vehicles authorised under the applicants' operators' licences [63(2)]. Notifiable applications are published in *Applications and Decisions* [1737/77/7].

In deciding on an application for an operator's licence the Licensing Authority shall consider whether the following requirements are satisfied:

(a) that the applicant is a fit person to hold a licence having regard to notified convictions;

(b) arrangements for ensuring that drivers' hours will be observed and for preventing overloading;

(c) that facilities and arrangements for maintaining vehicles are satisfactory and the vehicles' operating centre is suitable for that purpose;

(d) that the applicant has sufficient financial resources to provide (c) above [64(1), (2)].

In considering point (d) the Licensing Authority can call upon an assessor drawn from a panel appointed by the Minister for that purpose. If the Licensing Authority is not satisfied on any of these points, he must refuse the application, otherwise he must grant it either in the terms applied for or as modified [64(3), (4), (5)]. He can either authorise motor vehicles other than those applied for or reduce or increase the number, or vary the type of motor vehicles or trailers sought to be authorised and/or forbid the addition of vehicles to the licence [64(4)].

The Licensing Authority may hold a public inquiry into an application or variation [87] and an applicant is entitled to be heard in person or be represented by a barrister or solicitor or, if the Licensing Authority permits, by any other person [1737/77/10]. If a grant or variation is refused the Licensing Authority must give his reasons to the applicant or any objector [10(3)]. The date and place of any public inquiry must be published in *Applications and Decisions* [7].

Objections to applications may be lodged by a prescribed trade union or association whose members hold operators' licences or the employees of such licence holders, the police and a local authority [63(3)].

The trade unions and associations which can object are the Road Haulage Association; Freight Transport Association; General and Municipal Workers' Union; National Union of Railwaymen; Transport and General Workers' Union; Union of Shop, Distributive and Allied Workers; and United Road Transport Union [1737/77/8]. A person authorised by a body entitled to object can inspect a copy of the information given in a notifiable application, at the Licensing Authority's office, till the application is determined and during the currency of any licence granted or varied as a result of that application [6].

Grounds of objection are that paragraphs (a) to (d) above are not satisfied by the applicant [63(3)].

The onus of proving an objection lies on the objector [63(5)].

An objection must be in writing, in a prescribed form and must reach the Licensing Authority within 3 weeks of the publication of the application in *Applications and Decisions*. The objector must also supply the applicant with a copy of the objection [1737/77/9].

VARIATION OF LICENCES

The holder of an operator's licence can apply to the Licensing Authority who granted the licence for a variation of that licence during its currency. The Licensing Authority may: (a) increase the number of vehicles that may be specified or increase the number of trailers or of specified motor vehicles to be authorised or allow additional vehicles to be operated if the licence does not already cover them; (b) remove vehicles or reduce the maximum number allowed to be operated; (c) agree to changes relating to a standard licence holder's operations or transport manager; (d) alter or remove any condition attached to an operator's licence or (e) convert a restricted operator's licence into a standard operator's licence, or vice versa [Act 1968/68(1)].

Applications for variations will be published in *Applications and Decisions* unless they are of a kind referred to in (a) above and provided that there will not be a substantial increase in the number of vehicles authorised, or they are of a kind referred to in (b) above, or that they are of a trivial nature [68(4)]. Short-term variations, pending the determination of the substantive applications, may be granted [68(5)]. Temporary replacement of specified vehicles can be arranged with the Licensing Authority without going through the full procedure [1737/77/12].

An application to convert a restricted operator's licence into a standard licence is subject to the same requirements as a new application for a standard licence [1462/77/7(1)]. If the holder of a standard licence covering national transport operations applies for the licence to be varied to cover international transport operations he must give particulars of his own or his transport manager's professional competence covering both types of operation [7(2)(a)]. Unless the Licensing Authority is satisfied with these competence qualifications he must refuse the variation [7(2)(b)].

LICENCE CONDITIONS

Conditions may be attached on the grant of a licence by the Licensing Authority. He may require the licensee to inform him of any change in the organisation, management or ownership of the business or, in the case of a company, any changes in shareholders or of any other relevant circumstances [Act 1968/66(1)].

When granting a standard operator's licence the Licensing Authority must attach conditions requiring the holder to notify him of any of the above events which (a) occurs during the currency of the licence, (b) affects the licence holder or transport manager and (c) is relevant to the performance of the duties of a Licensing Authority [1462/77/6(1)]. Where a licence holder is a company notice of a change in shareholding does not have to be given unless it causes a change in the control of the company [6(3)].

LICENCE CURRENCY PERIODS

Every operator's licence must specify the date when it comes into force [Act 1968/67(1)]. Basically, a licence will be current for 5 years but a shorter period will apply if it appears appropriate to the Licensing

Authority in the case of any applicant. For administrative purposes, a Licensing Authority may issue a licence for over or under 5 years [67(2), (3)]. If a licence expires when an application for renewal has been made or if an appeal is pending, it will continue in force until the application or appeal has been determined [67(4)]. A short-term licence may be granted to a newcomer pending the determination of the application [67(5)]. Licences expire on March 24 and the last day of all other months [1737/77/17].

LICENCE REVOCATION OR SUSPENSION

A Licensing Authority can revoke, suspend, prematurely terminate or curtail an operator's licence he has granted. Grounds for such action are: contraventions by the licence holder of the provisions of Section 65, which relates to transport managers, or of Section 66, which concerns certain licence conditions; convictions during the preceding 5 years for the offences listed on page 132 [Act 1968/69(1), (4)]. If the holder of a restricted operator's licence is convicted on more than one occasion in a five-year period of using a vehicle for hire or reward the Licensing Authority must revoke the licence [69(3A)].

Where a Licensing Authority revokes a licence, he can disqualify the holder from obtaining another licence for any period he thinks fit [69(5)]. Where the licence holder is a company, its directors or those holding a controlling interest can be disqualified or, if the licence holder is a partnership, the partners can be disqualified [69(6)]. In suspending or curtailing a licence the Licensing Authority can order that a vehicle specified in the licence may not be used under any other licence, regardless of any hiring margin. This ban may last for up to 6 months or, if earlier, till the affected licence ceases to be in force [69(7A)]. No such penal action may be taken by the Licensing Authority without first holding an inquiry, if requested to do so [69(9)]. The Licensing Authority may suspend the effect of such directions or orders until after the time in which to appeal to the Transport Tribunal has passed or, if an appeal is lodged, until after it has been determined. If he does not do so the operator can apply to the Transport Tribunal for the Authority's decision to be suspended and it must give its decision on that point within 14 days [69(10)]. A person holding a controlling interest in a company is one who is the beneficial owner of more than half of its equity share capital [69(11)].

At a Section 69 inquiry the operator is entitled to be heard or represented [1737/77/10] and any direction to revoke, suspend or curtail a licence must be published in *Applications and Decisions* [7].

If, during the currency of a standard operator's licence, it appears to the Licensing Authority that the licence holder (a) is not of good repute, (b) does not have appropriate financial standing or (c) is not professionally competent and does not have one or more transport managers who are of good repute and professionally competent he must revoke the licence [1462/77/8(1)]. Before taking such action the Licensing Authority must notify the operator of his intention, specify the grounds for revocation, a time within which written representations can be made by the operator and he must consider any such representations made within the time allowed [8(2)].

In the event of the death or physical or mental incapacity of a licence holder or transport manager the Licensing Authority is not required to revoke the licence during a period of up to six months after the event or up to a further six months, both periods being such as the Authority may determine [8(4)]. In a case where for any other reason a transport manager ceases to be employed by the licence holder the Licensing Authority is not required to revoke the licence for such period, not over six months, as the Authority considers reasonable to enable the operator to engage a new transport manager or make alternative arrangements [8(5)].

A direction to revoke a licence under these provisions is regarded as given under Section 69(1) of the Act [8(3)].

OPERATOR'S LICENCE APPEALS

An applicant for an operator's licence, or for the variation of such a licence, who is aggrieved by the refusal or by the conditions attached to it, or of a variation, can appeal to the Transport Tribunal. So, too, can a licence holder who is dissatisfied with a Licensing Authority's decision to revoke, suspend, prematurely terminate or curtail his licence, order a vehicle not to be used under another licence or disqualify him as an operator. An objector, aggrieved by the grant of a licence or variation to which he has objected, can also appeal [70(1)]. No appeal can be based merely because a licence is granted for more or less than 5 years for the purpose of administrative convenience [70(2)]. The Transport Tribunal appeal procedure is given on page 141.

LICENCES, DISCS, ETC.

An identity disc is issued in respect of each motor vehicle specified on an operator's licence [1737/77/11]. At all times while a vehicle is specified on an operator's licence the identity disc must be displayed in a waterproof container adjacent to the place where the vehicle's excise licence is required to be displayed [11(3)].

The holder of an operator's licence must produce it if required by a police officer, certifying officer or traffic examiner and may elect to produce it at his operating centre, head office or principal place of business within the issuing traffic area [14]. If a licence or disc is lost, defaced or destroyed the holder must notify the Licensing Authority who can issue a copy. If the original licence or disc is found it must be returned to the Licensing Authority [15]. If the licence holder ceases to be the user of a specified vehicle he must, within 3 weeks, notify the Licensing Authority, return the licence for variation and return the vehicle's identity disc [16(1)]. If a licence is varied the holder must, when required by the Licensing Authority, return the licence and, if the number of vehicles has been reduced, return the identity discs of those vehicles [16(2)]. If a licence is revoked, suspended or curtailed, or a condition is to be attached to it, the holder must, within 5 days of receiving notification, return the licence and any identity discs which the Licensing Authority may specify [16(3)]. The Licensing Authority must be notified within 3 weeks of any change of address of the licence holder [13].

FEES

The fee for an operator's licence, other than an interim licence granted under Section 67(5), is calculated at the rate of £12 for each specified motor vehicle for each year [2060/74/3 and 460/76]. When the number of specified vehicles is reduced the licence holder is entitled, if he applies in writing within 3 months of the reduction, to a refund of £3 for each whole three-month period of the unexpired term of the licence or £1·25 in the case of a vehicle specified on the licence before January 1, 1975 [3(3)]. An identity disc will not be issued till the licence fee has been paid [3(4)(a)], and a refund will not be made till the identity disc is returned [3(4)(b)].

The fee for an interim licence granted under Section 67(5) is £2 for each specified motor vehicle and payment is due when the licence is applied for [4].

FOREIGN VEHICLES

Operators' licensing does not apply to foreign goods vehicles brought temporarily into Great Britain provided specified conditions are complied with. No such vehicle can remain in Great Britain more than 3 months, engage in transport between points within the United Kingdom and some part of the carriage of goods by the vehicle must take place outside the United Kingdom. Additional, and different, conditions apply in respect of vehicles from particular countries with which Britain has bilateral road transport agreements. The countries and conditions are contained in the Goods Vehicles (Operators' Licences) (Temporary Use in Great Britain) Regulations 1975.

An operator's licence is not required for a Northern Ireland or foreign goods vehicle used for carrying goods between member states of the E.E.C.

    (a) where the vehicle is
        (i) loaded or unloaded at a place not more than 25 km from the coast of Great Britain and unloaded or loaded at a place not more than 25 km from the coast of another Member State but the straight-line distance between the two places (disregarding sea travel on a regular lorry-carrying ferry) not exceeding 100 km, or
        (ii) a motor vehicle or trailer drawn by a foreign goods vehicle having a gross weight limit not over 6 metric tons or a permissible payload not over 3·5 metric tons, or
    (b) where the goods are
        (i) required for medical or surgical care in emergency relief, or
        (ii) carried in security vehicles accompanied by guards, or
        (iii) refuse or sewage.

[1046/75/5 and 1110/78/3]

Exemption from operators' licensing is also given to a vehicle used under an E.E.C. permit or an E.C.M.T. licence provided the permit or licence is carried on the vehicle [6].

TRANSPORT TRIBUNAL

The constitution, powers and procedure of the Transport Tribunal, which has High Court status, are set out in the Tenth Schedule of the Transport Act 1962.

An appeal to the Transport Tribunal by a person aggrieved by the decision of a Licensing Authority must be in the prescribed form [1687/65/12]. The appeal must be lodged with the Tribunal, with the appropriate fee, not later than one month after the date of publication of the issue of Applications and Decisions in which the decision was published or, if not published, the date of the Authority's notification to the aggrieved person. The appeal must be in writing, indicate precisely the decision appealed against, the grounds for appeal and give the names and addresses of every person to whom a copy of the appeal is sent [12A(1), (2)]. Six copies of the appeal must be sent to the Tribunal and at the same time, or soon afterwards, a copy must also be sent to (a) the Licensing Authority and (b) in the case of an application for, or variation of, a licence to every person who made an objection to the application or (c) in the case of an appeal by an objector, to the licence applicant [12A(3)]. The appeal may be amended by leave of the Tribunal [12A(4)].

Except for interlocutory proceedings or preliminary points of law, proceedings in the Tribunal must be in open court [23] and the appellant is heard first [24]. If the appellant fails to attend the court hearing the Tribunal may dismiss or adjourn the proceedings or proceed in his absence [25]. At the hearing the appellant may not depart from his notified grounds of appeal except by leave of the Tribunal [26]. A party to the hearing may appear and be heard in person or by counsel or solicitor [27]. New evidence may not be adduced at the hearing of an appeal except by leave of the court [30(2)]. In practice the court does not give leave to produce new evidence.

The Tribunal's judgment may be given orally or in writing and must give the reasons for the decision. An oral judgment takes effect when it is pronounced in open court and a written judgment takes effect on a day given in the judgment [38] but the Tribunal can lengthen or shorten any time prescribed in its rules [42].

The award of costs is in the discretion of the court but no order for costs can be made unless the court considers the proceedings or any objection or representation were frivolous or vexatious [43].

The fee for lodging an appeal is £2 and for the hearing it is £2 for a half day or part of a half day [59 and 2nd Sched.].

An appeal against the Tribunal's decision may be made, on a point of law only, to the Court of Appeal or, in Scotland, to the Court of Session [Act 1962/10th Sched./15].

PLATING AND TESTING

Road Traffic Act 1972
Motor Vehicles (Tests) (Extension) Order, **No. 973/66**
Goods Vehicles (Plating and Testing) Regulations, **No. 352/71**
Goods Vehicles (Plating and Testing) (Amendment) Regulations, **No. 2074/71**
Goods Vehicles (Plating and Testing) (Amendment) Regulations, **No. 195/72**
Goods Vehicles (Plating and Testing) (Amendment) (No. 2) Regulations, **No. 806/72**
Goods Vehicles (Plating and Testing) (Amendment) Regulations, **No. 1105/73**
Goods Vehicles (Plating and Testing) (Amendment) Regulations, **No. 99/74**
Goods Vehicles (Plating and Testing) (Amendment) Regulations, **No. 36/75**
Goods Vehicles (Plating and Testing) (Amendment) Regulations, **No. 242/76**
Motor Vehicles (Tests) Regulations, **No. 1977/76**
Goods Vehicles (Plating and Testing) (Amendment) Regulations, **No. 867/78**
Goods Vehicles (Plating and Testing) (Amendment) (No. 2) Regulations, **No. 1018/78**
Motor Vehicles (Construction and Use) Regulations, **No. 1017/78**

Most heavy goods vehicles and trailers are subject to a first examination at a Department of the Environment goods vehicle testing station 12 months after first registration or, in the case of trailers, 12 months after being supplied by retail. The first examination consists of a plating examination in which the vehicle's axle and gross weights are assessed and recorded on a plate, followed by a test of roadworthiness. The vehicles are then subject to a roadworthiness test every 12 months afterwards.

Light goods vehicles, dual-purpose vehicles and passenger vehicles, with specified exceptions, are subject to a roadworthiness test at an approved garage 3 years after first registration and then every 12 months afterwards (page 153).

Public service vehicles require a certificate of fitness. This is dealt with in a following chapter (page 186).

APPLICATION

Plating and testing applies to the following vehicles:
(a) heavy motor cars and motor cars constructed or adapted to form part of an articulated vehicle,
(b) other heavy motor cars,
(c) other motor cars which are over 1525 kg unladen,
(d) semi-trailers,
(e) other trailers over 1020 kg unladen,
(f) converter dollies not over 1020 kg unladen and manufactured on or after January 1, 1979.

[352/71/4 and 1018/78]

EXEMPTIONS

1. Dual-purpose vehicles not forming part of an articulated vehicle.
2. Mobile cranes subject to restricted use on public roads and not carrying or hauling any load.
3. Breakdown vehicles.
4. Engineering plant.
5. Trailers designed for the production of asphalt, tarmacadam, etc.
6. Tower wagons.
7. Road construction vehicles and road rollers.
8. Vehicles designed for fire-fighting and salvage purposes.
9. Works trucks, straddle carriers used only as works trucks, and works trailers.
10. Electrically propelled vehicles.
11. Motor vehicles used only for clearing frost, ice or snow from roads by means of a snow-plough or similar contrivance, whether forming part of the vehicle or not.
12. Vehicles made or adapted and used only for spreading grit, etc., on icy roads.
13. Motor vehicles used only for the haulage of lifeboats and carrying the necessary lifeboat gear.
14. Living vans.
15. Vehicles equipped and used mainly for medical, dental, health, educational or display purposes and not used for direct sales.
16. Trailers which have only parking and overrun brakes.
17. Vehicles (and any trailer drawn) exempt from duty because they are used only on public roads to pass from one part to another part of land in the licensee's occupation and not travelling more than 6 miles in any week.
18. Land implements, land locomotives and land tractors.

19. Agricultural trailers drawn on roads only by a land tractor.
20. Hackney carriages, and public service vehicles.
21. Vehicles used solely for funeral purposes.
22. Vehicles going to a port for export and those in use by a visiting force or of a headquarters.
23. Vehicles used by a vehicle manufacturer or importer for testing new or improved types of equipment.
24. Foreign-based motor vehicles brought temporarily into Great Britain within the last 12 months.
25. Motor vehicles currently licensed in Northern Ireland.
26. Vehicles based in the islands of Arran, Bute, Great Cumbrae, Islay, Mull or North Uist.
27. Foreign-based trailers brought temporarily into Great Britain within the last 12 months.
28. Track-laying vehicles.
29. Steam-propelled vehicles.
30. Motor vehicles first used before 1940 used unladen and not drawing a laden trailer, and trailers made before 1940 and used unladen.
31. Three-wheeled street cleansing, refuse disposal or gully cleaning vehicles.
32. Vehicles designed for servicing, controlling, loading or unloading aircraft and not laden or drawing a laden trailer when on roads outside an aerodrome.
32A. Aerodrome vehicles used for road cleansing, refuse disposal or gully cleaning.
33. Police vehicles maintained in workshops approved by the Secretary of State.
34. Articulated drawing units used only for drawing a trailer referred to in 14, 15 or 16 above or a trailer authorised under the Special Types Order. [352/71/4 and Sched. 2]

A vehicle is exempted from having a plating certificate when used for taking it to or away from a first examination, or appeal arising therefrom, or during the course of such an examination [352/71/56(2)]; while used under trade plates [56(3)]; in the case of an imported vehicle, from the place where it is imported to the place where it is to be kept [56(4)]; while authorised under the Special Types Order [56(5)]; while being removed under a statutory power of removal [56(6)]; while seized or detained by police [56(7)]; or while removed, seized, detained or condemned under the Customs and Excise Act [56(8)].

A vehicle is exempted from having a test certificate when used for taking it to or away from a first examination, periodical test, a test following a notifiable alteration, or any appeal arising therefrom, or during the course of such an examination [352/71/57(2)]. A test certificate is not required while the vehicle is used for any of the purposes described in Regulation 56(3) to (8) above [57(3)].

Plating and test certificate requirements do not apply to any island or area mainly surrounded by water from which vehicles cannot be conveniently driven to any other part of Great Britain due to the absence of a bridge, tunnel, ford or other suitable way. This exemption does not apply though to the Isle of Wight or the islands of Lewis, Mainland (Orkney), Mainland (Shetland) or Skye [352/71/58].

TEMPORARY EXEMPTION

A certificate of temporary exemption from plating and testing can be issued by the person in charge of a testing station or the Goods Vehicle Centre, Swansea, when, by reason of exceptional circumstances, an examination cannot be completed by the prescribed date. The exceptional circumstances are defined as an accident, fire, epidemic, severe weather, failure in the supply of essential services or other unexpected happening (except a breakdown or mechanical defect in a vehicle or non-delivery of spare parts). A certificate can last for up to three months [352/71/60, 2074/71].

GENERAL CONDITIONS

The purpose of a goods vehicle test is to ensure that prescribed construction and use requirements relating to a motor vehicle or trailer are complied with. The prescribed requirements are set out in Schedule 3 of the Regulations [352/71/5]. Every examination must be carried out by or under the direction of a goods vehicle examiner [6] and he is authorised to drive the vehicle, whether on a road or not [7]. The driver must, unless permitted otherwise, remain with the vehicle during its examination and drive it or operate its controls as directed [8].

Examiners at testing stations can refuse to examine vehicles and trailers in the following cases:

If not submitted for examination at the appointed time;
Where the applicant, after being requested to do so, fails to produce the examination appointment card (if any) and, in the case of motor vehicles, the registration book or other evidence as to the date of first registration and, for trailers, evidence of the date of manufacture;

Where the particulars shown on the application form are found to be substantially incorrect;

Where a motor vehicle stated to be used to draw a trailer is not, if previously required, accompanied by a trailer;

Where a trailer is not accompanied by a motor vehicle suitable to draw it;

If a motor vehicle is not marked with the chassis or serial number shown in the registration book or where it bears no identification mark allotted by the Ministry or where that number or mark is not permanently affixed to the chassis in such a position as to be readily legible;

A trailer bearing no Ministry identification mark allotted to it or where that mark is not affixed to it in such a position as to be readily legible;

A motor vehicle or trailer in such a dangerous or dirty condition as to make it unreasonable for an examiner to carry out his work. The examination appointment card may require that, for vehicles or trailers which carry toxic, corrosive or inflammable loads, a certificate must be provided to show that they are safe;

A motor vehicle without sufficient fuel and oil for it to be driven on a road for any test which may not be practicable at the testing station or, where a trailer is to be examined, if it is not accompanied by a currently taxed motor vehicle with adequate fuel and oil supplies;

Where a motor vehicle or trailer has no load although one was specified on the last examination appointment card, or *vice versa* [601/68/8, 9];

Where a motor vehicle or trailer examination cannot be completed due to the failure of any part which renders the vehicle or trailer incapable of being moved safely under the vehicle's own power;

Where the driver of a motor vehicle submitting a vehicle or trailer for a periodical test or Part III re-test does not produce the last plating certificate (or a photo-copy of it) and the last goods vehicle test certificate (or a photo-copy) issued for that vehicle or trailer [352/71/9, 10].

FIRST EXAMINATION

Apart from motor vehicles registered before April 1, 1970 (for which special arrangements were made), a motor vehicle must be submitted for a first examination not later than the end of the month in which falls the first anniversary of its registration. Apart from trailers sold or supplied by retail before April 1, 1970 (for which special arrangements were made), a trailer must be submitted for first examination not later than the end of the month in which falls the first anniversary of the date on which it was supplied or sold by retail. A motor vehicle or trailer made after January 1, 1970, and which is not registered or sold or supplied by retail before July 1 of the year following the year of manufacture must be submitted for first examination by the end of that following year [352/71/11].

An application for a first examination must be made at least one month before the desired test date but not more than three months before the date by which it is required to be examined. Application should be made to the Goods Vehicle Centre, 91/92, The Strand, Swansea, on form VTG 1 for motor vehicles or form VTG 2 for trailers but, in the case of trailers, application can be made direct to a testing station if the Swansea Centre consents. If an application is not made at the correct time it can still be dealt with if there are reasonable grounds for the variation [352/71/12, 13]. The required fee must accompany the application and the fees are £12.50 for a motor vehicle and £7 for a trailer [12(2), Sched. 4 and 867/78].

The applicant will be notified of the time, date and place of the examination and regard will be taken of his choice of time and place [14].

STANDARD VEHICLES

When a vehicle submitted for examination is found to be of a make, model and type included in the Standard Lists of Motor Vehicles (copies of these are obtainable from H.M. Stationery Office), the examiner must determine its plated gross and axle weight and the equivalent design weights. Plated weights higher than the current legal maxima will not be given, even if the vehicle is designed for above legal weights [15, 16].

NON-STANDARD VEHICLES

In determining the plated weights to be applied to any vehicle not in the Standard Lists, an examiner must have regard to any information the Secretary of State supplies about similar vehicles; to its design, construction and equipment and the stresses to which it is most likely to be subjected; any information about the weights it was originally designed for; and the specified brake requirements and the need for the vehicle to comply with current legal weight limits [17].

ISSUE OF CERTIFICATES

When the plated weights have been determined, a plating certificate will be issued unless the vehicle fails the goods vehicle test [18]. After this examination the vehicle must undergo a goods vehicle test. For a vehicle complying with the prescribed construction and use requirements, a goods vehicle plating certificate will be issued. In the case of a vehicle which does not comply with these requirements, notice of a refusal to issue both certificates will be given [19].

The prescribed construction and use requirements are set out in detail and cover virtually everything from brakes and steering to the spare wheel carrier and bumpers [3rd Sched.].

RE-TESTS

An operator whose vehicle does not pass the test the first time can either send the vehicle in for a re-test—referred to as a Part II re-test—[352/71/20], or he can appeal against the refusal of a test certificate (and plating certificate) to the area mechanical engineer [26].

Two types of Part II re-test are available. The first is the re-test at the same station or, if the first examination was at an auxiliary station, at that or a different station within 14 days from when the vehicle was first submitted. Arrangements for such a re-test can be made direct with the station [20(2)]. The second is a re-test at the same station after 14 days or at a different station. Arrangements for these re-tests must be made on a prescribed form 7 days before the re-test is required at any vehicle testing station chosen [20(3)]. When a further re-test is desired within 14 days at the station of its last re-test or, where that station is an auxiliary station at that or a different station, arrangements can be made direct with the station concerned [20(4)]. If a vehicle passes a re-test, the necessary certificate will be issued; if it does not, the operator can go through the whole procedure again or he can appeal.

FEES FOR RE-TESTS

No fee is payable for a Part II re-test which is made either on the same day as the first test or on the next day the station is open and it is the first re-test and due only to a minor defect, as defined. For other

Part II re-tests within 14 days fees payable are £7 for a motor vehicle and £4.50 for a trailer. Fees for Part II re-tests after 14 days or at a different station (apart from the auxiliary station provision) are the same as for the first examination [352/71/21, 4th Sched. and 867/78].

APPEALS

An appeal can be made to the area mechanical engineer by a person aggrieved by the result of the first examination or the refusal of a test certificate on either the first examination or a Part II re-test. The appeal must be lodged at the office of the traffic area concerned not later than 10 days after the examination was made. Every appeal, which must be made on an approved form, must be accompanied by a fee of £15.

The engineer will then send the applicant a notice stating when and where the re-examination will take place. It may be at a testing station or any other place he considers convenient. If required, the plating certificate or refusal notice, whichever is in dispute, must be produced. Information can also be sought about any alterations, repairs, accident or anything else which may have affected the vehicle since the date of the test appealed against. The list of conditions applicable to the first examination—embodying the production of documents and the state of the vehicle—apply equally to examinations on appeal [352/71/26].

An operator who does not agree with the area mechanical engineer's findings can appeal to the Secretary of State. This appeal must be lodged at the Goods Vehicle Centre, Swansea, within 14 days and be accompanied by a fee of £25. The operator will be notified of the time and place of the re-examination to be made by an officer appointed by the Minister for the purpose. The procedure governing his examination is the same as that governing the area mechanical engineer's examination and he can adopt the same courses on concluding his examination [27].

PERIODICAL TESTS

Generally a goods vehicle registered before January 1, 1968, must be submitted for a periodical test not later than the end of the month in each year in which falls the anniversary of the vehicle's registration [352/71/28(1)]. In the case of a trailer made before January 1, 1968, the end of the month by which it has to be submitted for a periodical examination in each year is indicated by the last two figures in the identification mark allocated to the trailer on its first examination. For example, if the last two figures are 10, the trailer must have an annual test by the end of October in each year [28(2)]. In the case of newer vehicles, a periodical test must be made by the end of the month in each year in which falls the anniversary of the date of issue of the vehicle's first test certificate [29].

Provision is made for an expedited test certificate to be issued for a motor vehicle or trailer more than two months before a certificate already in force for the vehicle is due to expire [352/71/30(1), 2074/71]. Where an expedited certificate is issued the vehicle's next periodical test is due by the end of the month in which falls the anniversary of the date of issue of the expedited certificate [30(2)].

Application for a periodical test, the fees payable and notification of test appointment are the same as for a first examination [31, 32, 33].

After a periodical test has been carried out the examiner shall either issue a test certificate or a notification of refusal [34]. If a refusal notice is given the operator can have a Part III re-test, which involves the same procedure as a Part II re-test, or he can go through the same appeal procedure as applies to Part II tests [35-40].

NOTIFIABLE ALTERATIONS

If alterations to a vehicle or its equipment come within the definition of 'notifiable alterations', an operator must declare details of the alterations on an approved form to the Goods Vehicle Centre at Swansea before the vehicle can legally be used on a road. The sender can ask for the plating certificate to be amended [351/71/42].

Notifiable alterations are defined as: alterations made to the vehicle or its fixed equipment which varies the carrying capacity; alterations adversely affecting the braking system; or alterations made to the vehicle or its fixed equipment which would render the vehicle unsafe to operate at its plated weights [41].

If a request is made for the plated weights to be amended, the Centre will notify the operator as to the time and place where a re-examination will take place [42, 43]. The re-examination fee is £6 [45 and 867/78]. Re-examination may be required if no such request has been made but, if this is done, no fee is payable [43(2), 45].

Where any particular on a plate becomes no longer applicable to the vehicle, otherwise than by a notifiable alteration, the operator can apply for that particular to be amended. The application to the Centre must be accompanied by a £6 fee and the operator will be notified of a re-examination in the usual manner [44, 45 and 867/78].

Vehicles submitted for re-examination must be in the prescribed condition. Examination will be confined to the plating aspect. On completion, the examiner will either notify the operator in writing that the alterations have not changed the plated rating, or amend the certificate to show new weights, or issue a new certificate [47].

Any person aggrieved by the result of the re-examination can appeal to the area mechanical engineer and, subsequently, to the Minister in the manner described for Part II re-test appeals [48].

PAYMENT OF FEES

Except in cases where fees can be paid in cash, they must be paid by cheque, money order or postal order [352/71/49].

The fee for a first examination, periodical test, re-test or re-examination is payable even if the vehicle is not presented for test at the appointed time. But, if (a) the applicant gives the testing station concerned at least 7 days' notice before the appointment that he does not propose to keep the appointment or (b) that due to exceptional circumstances (as defined earlier) occurring not more than 7 days before the appointment (and of which the Centre is notified within 3 days) he cannot or could not keep the appointment then, within 28 days of the notice, the applicant can (1) request that the fee be used for another examination or (2) state that no other examination is required, in which case the fee will be repaid, less 75p [50, 2074/71 and 36/75].

If the vehicle is presented at the Centre and is not examined because the necessary documents are not produced, or it is not in a clean condition and the test is refused, the fee is forfeited [51].

Appeal fees can be repaid to the operator, either wholly or partly, at the discretion of the Secretary of State where it appears to him that there were substantial grounds for appealing.

If a vehicle to be re-examined following an appeal is not submitted for examination, the fee is lost. But if at least 2 days before the examination the operator notifies the office where the appeal was lodged that the vehicle will not be submitted for re-examination the fee will be repaid unless another time is arranged for the re-examination [52].

In calculating the number of days' notice to be given in the various parts of the Regulations, no account has to be taken of Saturdays, Sundays and public holidays [54].

REPLACING LOST PLATES

If a plate, plating certificate, test certificate or Ministry test date disc is lost or damaged a replacement can be obtained from the Centre at Swansea. They cost £1 each [352/72/53 and 867/78].

TEST DATE DISC

When a test certificate is issued for a trailer a test date disc is issued with it. The disc contains the trailer's identification mark, the date of expiry of the certificate and the number of the testing station issuing the certificate. The disc must be carried in a readily accessible position so that it is clearly visible from the nearside of the road. It must not be displayed after the test certificate to which it relates has expired or after the date a new certificate is issued [1017/78/149].

DISPLAY OF PLATE

When a plating certificate has been issued for a goods vehicle the Ministry plate issued with it must be securely fixed in the cab of the vehicle in a conspicuous and readily accessible position or, if the vehicle does not have a cab, in a conspicuous and readily accessible position elsewhere on the vehicle [1017/78/148].

MARKING OF WEIGHTS

Maximum permitted gross weights may be marked on the sides of a vehicle which has been Ministry plated [1017/78/151]. (Section 172 of the 1972 Act prohibits the unauthorised marking of weights on Ministry plated vehicles.)

The weights shown in column 2 of the Ministry plate (page 158) must not be exceeded when the vehicle is used on a road in Great Britain [1017/78/150]. They take effect on the date by which the vehicle is required to be submitted for its plating examination [150 and Act 1972/46(1)].

TESTS FOR LIGHT GOODS VEHICLES AND CARS

Subject to specified exceptions, all motor vehicles registered for more than three years must, at any time when used on a road, have in force a test certificate issued during the preceding 12 months [Act 1972/44, 973/66]. If a vehicle is used on roads, whether in Great Britain or elsewhere, before being registered the three years counts from the time of first use but any use of the vehicle before being sold or supplied by retail is disregarded [44(2)(b), (3)(a)].

Vehicles which are exempt are public service vehicles adapted to carry eight or more passengers [44(4)] and the following:

(a) locomotives and motor tractors,
(b) tracked vehicles,
(c) goods vehicles over 1525 kg unladen (excluding dual-purpose vehicles and motor caravans),
(d) vehicles forming part of an articulated vehicle,
(e) works trucks,
(f) pedestrian-controlled vehicles,
(g) certain invalid carriages,
(h) licensed Metropolitan taxis,
(i) vehicles going to a port for export, vehicles of visiting forces and land tractors,
(j) vehicles temporarily in Great Britain,
(k) vehicles licensed in Northern Ireland,
(l) vehicles exempt from duty due to travelling less than 6 miles a week on public roads,
(m) certain taxis tested on behalf of local authorities,
(mm) certain hire cars tested on behalf of local authorities,
(n) police vehicles maintained in approved workshops,
(o) imported military vehicles,
(p) electrically propelled goods vehicles not over 1525 kg unladen.   [1977/76/30].

A test certificate is not required for a vehicle being taken to a test previously arranged, being brought away from a test or during a test; a vehicle authorised under the Special Types Order; an imported vehicle while on the journey from the point of importation to the residence of the owner or driver; a vehicle being removed under a statutory power of removal; a vehicle detained or seized by police; a vehicle detained or seized under the Customs and Excise Act; or a vehicle being tested by a motor trader during or after repairs to the vehicle [1977/76/31]. A test certificate is not required for the use of a vehicle in any island or area mainly surrounded by water, except the Isle of Wight, Arran, Bute, Great Cumbrae, Islay, Lewis, Mainland (Orkney), Mainland (Shetland), Mull, North Uist, and Skye [32].

For the purposes of this kind of test motor vehicles are divided into the following five classes:

Class I: light motor bicycles,
Class II: motor bicycles,

Class III: light motor vehicles (i.e. motor cars
                              not over 408 kg unladen and motor
                              tricycles),
Class IV: heavy motor cars and motor cars
                              (not in Class III or V),
Class V: large passenger carrying vehicles
                              (i.e. vehicles constructed or adapted
                              for more than 12 passengers, exclud-
                              ing the driver, and which are not
                              p.s.v.s.).   [1977/76/4(4)].

An application for an authorisation to carry out tests may be made to the Secretary of State by an individual, a partnership or a company [5]. The applicant may then be authorised to carry out examinations of vehicles of a particular class or classes [8]. In practice very few privately owned garages are authorised to test Class V vehicles. Such tests are generally carried out at Department of Transport h.g.v. testing stations. A list of testing stations authorised to test Class V vehicles can be obtained from a person's area traffic office.

Examiners have to comply with specified conditions. These include exhibiting in the test station in a conspicuous place the testing station authorisation and a list of names of persons authorised to carry out or supervise examinations and to sign test certificates. A prescribed sign must be fastened to a wall outside the testing station [9].

A person who wishes to have a vehicle examined can apply by telephone, in person, or in writing to an authorised examiner, a designated council or the Secretary of State at the vehicle testing station concerned for a test appointment. He can also submit the vehicle for examination at the testing station of an examiner or a designated council without a prior appointment [11(1), (2)]. Authorised examiners and councils must ensure that

(a) where a test appointment is requested an appointment is offered at the earliest time which is reasonably practicable for the examination to be carried out;
(b) where a vehicle is submitted without prior appointment, the applicant is informed that the test can be carried out forth-with or, if not, of the earliest time which is reasonably practicable to carry out the test;
(c) except in circumstances beyond the control of the examiner or council, examinations are carried out in accordance with

the appointment or at another time agreed between the parties [11(4)].

The time and date of an appointment or arranged time for the test and the name of the person who asked for it must (except where no appointment is made) be recorded by the authorised examiner or designated council [11(5)]. Whilst an examination may be carried out even though the conditions in Regulation 11 are not complied with [11(6)] nothing in the Regulation is to be taken as entitling an examiner to test vehicles of a class not specified in his authorisation [11(7)].

An examiner is not obliged to carry out an examination:

(i) where on submission of the vehicle for test the applicant does not, on request, produce the vehicle's registration document or other evidence of its date of first registration or manufacture;

(ii) where the vehicle or any part is in such a dirty condition as to make examination unreasonably difficult;

(iii) where the test cannot be carried out without the vehicle being driven and it does not have enough fuel and oil;

(iv) where goods on the vehicle are required by the examiner to be removed or secured and they are not removed or secured [12].

Methods to be used and apparatus required for testing brakes, steering, lighting equipment, seat belts, tyres, wipers and washers, exhausts and bodywork are specified [13 and Sched. 3].

Where a vehicle is submitted for examination the examiner, designated council or Secretary of State, as the case may be, has responsibility for loss of or damage to the vehicle and loss of or damage to any other property or personal injury arising in connection with the examination as if a contract, with no provision as to liability, existed between the parties [14(1)]. A person submitting a vehicle for test must not be requested or required by an examiner, a designated council or the Secretary of State to accept responsibility for, or to give any release or indemnity in respect of, any loss, damage or injury for which the examining body is responsible under Regulation 14(1) [14(2)]. These provisions do not prevent a person being requested or required to accept responsibility for (a) loss of or damage to the vehicle while still in possession of the examiner but after the time it should have been removed from the premises under Regulation 20(1) (explained below) or (b) loss, damage or injury arising while repairs are carried out at the request of the person submitting the vehicle for test [14(3)].

If the vehicle condition conforms to statutory requirements [Sched. 2] a test certificate, in the prescribed form, is issued. If the requirements are not met, a notification of the refusal of a test certificate is issued with reasons for its refusal. Test certificates and notifications of refusals should be issued on the same date as the examination. Where this is not practicable, they must be issued not later than the next day (not a Sunday or a public holiday) provided that between the issue and when the vehicle examination is completed, the vehicle has remained in an unaltered condition at the testing station [15].

When, during an examination, it is found that the construction or condition of a vehicle or its equipment or accessories is so defective that a brake test would be likely to cause danger or damage the examiner can refuse to carry out the braking test but must continue with the rest of the examination. In such circumstances a test certificate will be refused [16].

Fees payable on an application for examination are £2.50 for solo motor bicycles and £4.10 for any other vehicle [17 and Sched. 5]. Where the statutory requirements are not complied with or where a brake test cannot be carried out then (a) if the vehicle is left at the same testing station for repair no further test fee is payable on completion of those repairs and (b) if the vehicle is removed from that testing station but within 14 days is taken to the same or another testing station for repair the test fee payable on completion of those repairs is half the above figure [Sched. 5].

An appeal by any person aggrieved by the refusal or the grounds for refusal of a test certificate can be made to the Secretary of State and must be lodged with an area traffic office not later than 14 days after receiving the notification of refusal [18]. The fee for an appeal, which must accompany the notice, is £2.50 for a motor bicycle and £4.10 for any other vehicle. All or part of such fee can be refunded where the Secretary of State finds there were substantial grounds for contesting the whole or part of the decision appealed against [19].

A person who submits a vehicle for test must remove it from the custody of the examiner, designated council or Secretary of State:

(a) where an appointment was made for carrying out the test on a particular day and it has been completed on or before that day, before the end of the second day after the appointed day, or

MINISTRY PLATE

| PLATE | DEPARTMENT OF TRANSPORT | Serial No. |

Road Traffic Act 1972, Sections 40 and 45
Examination of Goods Vehicles

REGISTRATION/IDENTIFICATION MARK (where applicable)	CHASSIS/SERIAL No. (where marked on vehicle)	YEAR OF ORIGINAL REGISTRATION (where applicable)	YEAR OF MANUFACTURE	MAKE	MODEL (where applicable)

(1) DESCRIPTION OF WEIGHTS APPLICABLE TO VEHICLE		(2) WEIGHTS NOT TO BE EXCEEDED IN GREAT BRITAIN KILOGRAMS	(3) DESIGN WEIGHTS (if higher than shown in col. (2)) KILOGRAMS	Space for Authenticating Stamp
AXLE WEIGHT (Axles numbered from front to rear)	AXLE 1			
	AXLE 2			
	AXLE 3			
	AXLE 4			
GROSS WEIGHT (see warning opposite)				DATE OF ISSUE OF PLATING CERTIFICATE
TRAIN WEIGHT (see warning opposite)				

WARNING

1. A reduced gross weight may apply in certain cases to a vehicle towing or being towed by another.
2. A reduced train weight may apply depending on the type of trailer drawn.
3. All weights shown are subject to fitting of correct tyres.

Notes: 1. A Ministry Plate may contain the words 'MINISTRY OF TRANSPORT' or 'DEPARTMENT OF TRANSPORT', and may contain the words 'DEPARTMENT OF THE ENVIRONMENT' instead of the words 'DEPARTMENT OF TRANSPORT', Sections 8 and 9' instead of the words 'Road Traffic Act 1972, Sections 40 and 45'. It may also contain additional columns in Columns (2) and (3) showing the weights in tons.

2. Entries in respect of train weight are required only in the case of motor vehicles constructed or adapted to form part of an articulated vehicle.

3. A Ministry Plate may, in a space provided for the purpose, show the DOE (Department of the Environment) or DTp.

(b) in any other case, before the end of the second day after the day on which he receives notice (written or verbal) (i) that the test has been carried out or (ii) that the test has not been carried out for reasons under Regulation 12 and he is to remove the vehicle [20].

Duplicate certificates to replace lost or defaced originals can be obtained on application to the authorised station or authority issuing the originals for a fee of 50p [23].

POWERS OF POLICE, EXAMINERS, ETC.

Road Traffic Act 1960
Weights and Measures Act 1963
Road Traffic Regulation Act 1967
Road Traffic Act 1972 as amended by *Road Traffic Act 1974* and *Transport Act 1978*
Road Traffic (Foreign Vehicles) Act 1972
Heavy Commercial Vehicles (Controls and Regulations) Act 1973
Public Service Vehicles (Arrest of Offenders) Act 1975
P.S.V. (Drivers' and Conductors' Licences) Regulations, **No. 1321/34**
P.S.V. (Licences and Certificates) Regulations, **No. 900/52**
Removal and Disposal of Vehicles Regulations, **No. 43/68**
Functions of Traffic Wardens Order, **No. 1958/70**
Road Vehicles (Registration and Licensing) Regulations, **No. 450/71**
Goods Vehicles (Prohibitions) (Exemptions and Appeals) Regulations, **No. 2020/71**
Motor Vehicles (Driving Licences) Regulations, **No. 1076/76**
Heavy Goods Vehicles (Drivers' Licences) Regulations, **No. 1309/77**
Goods Vehicles (Operators' Licences) Regulations, **No. 1737/77**
Motor Vehicles (Construction and Use) Regulations, **No. 1017/78**
Weighing of Motor Vehicles (Use of Dynamic Axle Weighing Machines) Regulations,
    No. 1180/78

INSPECTION OF VEHICLES

An authorised examiner can test any motor vehicle or trailer on a road to check that legal requirement as to brakes, silencers, steering gear, tyres, lighting equipment and reflectors, smoke, fumes and vapour are being complied with and for this purpose he may drive the vehicle [Act 1972/53(1)].

Authorised examiners are Department of the Environment examiners, London taxi examiners, authorised police officers and persons appointed by a police chief for the purposes of this Section [53(2)]. When an examiner wishes to test a vehicle under this section the driver can elect for a deferred test unless an accident has occurred due to the vehicle's presence or if it appears to a constable that the vehicle is so defective it ought not to proceed [53(3)]. In electing for a deferred test the vehicle owner should specify a period of 7 days in the next 30 days when the test can be made and the premises where it can be done. The examiner must then give at least 48 hours' notice of the time he proposes to test the vehicle. The place and time of the test can be varied by agreement between the examiner and owner [Schedule 3]. It is an offence to obstruct an examiner or fail to comply with a requirement of the Section [53(4)].

A D.o.E. examiner, London taxi examiner, police officer in uniform or person appointed under Section 53 of the 1972 Act can test and inspect the brakes, silencer, steering gear, tyres, lighting equipment and reflectors of a motor vehicle or trailer on premises, if the owner of the premises consents [1017/78/145]. This power cannot be used unless the owner of the vehicle consents or he has been given at least 48 hours' notice of the test but this restriction does not apply if the vehicle has been involved in a notifiable accident [145(2), (3), (4)].

To ensure that goods vehicles are maintained in a fit and serviceable condition a D.o.E. examiner may, at any time, enter and inspect any goods vehicle and may also, at a reasonable time, enter premises on which he believes a goods vehicle is kept [Act 1972/56(1)(2)]. It is an offence to obstruct an examiner acting under these provisions [56(3)]. An examiner or police officer in uniform can require the driver of a stationary goods vehicle to take the vehicle to a place for inspection up to 5 miles away [56(4), (5)].

A p.s.v. certifying officer can enter and inspect any p.s.v. and for this purpose may require the p.s.v. to be stopped. He can also, at any reasonable time, enter premises on which he believes a p.s.v. is kept. It is an offence to obstruct an officer acting under these provisions [Act 1960/128].

An authorised examiner can, at any reasonable time, enter premises where used vehicles are sold, supplied or offered for sale or supply, exposed or kept for sale to ensure that such vehicles can be used on a road without contravening specified requirement. To test a vehicle he may drive it on a road. Authorised examiners are the same persons referred to in Section 53, above, and it is an offence to obstruct an examiner [Act 1972/61].

The examiner may enter at any reasonable hour premises where vehicles or vehicle parts of a class to be prescribed for type-approval purposes are sold, supplied, offered for sale or supply, exposed or kept for sale or supply. He can test the vehicle or part and to test a vehicle or trailer may drive it on a road [61(1A)].

WEIGHING

Department of the Environment examiners, persons authorised by a highway authority and police officers authorised by their chief constable can require the person in charge of any vehicle to take it to a weighbridge and allow it to be weighed. Failure to comply or to obstruct an authorised person is an offence [Act 1972/160(1)]. The requirement can apply to vehicles on harbour premises [160(7)]. It is unlawful for such a person to require or allow the vehicle to be unloaded for it to be weighed unladen [160(1) proviso]. Regulations may be made as to how a vehicle is to be weighed and the limits within which, unless the contrary is proved, a weight is to be presumed accurate [160(1A)]. An authorised person can require the driver of a vehicle to drive it or do any other thing in relation to the vehicle or load for the purpose of weighing it in accordance with those regulations [160(1B)].

If the vehicle is more than 5 miles from the weighbridge when the requirement is made and the vehicle is found not to be overloaded the operator can claim for any loss he sustains [160(2)]. When a vehicle is weighed under these provisions the driver must be given a certificate of weight (whether the vehicle is overloaded or not) and this exempts the vehicle from being weighed again on the same journey with the same load [160(3)].

A prescribed form of certificate required by an authorised person stating the weight of a vehicle weighed under Section 160(1) is evidence of the matters it states [160(5)]. If, in connection with weighing a vehicle under Section 160(1) an authorised person (a) drives or does anything in relation to the vehicle or its load or (b) requires the driver to drive in a particular way, to a particular place or do anything in relation to the vehicle or load neither he nor the driver shall be liable in respect of any damage or loss to the vehicle or load unless it is shown he acted without reasonable care [160(6)].

Where a vehicle is weighed on a dynamic axle weighing machine the weighing shall be made by causing the vehicle to be driven across the weighing platform in accordance with the instructions of an authorised person in a manner and at a steady speed to ensure that (a) the machine can show successively each axle weight and (b) if the machine does not print a record of each weight, so that the authorised person can record the weights [1180/78/3]. Unless the contrary is proved, the weights determined by a dynamic axle weigher will be presumed accurate to within plus or minus 150 kilograms for each axle [4]. A certificate of weight is prescribed for the purposes of Section 160(5) of the 1972 Act [5]. Section 160(5) provides that a prescribed certificate signed by an authorised person and which gives any weight of a vehicle following a weighing under Section 160 will be evidence of the matter it states.

When, under the Weights and Measures Act 1963, a conveyance note has to be carried on a vehicle and the quantity of goods is stated, an inspector of weights and measures can require the vehicle to be taken to a weighbridge and weighed, require the driver to have it check-weighed (both gross and tare) and/or require goods to be unloaded [Act 1963/30(3)] but these powers may be exercised only if reasonably necessary to enforce the Act.

The Secretary of State can, on giving 7 days' notice in writing, require an owner to produce a goods vehicle (including any alternative or additional body and any alternative parts which are required to be included in its unladen weight) at any given time at a specified weighbridge for the purpose of weighing the vehicle in the presence of an officer of the council [450/71/45].

PROHIBITIONS

If on inspecting a goods vehicle it appears to a goods vehicle examiner that the vehicle is unfit or likely to become unfit for service he can prohibit the driving of the vehicle on a road either absolutely or conditionally [Act 1972/57(1)]. The prohibition must be given in writing to the driver and it must state whether it is immediate or delayed [57(2)]. If the vehicle is an immediate risk to public safety the prohibition comes into operation forthwith [57(3)] and in any other case can be delayed subject to conditions specified by the examiner [57(4),(5)]. A prohibition may be made irremovable till the vehicle is inspected at a testing station [57(4A)]. When a notice has been given an examiner may vary or suspend it [57(6)].

When a goods vehicle has been weighed under Section 160, above, and found to exceed a weight limit a goods vehicle examiner or authorised person can prohibit the use of the vehicle on a road until the weight is reduced to the appropriate limit and official notification is given that the vehicle can proceed. The prohibition notice may direct the removal of the vehicle to a specified place and subject to specified conditions and during such removal the prohibition does not apply [Acts 1972/57(7), (7A) and 1973/3].

When a prohibition is made under Section 57(2) or (7) the vehicle owner and, in the case of a vehicle on an operator's licence, the Licensing Authority must be informed [57(8)].

It is an offence for a person to drive, or cause or permit to be driven, a vehicle in contravention of a prohibition or to refuse or neglect to comply with a direction under Section 57(7) [57(9)]. Exemptions are provided for taking a prohibited defective vehicle to a place for a previously arranged examination [2020/71/4].

A prohibition may be removed when an examiner is satisfied the vehicle is fit for service again [Act 1972/58(1)]. If he refuses to remove a prohibition an appeal procedure is provided [58(2), (3) and 2020/71/5].

On inspecting a p.s.v. a certifying officer can revoke the vehicle's certificate of fitness if the vehicle does not comply with prescribed conditions and if he does so the vehicle's p.s.v. licence is of no effect until a new certificate is obtained [Act 1960/129(5)]. He can also suspend the vehicle's p.s.v. licence if the vehicle is unfit or likely to become unfit for service through any defect [133(1)]. If a p.s.v. examiner refuses to remove a suspension the operator can appeal to the Traffic Commissioners [133(4)] and then to the Secretary of State [143(4)].

Under the Road Traffic (Foreign Vehicles) Act 1972 (as amended by the Transport Act 1978) if the driver of a foreign goods or public service vehicle obstructs an examiner in carrying out his duties in inspecting the vehicle or it appears that the law governing operators' licensing, drivers' hours and records, construction and use of vehicles or lighting would be contravened by the vehicle he can prohibit its use on a road either absolutely or conditionally. Such a prohibition for construction and use or lighting defects may be made irremovable till the vehicle is inspected at a testing station.

If the vehicle has been weighed and found to be overloaded or the driver obstructs an authorised person or fails to allow the vehicle to be weighed the vehicle can again be prohibited. Such a prohibition may be against driving the vehicle on a road till the weight is reduced and official notice given that it can proceed.

Where a vehicle is prohibited the driver can be directed to take the vehicle to a specified place. If a person drives a vehicle, or causes or permits it to be driven, in contravention of a prohibition or fails to comply with a direction he commits an offence and may be arrested by a police officer in uniform.

An examiner can require the driver of a foreign goods vehicle to produce a permit or own-account document (if he is required to carry one) and the driver of a foreign p.s.v. to produce a control document. If the driver fails to comply the examiner can prohibit the use of the vehicle.

Foreign goods and public service vehicles are those not registered in the United Kingdom, including any trailer drawn.

A traffic examiner has power under the International Road Haulage Permits Act 1975 to prohibit a vehicle from leaving the United Kingdom if a prescribed document is not carried on the vehicle—see page 238.

PRODUCTION OF LICENCES, ETC.

A constable can require the following to produce a driving licence: (a) a person driving a motor vehicle on a road, (b) a person believed to have been the driver when an accident occurred or when a traffic offence was committed or (c) a person who supervises a provisional licence holder in (a) or (b). He can also require such a person to give his date of birth if (1) he fails to produce his licence forthwith or (2) produces a licence (a) granted by a local authority; (b) which the constable suspects was not granted to him, was granted in error or is altered with intent to deceive; or (c) in which the driver number has been altered, removed or defaced [Act 1972/161(1) and 1076/76/24]. A certifying officer or examiner is given the same powers in respect of a goods vehicle [163]. A person is allowed 5 days in which to produce his driving licence at a police station he specifies [161(4)]. If a licence has been revoked or obtained by a false statement a constable can require its production [161(2),(3)].

A constable can require a person driving a motor vehicle on a road, or a person believed to have been driving at the time of an accident or traffic offence, to give his and the owner's name and address and to produce a certificate of insurance or security, a test certificate (in the case of a three-year-old vehicle) and, in the case of a goods vehicle, a plating certificate or goods vehicle test certificate [162(1)]. A certifying officer or examiner is given the same power in respect of goods vehicles [163]. A person who supervises a provisional licence holder in the above circumstances can be required by a constable to give his own and the vehicle owner's name and address [162(3)].

A chief officer of police can require the owner of a vehicle to give third-party insurance details in any case where the driver fails to produce a certificate or if a certificate is not produced following an accident involving injury [Act 1972/167]. He can also require a vehicle owner to state who the driver was when a specified traffic offence was committed. But it is a defence for the owner to show that he did not know and could not with reasonable diligence have discovered the driver's identity [168].

The driver of a heavy goods vehicle, and a person who accompanies a learner-driver, must produce his h.g.v. driver's licence when required by a constable or an examiner and the examiner can require him to sign his (the examiner's) record sheet [1039/77/15]. A constable can also require a h.g.v. licence to be produced by a person believed to have been the driver when an accident occurred or a traffic offence was committed and by a person supervising a learner under such circumstances [15(2)]. A constable or examiner may require the holder of a h.g.v. licence which has been suspended or revoked to produce it and he may then take possession of it [15 (3), (4)]. He can also require production of a licence obtained by making a false statement [15 (5)]. In any of the above circumstances, if production is required by a constable the holder is allowed 5 days in which to produce it at a police station he specifies or, if it is required by an examiner, the holder is allowed 10 days in which to produce it at a D.o.E. traffic office [15(6)]. A Licensing Authority can require the holder of a h.g.v. licence to produce it to him, together with his ordinary licence, within 10 days [15(7)]. Above references to a licence include a Northern Ireland licence.

A driver or conductor of a public service vehicle must, when required by a constable, certifying officer or examiner to produce his p.s.v. driver's or conductor's licence, either produce it or state the address at which, in the next 5 days, it can be inspected [1321/34/11].

The holder of a road service licence, backing or certificate of fitness must produce it for examination at his principal place of business when so required by a constable, certifying officer or examiner [900/53/9].

The holder of an operator's licence must produce it when required by a constable, certifying officer or examiner and may elect whether to produce it at his operating centre, head office or principal place of business [1737/77/14].

On a p.s.v. carrying passengers at separate fares but which is regarded as a contract carriage, by virtue of Section 118(2) and Part III or IV of the 12th Schedule to the 1960 Act, the driver must keep a work ticket which must be produced when required by a constable, certifying officer or examiner [Act 1960/12th Sched. 14(3)]. The holder of a p.s.v. licence must keep such work tickets for 6 months and produce them when required by a person authorised by the Traffic Commissioners [14(4)].

RECORD SHEETS AND TACHOGRAPHS

The powers to enable production and inspection of record books, registers and other documents in connection with the drivers' hours law are described on page 80. The powers to require production and enable inspection of record sheets produced by tachographs fitted in vehicles from other E.E.C. countries and fitted voluntarily in British-based vehicles are given on page 86.

REMOVAL OF VEHICLES

If a vehicle has broken down or been left on a road so as to cause obstruction or danger or in contravention of a parking restriction a constable can require the driver or owner to remove it in accordance with any directions which may be given [43/68/3]. In the above circumstances or if a vehicle appears to have been abandoned a constable may himself remove it or arrange for it to be removed [4]. A local authority has power to remove vehicles which appear to be abandoned [5].

EYESIGHT TEST

If a constable suspects that a person is driving a vehicle when he cannot perform the driving test eyesight requirement—reading a number plate having $3\frac{1}{2}$ in or $3\frac{1}{8}$ in figures at 75 ft and 67 ft respectively—he can require that person to take such an eyesight test [Act 1972/91].

ARREST

A constable may arrest a person who is in charge of, driving or attempting to drive a motor vehicle on a road or other public place if he is unfit to drive through drink or drugs [Act 1972/5]. A constable may arrest a person who takes a breath test and the device used indicates that the person's proportion of alcohol in the blood exceeds the prescribed limit. He may also arrest a person who fails to take a breath test but who he believes to have alcohol in his body [8(4), (5)]. A person who has been arrested under these provisions and required to provide a specimen of blood or urine may be detained at a police station till he takes a breath test which shows his blood/alcohol level to be below the prescribed limit [11].

A constable can arrest the driver of a motor vehicle who, within his view, commits an offence of dangerous, careless or inconsiderate driving unless the driver either gives his name and address or produces his ordinary driving licence for examination [Act 1972/164(2)]. A constable in uniform can arrest any person driving or attempting to drive a motor vehicle on a road and whom he suspects is a disqualified driver [100].

A constable may require a person whom he has reason to suspect of contravening the Public Service Vehicles (Conduct of Drivers, Conductors and Passengers) Regulations to give his name and address and if the person (a) refuses his name and address or (b) gives his name and address but does not satisfactorily answer any of the constable's questions about it he may be arrested [Act 1975/1].

TRAFFIC WARDENS

A police authority may appoint traffic wardens [Act 1967/81] and they may be employed in enforcing the law with respect to an offence of (a) parking without lights or reflectors, (b) a vehicle obstructing a road or waiting, parking, loading, or unloading on a road or other public place, (c) contravening the Vehicles (Excise) Act, or (d) parking meter charges. They may also give out fixed penalty notices (except for obstruction and leaving a vehicle in a dangerous position); be employed as attendants at street parking places, at car-pounds and as school crossing patrols; and may be employed in making inquiries about the identity of a driver and in regulating traffic (but not from a moving vehicle) [1958/70/Schedule].

In carrying out the above functions traffic wardens are given the same powers as a constable in preventing obstruction in the Metropolitan and City of London areas; in giving directions to drivers and pedestrians when engaged in the regulation of traffic; and to require a pedestrian who ignores a traffic direction to give his name and address [3(2)].

A traffic warden can require a driver, or person believed to have been a driver, to give his name and address if he has reasonable cause to believe that an offence has been committed (a) of parking without lights or reflectors, (b) by a vehicle obstructing, waiting, parking, loading, or unloading, (c) of failing to comply with a traffic sign or direction when engaged on traffic regulation, (d) against the Vehicles (Excise) Act, or (e) in relation to parking meter charges [3(3)].

The production of a driving licence can be required by a traffic warden employed at a car-pound but only if he has reasonable cause to believe that an offence has been committed by the vehicle obstructing, waiting, being parked, loaded or unloaded in a road [3(4)].

A traffic warden has no power to require production of insurance or test certificates.

P.S.V. CONDUCT, ETC.

P.S.V. (*Conduct of Drivers, Conductors and Passengers*) *Regulations*, **No. 619/36**
P.S.V. (*Conduct of Drivers, Conductors and Passengers*) (*Amendment*) *Regulations*, **No. 461/75**
P.S.V. (*Lost Property*) *Regulations*, **No. 1268/34**
P.S.V. (*Lost Property*) (*Amendment*) *Regulations*, **No. 2262/58**
P.S.V. (*Lost Property*) (*Amendment*) *Regulations*, **No. 2397/60**
London Transport (*Lost Property*) *Regulations*, **No. 2125/71**
P.S.V. *and Trolley Vehicles* (*Carrying Capacity*) *Regulations*, **No. 1612/54**
P.S.V. *and Trolley Vehicles* (*Carrying Capacity*) (*Amendment*) *Regulations*, **No. 472/58**
P.S.V. *and Trolley Vehicles* (*Carrying Capacity*) (*Amendment*) *Regulations*, **No. 674/66**

DUTIES OF P.S.V. STAFF

Every p.s.v. driver and conductor, when on duty, must behave in a civil and orderly manner; must not smoke in or on a vehicle during a journey or when it has passengers on board; must take all reasonable precautions to ensure the safety of passengers; must not wilfully deceive or refuse to inform any passenger or intending passenger as to the destination or route of the vehicle, or as to the fare for any journey; must, on request by a police constable or other person having reasonable cause, give particulars of his licence and name and the name and address of his employer; must not obstruct or neglect to give all reasonable information and assistance to any person having authority to examine the vehicle [619/36/4].

The conductor must not distract the driver's attention without reasonable cause when the vehicle is in motion, or speak to him unless it is necessary to do so in order to give directions as to the stopping of the vehicle. He must take all reasonable precautions to ensure that the route, destination and fare indicators where provided are correctly and clearly displayed [619/36/6].

Bus drivers and conductors should bear in mind that if they are called upon to remove a passenger from a vehicle for contravening the regulations [619/36/12(a)] no more force should be used than is absolutely necessary; if undue force is used, the passenger might be able to bring an action for assault.

PASSENGERS' CONDUCT

The following are some of the things which a passenger in a public service vehicle must *not* do: use obscene or offensive language; conduct himself in a riotous or disorderly manner; wilfully and unreasonably impede other boarding or alighting passengers; enter or remain on the vehicle when asked by the driver or conductor to leave on the grounds that the vehicle is full or is not allowed to pick up at the point in question; travel in the upper deck of a vehicle without occupying a seat or in any part not provided for carrying passengers; do anything likely to interfere with the working of the vehicle or to cause injury or discomfort to any person; distract the driver's attention when the vehicle is in motion or speak to the driver unless it is necessary to do so in order to give directions as to stopping; give any signal which might be interpreted by the driver as a signal from the conductor to start; spit on or from the vehicle or damage, soil or defile any part of the vehicle [619/36/9].

Other offences relate to the distribution of printed matter or articles 'for the purpose of advertising'; causing annoyance by operating a noisy instrument or, with others, singing or shouting; removing, damaging or altering route indicators, fare tables or advertisements; smoking where prohibited; causing danger by throwing things out of the vehicle; obstructing the crew or other authorised person, and so on [619/36/9]. Except in a contract carriage, it is an offence to beg, sell or offer any article for sale [9(xvii)].

A passenger on a stage or express carriage must not use or attempt to use an altered or defaced ticket, a non-transferable ticket issued to another person or, without reasonable excuse, an expired season ticket [619/36/11(a) and 461/75]. Such a passenger must (i) declare his journey if asked, (ii) unless he has a ticket pay his fare, (iii) if required by an authorised person produce his ticket or pay his fare, (iv) leave the vehicle at the end of the journey he has paid for or pay for continuing the journey, (v) at the end of a journey give up his ticket if required and (vi) surrender an expired season ticket if required [11(b)]. A passenger must not, without reasonable excuse, leave or attempt to leave the vehicle without having paid the fare for the journey [11(c)].

REMOVAL FROM VEHICLE

Any passenger contravening the Regulations may be removed from the vehicle by the driver or conductor or, at their request, by any police constable [12(a)]. A suspected offender must give his name and address, on demand, to the police or to the driver or conductor [12(b)].

For police power of arrest see page 167.

LOST PROPERTY

Two main sets of Regulations—one for London Transport—cover the country.

It is laid down in the general Regulations that anyone finding property left in a public service vehicle must at once hand it to the conductor [1268/34/4] who, in turn, must hand it in at his depot. If the conductor leaves the vehicle before it goes to the depot, he must pass the property on to his relief and obtain a receipt from the conductor who takes over. At the end of each journey the vehicle must be searched for lost property [5].

When property is claimed before being handed in and the claimant satisfies the conductor as to ownership, it must be returned forthwith without fee or reward. The conductor must then report the fact, giving the claimant's name and address and a description of the property [5].

Operators must keep appropriate records [6] and retain the property in safe keeping. Official books or documents must be sent to the appropriate office. If the owner's name and address are ascertainable from the property he must be notified [7].

After 3 months, unclaimed property must be given to the conductor or sold, at the operator's discretion. If any article realises more than 10p on being sold, the conductor is entitled to a reward of one-twelfth of the proceeds [8], subject to a maximum reward of £4[2262/58/2]. If the property is claimed after being handed in, the operator may charge a fee not exceeding 5p [2262/58/2], and if its value exceeds 10p the conductor is entitled to be rewarded as before. Disputes as to value must be settled by a licensed appraiser, the claimant paying his fee [1268/34/9].

Perishables may be disposed of as the operator thinks fit. If sold, the conductor is entitled to his reward [10].

The conductor into whose possession the property first came is alone entitled to any reward [11].

The foregoing Regulations do not apply to lost property found in London Transport vehicles [2397/60/2].

Provisions of the London Transport Regulations are similar to the general Regulations. The main differences relate to the amount of fees charged for property claimed and the disposal of unclaimed property.

If a person claims property before it is delivered to a Lost Property Office of the London Transport Executive he must pay a fee related to the nature of the property. The fees are set out in a schedule to the Regulations and range from 15p for small items such as hats, umbrellas, etc., to 45p for bicycles and prams. If property is claimed from the Lost Property Office the charges are doubled [2125/71/8]. Property may be disposed of by the Executive after it has been at the Lost Property Office for 1 month or, in the case of property valued at over 50p, 3 months [9].

STANDING PASSENGERS

Not more than 8 standing passengers, or one-third of the seating capacity (whichever is the less) may be carried in a single-decked public service vehicle or trolley-bus, or on the lower deck of a double-decked p.s.v. or trolley-bus if the vehicle is a stage carriage with a conductor. The permission applies only during 'hours of peak traffic' (not defined) or in circumstances in which undue hardship would otherwise be caused to the persons concerned [1612/54/3].

The same number of standing passengers can be authorised by the Traffic Commissioners in respect of any p.s.v. when used as an express carriage [1612/54/5].

No standing passengers are allowed (a) in any gangway forward of the rearmost part of the driver's seat [674/66], (b) in any half-decker, (c) on the top deck of a double-decker or (d) on any vehicle not carrying a conductor other than on any vehicle on a service when the Traffic Commissioners have certified that a conductor is not required [1612/54/4 to 7 and 674/66].

No standing passengers may be carried on a p.s.v. with 12 or fewer seats for which the first certificate of fitness was issued on or after April 11, 1958, unless the vehicle is specially constructed or adapted to carry standing passengers and their carriage is authorised by the Traffic Commissioners [472/58/2(3)].

Where only children not over 15 years of age and not more than six necessary attendants are carried on a public service vehicle, any three children may, so long as they are sitting passengers only, be reckoned as two passengers [1612/54/3]. On vehicles with not more than 12 seats for which a certificate of fitness was first issued on or after April 11,

1958, the maximum number of children which can be reckoned on this basis is nine [472/58/2(2)].

Specially constructed or adapted vehicles, other than p.s.v.s when used as express or contract carriages, may carry standing passengers up to the number the Ministry's certifying officer certifies that the vehicle is constructed or adapted and fit to carry. Permission may be granted in respect of specified routes or areas [1612/54/6(1) and 674/66].

The Traffic Commissioners may prohibit or restrict the carriage of standing passengers on any service [1612/54/7(2)].

Where a vehicle owner is aggrieved by the refusal of a certificate permitting him to carry standing passengers, by the limitation of the number to be carried, or by variation, suspension or revocation of a certificate issued, he can appeal to the Minister of Transport whose decision will be binding [1612/54/6(2)].

P.S.V. FITNESS, EQUIPMENT AND USE

Road Traffic Act 1960
Minibus Act 1977
Public Service Vehicles (Conditions of Fitness, Equipment and Use) Regulations, **No. 751/72**
Public Service Vehicles (Conditions of Fitness, Equipment and Use) (Amendment) Regulations, **No. 726/76**
Minibus (Conditions of Fitness, Equipment and Use) Regulations, **No. 2103/77**

Before a passenger vehicle adapted to carry eight or more passengers can be licensed as a public service vehicle a certificate of fitness must be in force for it [Act 1960/129]. The certificate is issued by a certifying officer appointed by the Secretary of State [128(1)] if conditions as to fitness prescribed in Part II of the 1972 Regulations are fulfilled [751/72/5]. A certificate is normally in force for seven years but it can be issued for a shorter period [Act 1960/129(4)]. A certificate can be revoked and if it is any p.s.v. licence in force for the vehicle ceases to have effect until a new certificate is obtained [129(5)].

Vehicles of specified ages are exempt from many of the fitness requirements. The exemptions will be given below only where it is likely that vehicles of a particular age are still in normal service. The full list of exemptions is contained in Schedule 2 of the 1972 Regulations.

Conditions for minibuses authorised under the Minibus Act 1977 are given at the end of this chapter (page 180).

FITNESS

STABILITY

Every public service vehicle must pass a stability test.

For a double-decker this consists of tilting to an angle of 28 degrees without overturning. When undergoing the test, the vehicle must be complete and fully equipped for service and loaded with weights (at the rate of 140 lb per person) to represent a full complement of passengers on the top deck only, plus the driver and conductor, if carried.

Single-deckers and half-deckers must be tilted to 35 degrees without overturning. This test must be made when the vehicle is complete and fully equipped for service under any conditions of load.

Any wheel stop used when carrying out these tests may not be higher than two-thirds of the height of the appropriate wheel rim above ground level [751/72/6].

SUSPENSION

Every p.s.v. must have a suspension system which does not permit excessive body sway. Construction of vehicles registered on or after April 1, 1959, must be such that a failure of a spring, torsion bar or other resilient component of the suspension system is not likely to cause the driver to lose steering control of the vehicle. A tyre is not regarded as forming part of a suspension system [751/72/7].

TURNING CIRCLE

Every p.s.v. first registered on or after April 1, 1959, and with an overall length of not more than 27 ft, must be capable of turning in a swept circle ('a circle which, traced at ground level by a vertical line passing through any part of the vehicle included in the overall length and overall width of the vehicle') not exceeding 65 ft; if the overall length of the vehicle exceeds 27 ft but is not more than 36 ft, the maximum turning circle may be 71 ft and if the vehicle exceeds 36 ft the turning circle may be up to 78 ft. Vehicles first registered after January 1, 1932, and before April 1, 1959, which cannot satisfy these requirements, must, if registered between January 1, 1932, and June 1, 1950, be capable of turning in a circle (measured at the extreme outer edge of the wheel track) of not more than 60 ft in diameter or 66 ft for those over 26 ft long. For vehicles first registered on or after June 1, 1950, and before April 1, 1959, a vehicle with an overall length of not more than 27 ft must turn within a circle (measured at the extreme outer edge of the wheel track) of 60 ft, and a vehicle over 27 ft in length in a 66 ft circle [751/72/8].

GUARD RAILS

Between the front and rear wheels on each side there must be an effective guard extending to within 9 in of the front wheel and 6 in of the rear wheel and leaving a space of not more than 12 in above ground level when the vehicle is empty [751/72/9].

SIDE OVERHANG

No part of a vehicle may project more than 6 in (7 in for 12-seaters and smaller vehicles) beyond the wall of the rear outer tyre on the same side. This does not apply to vehicles first registered on or after December 1, 1932, and before April 1, 1959, unless used as stage carriages [751/72/10].

BRAKES

A brake acting through the transmission gear is not allowed on a public service vehicle except on a vehicle registered before 1955 or in the case of a handbrake which operates without any hydraulic, electric or pneumatic intervention so long as there is no universal joint between the brake and the wheels, failure of a brake part would not cause a wheel to become detached and all the wheels of the vehicle have brakes which can be operated by one means [751/72/11]. One of the braking systems of a vehicle must be operated by a pedal [11(3)].

STEERING GEAR AND HUBS

The steering gear of public service vehicles must be arranged so that no overlock is possible, and the wheels do not foul any part of the vehicle in any circumstances [751/72/12]. If brake or steering connections are secured by bolts or pins, these must be threaded, effectively locked, and, if fitted otherwise than horizontally, their heads must be uppermost [13].

No part of a wheel or its fittings may project more than $3\frac{1}{2}$ in beyond the outer face of the tyre [14].

FUEL TANK

On single-deckers with 13 or more seats, half-deckers, and the lower deck of double-deckers, no fuel tank may be placed under any part of any gangway or, on vehicles first registered on or after April 1,

1959, any passage leading to an emergency exit, which, in either case, is within 2 ft of any entrance or exit [751/72/15(1)]. It is not illegal, however, to fit a fuel tank under a passage leading to a secondary emergency exit.

On single-deckers with 12 or fewer seats registered before October 28, 1964, no fuel tank may be placed under any entrance or exit and no tank filling point may be under or immediately adjacent to any entrance or exit [Sched. 2(7)].

On similar vehicles first registered on or after October 28, 1964, no fuel tank may be placed under or within 12 in of any entrance or exit and no filling point may be situated at the rear of the vehicle [15(2)].

No part of any fuel tank or fuel supply apparatus may be placed in any compartments or spaces provided for the driver or passengers on vehicles first registered on or after April 1, 1959 [15(3)].

Every tank and 'all apparatus supplying fuel to the engine' must be so placed or shielded that no leaking fuel can fall on to any part of the vehicle where it can be readily ignited or into any receptacle where it can accumulate [15(4)].

All filling points must be outside the body, with caps that can be securely fixed. The vent hole, if any, must be of the non-splash variety, and protected from danger of penetration by fire [15(5)].

A device must be provided which can readily cut off the supply of petrol or diesel to the engine. The means of operation must be accessible from outside the vehicle and, except for a diesel-engined vehicle, must be visible from outside the vehicle. Where it is visible the 'off' position must be marked and where it is not visible its position must be marked together with the means of operation. This requirement does not apply to a diesel-engined vehicle registered before April 1, 1959, or to a petrol-engined vehicle registered before this date if it has a cock to cut off the supply of petrol to the carburettor and its 'off' position is marked on the outside of the vehicle [15(6), Sched. 2(7)].

EXHAUST PIPE

The exhaust pipe must be kept clear of any inflammable material on the vehicle and placed or shielded so that no such material can be thrown on to it from any other part of the vehicle. The outlet of the pipe has to be at the rear or on the off-side of the vehicle and far enough to the rear to prevent, as far as practicable, fumes from entering the vehicle [721/72/16].

LOCKING OF NUTS

Bolts or studs and nuts used in moving parts and parts subject to severe vibration must be fastened by lock nuts or split pins or similar means [721/72/17].

LIGHTING

In public service vehicles adequate artificial illumination must be provided for each deck with a permanent top and at least one lamp as near as is practicable to the top of every staircase leading to an upper deck without a permanent top.

On vehicles first registered on or after April 1, 1959, entrance or exit steps or platforms (other than emergency exits) must be adequately lighted. On vehicles first registered on or after October 28, 1964, circuits must be so arranged that an electrical failure in any sub-circuit cannot extinguish all lights on any deck [751/72/18].

All electric leads must be adequately insulated [19(1)].

In every electrical circuit (other than high-tension) of over 100 V there must be an isolating switch in each pole of the main circuit and readily accessible to the driver or conductor but this does not apply to a vehicle registered before June 19, 1968, if a 100-V circuit has been installed in the vehicle after that date [19(2), Sched. 2(9)]. The isolating switch must not be capable of disconnecting the vehicle's obligatory front and rear lamps [19(2)].

BODY

The body of a vehicle must be securely fixed to the chassis, trap-doors must be secure against vibration and their lifting devices must not project above the level of the floor [751/72/20].

General construction requirements, which are usually incorporated when a vehicle is built, are also specified. These include requirements as to the height of the body sides [21]; steps, platforms and stairs [22]; entrances and exits [23, 24]; doors [25 and 726/76]; emergency exits [26]; access to exits [27]; gangways [28, 29]; seats [30]; and driver's accommodation [34].

WINDSCREEN AND WINDOWS

Unless the driver's windscreen can be opened to give him a clear view of the road ahead it must be fitted with an adequate demisting and defrosting device [751/72/35]. All transverse windows not made of safety glass must be guarded against breakage by passengers being thrown against them [31].

MISCELLANEOUS

Adequate ventilation must be provided for the passengers and driver without the need to open any main window or windscreen [751/72/33]. The vehicle must be marked with its seating capacity or its standing and seating capacity [32]. Except for vehicles adapted for less than 13 passengers, there must be means to enable passengers to signal to the driver [36]. Luggage racks must be designed and constructed so that if any article falls from them it is not likely to fall on the driver or interfere with his control of the vehicle [38]. A vehicle must comply in all respects with the Motor Vehicles (Construction and Use) Regulations and its bodywork, upholstery and fittings must be soundly and properly constructed of suitable materials, well finished and in good and serviceable condition [39].

EQUIPMENT

FIRE-EXTINGUISHER

A suitable and sufficient fire-extinguisher of a specified type must be readily available for use on a public service vehicle [751/72/41]. Five types of fire-extinguisher are specified from which the operator can choose. The types specified should comply with a British Standards Institution specification B.S. 740: Part I: 1948; B.S. 740: Part II: 1952; B.S. 138: 1948; B.S. 1382: 1948; or B.S. 1721: 1968 [41(2)].

FIRST AID

On an express carriage or contract carriage there must be a receptacle containing specified first aid dressings. The receptacle must be prominently marked and be readily available for use [42, Sched. 3].

MARKING

The name and address of the p.s.v. licence holder must be marked on the nearside of the vehicle in letters at least 1 in high which contrast with the colour of the bodywork [751/72/40].

USE

While passengers are being carried no person must cause or permit any unnecessary obstruction of an entrance, exit or gangway [751/72/43]. No person shall cause or permit any obstruction of the driver [44]. The body of a vehicle, windows, fittings and passengers' seats must be maintained in good and clean condition while passengers are being carried [45]. During the hours of darkness gangways leading to exits and exits must be adequately lit by interior lighting, except the upper deck of a double-decker if a barrier across the stairs prevents access to that deck [46]. Controls for power-operated doors can be used only by authorised persons except in cases of emergency [47]. While a vehicle engine is running a petrol filler cap must not be removed and petrol must not be put into the tank [48]. On a stage carriage with seating capacity for more than 20 a conductor must be carried except (a) if the vehicle seats not more than 32, the emergency exit and entrance are at the front in the driver's view and the driver can become aware if a person is trapped in a door or (b) if Traffic Commissioners certify that a conductor is not required [49]. Restrictions are also placed on the carriage of inflammable or dangerous substances [50].

If a radio or television installation is used in a motor coach a licence must be obtained. The Performing Rights Society (29–33 Berners Street, London, W.1, phone 01–580–5544) charges 2p per seat per month *if this fee is paid voluntarily*, otherwise the fee and damages may be claimed. For recorded music, whether discs or tapes are used, the charge is 6p per seat per month. The minimum charge is £4·80 per coach per year. All the charges are subject to a 35% surcharge.

Minibus conditions of fitness

Minibuses authorised under Section 1 of the Minibus Act 1977 have to comply with Regulations governing their fitness, equipment and use [2103/77]. If a contravention of these Regulations arises the minibus ceases to be treated, under Section 1(1), as not being a public service vehicle [Act 1977/3(2)].

In this section any reference to a minibus is to a minibus within Section 1 of the Minibus Act 1977. The given requirements do not apply to a minibus authorised under a p.s.v. licence or to a minibus which does not carry passengers for hire or reward.

The bulk of the Regulations do not apply (a) to minibuses first used before January 27, 1978, till January 27, 1983, and (b) to minibuses first used on or after January 27, 1978, till January 27, 1981

[2103/77/3(1)]. However, three of the fitness Regulations (16, 23 and 24) and all the equipment and use Regulations (26–34) apply now to a minibus of any age.

FITNESS

STABILITY

With weights of 63·5 kilograms placed in positions to represent the driver and passengers the minibus must not overturn when tilted 35 degrees from the horizontal on either side [5]. An efficient suspension system must be fitted so that there is no excessive body sway and a failure of a spring, torsion bar or other resilient component is not likely to cause the driver to lose control [6]. Brakes must act on the wheels and not through the transmission but a mechanical handbrake can act through the transmission as long as there is no universal joint between the brake and the wheel [7]. The steering mechanism must be such that no overlock is possible and the wheels must not foul any part of the vehicle [8].

FUEL TANK, PUMP AND PIPES

No fuel tank, pump or pipes must be placed in the driver's or passengers' compartments. They must be placed or shielded so that no overflowing or leaking fuel can fall or accumulate on any woodwork or other part of the vehicle where it might readily ignite or accumulate in a receptacle. Fuel tank filling points should be accessible only from outside the minibus. A fuel cut-off device must be provided on a minibus to that (a) in the case of a vehicle fitted with a fuel injection system, the position and means of operation are clearly marked on the outside of the vehicle and the means of operation is readily accessible from outside the vehicle and is clearly indicated and (b) in any other case, the device is readily visible and accessible from outside the vehicle and the 'off' position is marked [9].

EXHAUST PIPE

A minibus exhaust pipe must be fitted or shielded so that inflammable material cannot fall or be thrown on to it from the vehicle;

so that it is not likely to cause fire by being near inflammable material; and its outlet is either at the rear or on the offside and so far to the rear as to prevent fumes from entering the vehicle [10].

LOCKING OF NUTS

Moving parts and all parts subject to severe vibration and which are connected by bolts or studs and nuts must be fastened by lock nuts; nuts and spring or lock nut washers; castellated nuts and split pins; or some other efficient device to prevent their working loose [11].

ELECTRICAL APPARATUS

Electrical apparatus and circuits must be constructed and installed to guard against the risk of electric shock or fire. Electrical circuits which carry over 100 volts must be provided with an isolating switch inside the vehicle and in a place readily accessible to the driver [12].

ENTRANCES AND EXITS

The positioning of entrances and exits on a minibus depends on the location of the fuel tank. Where the fuel tank is behind the rear wheels the vehicle must have (a) an exit on the nearside and (b) an emergency exit on either the offside or rear face of the minibus. Where the fuel tank is not behind the rear wheels the minibus must have (a) an exit on the nearside and an emergency exit on the offside or rear face or (b) an exit and entrance on the rear face of the vehicle [13(1), (2)]. An exit must be at least 1·17 metres high and 530 mm wide [13(3)]. No entrance, other than the driver's entrance, may be on the offside of the vehicle [13(4)]. Grab handles must be fitted to every entrance and exit (other than an emergency exit) [13(5)].

Except for the driver's seat and any seat alongside his seat, there has to be unobstructed access from every seat in the minibus to every exit [14].

Doors must not obstruct clear access to any entrance or exit from inside or outside the vehicle. Means must be provided for keeping doors closed or open. Two devices must be provided for operating the means for securing each door in the closed position and one of these must be on the outside of the vehicle. The devices must be easily accessible to a person of normal height; if the device is not on the door it must be so placed as to be readily associated with the door; and a single movement of the device must open the door. The method of operation of a device and its position, if not on the door, must be indicated [15].

Emergency exits must be clearly marked on both the inside and outside of the minibus; their doors must open outwards, be readily accessible to passengers and not be power-operated [16].

SEATING

A length of 405 mm measured across the front of each seat is to be allowed for each seated passenger. If a seat is so placed that its occupant is liable to be thrown through any entrance or exit or down any steps an effective screen or guard must be provided to prevent that event occurring. No seat may be fitted to a door and all seat supports must be securely fixed in position [17].

DRIVER'S SEAT OR COMPARTMENT

A minibus must be so constructed that the seated driver has adequate room and can readily reach and operate the controls. Means must be provided, if necessary, of preventing the vehicle's interior lighting inconveniencing the driver. When access to the driver's seat is on the offside of the vehicle the opening must be at least 455 mm wide (discounting any wheelarch) and if its lower edge is more than 690 mm above ground level a convenient step must be provided. When a separate and enclosed compartment is provided for the driver and access is obtained from the offside of the vehicle an emergency exit at least 530 mm by 455 mm must be provided for him otherwise than on the offside [18].

MISCELLANEOUS

Luggage racks fitted in a minibus must be so designed that anything dislodged from them is unlikely to fall on the driver or interfere with his driving [19].

Internal lighting adequate to illuminate the exits and adequate ventilation must be provided [20, 21].

Transverse windows which are not made of safety glass, safety glazing or specified safety glass must be protected against being broken by passengers thrown against them [22].

Every minibus must be a single-deck vehicle and its length must not exceed 7 metres [24, 23].

A minibus must conform to the Construction and Use Regulations as regards construction, weight and equipment. Its bodywork and fittings must be soundly and properly constructed of suitable materials and be in good and serviceable condition. It must be designed to be capable of withstanding loads and stresses likely to be met with in the normal operation of the vehicle [25].

EQUIPMENT

SEATING CAPACITY

The seating capacity must be painted in characters not less than 25 mm high either (a) on the inside of the vehicle so as to be readily visible from the outside or (b) on the rear or nearside of the outside of the vehicle [26].

FIRE-EXTINGUISHER

A fire-extinguisher which is readily available for use must be carried. The types of extinguisher specified are the same as those specified for public service vehicles (page 179) [27]. First aid equipment of a specified kind (same as p.s.v.) must be carried in a prominently marked receptacle and be readily available for use [28].

USE

While passengers are carried no person must cause or permit any unnecessary obstruction of any entrance, exit or gangway [29]. No passenger shall unnecessarily obstruct the driver or divert his attention from controlling the vehicle [30]. While carrying passengers the windows of a minibus must be kept clean and in good condition [31].

While the engine is running no person must remove the petrol tank filler cap or put petrol into the tank [32]. No highly inflammable or otherwise dangerous substance may be carried unless carried in containers and so packed that damage or injury is unlikely [33]. A trailer may not be drawn unless all passengers have access to an exit on the nearside of the vehicle [34].

P.S.V. LICENSING

Road Traffic Act 1930
Public Service Vehicles (Travel Concessions) Act 1955
Road Traffic Act 1960
Transport Act 1968
Transport (London) Act 1969
Transport (London) Amendment Act 1969
European Communities Act 1972
Passenger Vehicles (Experimental Areas) Act 1977
Minibus Act 1977
Transport Act 1978
E.E.C. Regulation 117/1966
P.S.V. (Duration of Road Service Licences) Regulations, No. 414/57
P.S.V. (Duration of Road Service Licences) Regulations, No. 747/38
P.S.V. (Licences and Certificates) Regulations, No. 900/52
P.S.V. (Licences and Certificates) (Amendment) Regulations, No. 123/57
P.S.V. (Licences and Certificates) (Amendment) (No. 2) Regulations, No. 1118/57
P.S.V. (Licences and Certificates) (Amendment) Regulations, No. 2128/61
P.S.V. (Licences and Certificates) (Amendment) Regulations, No. 32/69
P.S.V. (Contract Carriage Records) Regulations, No. 1503/60
London Transport (Consent Appeals) Regulations, No. 1269/72
Road Transport (International Passenger Services) Regulations, No. 806/73
Public Service Vehicle Operators (Qualifications) Regulations, No. 1461/77
Public Service Vehicles (Definition of Express Carriage) Regulations, No. 1496/77
Passenger Vehicles (Experimental Areas) Designation Order, No. 1554/77
Minibus (Permits) Regulations, No. 1708/77
Minibus (Designated Bodies) Regulations, No. 1709/77

For the purpose of controlling road transport, Great Britain is divided into eleven traffic areas, one of these covering the whole of Scotland. The other ten cover England and Wales [Act 1960/119(1)], the boundaries being defined in three 'signed maps', two of which are deposited in the Houses of Parliament and one at the Ministry of Transport headquarters [Act 1960/252(3)].

Subject to provisions of the Transport Act, 1968, establishing Passenger Transport Areas, control of public service vehicles is vested in each area in the Traffic Commissioners. These comprise three members, one being a full-time chairman and the other two being drawn from panels of elected representatives of county councils and county boroughs and urban districts [Act 1960/120(1) and 121(4)]. In the Metropolitan Traffic Area Greater London is regarded as a county and the City of London as a borough for this purpose [Act 1969/24(3)]. The chairman of the Commissioners can, at his discretion, sit with only one of the elected representatives [Act 1960/153(3)]. The chairman of the Commissioners in each area acts also as Licensing Authority for goods vehicle licensing purposes [Act 1968/59]. Passenger transport in the Greater London area is controlled by the London Transport Executive [Acts 1969].

CLASSIFICATION OF VEHICLES

A 'public service vehicle' is a motor vehicle used for carrying passengers for hire or reward, and if not carrying passengers at separate fares, it has 8 or more seats. [Act 1960/117(1)].

Public service vehicles are divided into express, stage and contract carriages. An 'express carriage' is a p.s.v. used for carrying passengers at separate fares none of which is less than 21p [Act 1960/117(3) and 1496/77]. For this purpose a composite fare for more than one journey is not to be regarded as representing the aggregate of fares of any less amount, and no account is to be taken of any particular fare (e.g. for children, workmen, or students) in cases where the normal fare for other passengers is 21p [Act 1960/117(3)]. 'Fare' includes the price of a contract or season ticket [Act 1960/257(1)]. Any other vehicle carrying passengers at separate fares is a 'stage carriage' [117(2)].

A 'contract carriage' is a p.s.v. not carrying passengers at separate fares [Act 1960/117(4)]. A vehicle carrying passengers at separate fares in the circumstances set out in Part I, II, III or IV of Schedule 12 of the 1960 Act (set out below) will not be regarded as a public service vehicle unless it is constructed to carry 8 or more passengers [118(1)].

A p.s.v. carrying passengers at separate fares will be treated as a contract carriage and not as a stage or express carriage if the conditions set out in Parts III or IV of Schedule 12 are met [118(2)].

Schedule 12 of the Road Traffic Act 1960 as amended by Schedule 1 of the Transport Act 1978 is as follows:

PART I—RACE MEETINGS, PUBLIC GATHERINGS, ETC

1. The journey must be made on the occasion of a race meeting, public gathering or similar special occasion.

PART II—VEHICLES ADAPTED TO CARRY NOT MORE THAN
7 PASSENGERS

2. The number of passengers must not exceed 7; or 4 if any passenger is carried in the course of a passenger-carrying business.

3. Where passengers are carried in the course of a business of carrying passengers the making of the agreement for payment of separate fares must not have been initiated by the driver or owner of the vehicle, by a person who has let the vehicle for hire or by any person who receives any remuneration in respect of the arrangements for the journey.

4. The journey must be made without previous advertisement to the public of facilities for its being made by fare-paying passengers.

5. The facilities for the journey may have been previously advertised if the following conditions are satisfied:

    (a) the local authorities and traffic commissioners concerned have consented to the advertisement as being provided under a social car scheme, and their consents remain in force, and

    (b) the advertisement in each case contains a statement that these consents have been given.

Local authorities and traffic commissioners must not give consents for these purposes where it appears that the facilities are to be provided for a commercial purpose or for profit and a consent will only be given if the facilities are for meeting the social and welfare needs of one or more communities.

Before a local authority or traffic commissioners withdraw a consent they must consult with each other and a withdrawal of a consent must be by written notice to those arranging the facilities. The local authorities and traffic commissioners for these purposes are those in whose area any part of the journey is to be made. A 'local authority' is, in Greater London, the Greater London Council; elsewhere in England and Wales, a county council; and in Scotland, a regional or island council.

6. The journey must not be made in conjunction with, or in extension of, a service provided under a road service licence if the vehicle is owned by, or made available by arrangement with, the licence holder or any person who receives remuneration relating to the service.

PART III—OVERSEAS VISITORS

7. Every passenger must have been outside Great Britain at the time of concluding the arrangements to make the journey.

PART IV—ALTERNATIVE CONDITIONS

8. Arrangements for the bringing together of all the passengers for the purpose of making the journey have not been made by the holder of the p.s.v. licence, the driver or owner of the vehicle or anyone who receives any remuneration in respect of the arrangements.

9. The journey must not be advertised to the public.

10. All the passengers must be carried to the particular destination, or to the vicinity of it, or, in the case of a tour, for the greater part of the journey.

11. No differentiation of fares on the basis of distance or time is made.

12. In the case of a journey to a particular destination the passengers must not include anyone who frequently, or as a matter of routine, travels at or about the time of day at which the journey is made to or near that destination from a place from or through which the journey is made.

For the purposes of paragraphs 4 and 9 of Schedule 12 no account is taken of the following kinds of advertisement:

(a) a notice or announcement at any place of worship made in the normal way for persons attending that place;

(b) a notice in a periodical published for persons attending a particular place of worship or place of worship in a particular place and circulated wholly or mainly among persons who attend there or might reasonably be expected to attend there;

(c) a notice or announcement at a place of work with regard to journeys to be made from there by people who work there; or

(d) a notice or announcement at a club or voluntary association which (i) relates only to journeys incidental to other activities and (ii) is displayed or made in premises occupied or used by the club or association or in any periodical it issues [Act 1960/ Sched. 12/13 and Act 1978/Sched. 1].

A vehicle with 8 or more seats where passengers pay separate fares only remains a contract carriage if, besides fulfilling the conditions specified in Parts III or IV of Schedule 12, the p.s.v. licence holder makes, or causes to be made, a record of the journey and the circumstances in which it was arranged in the prescribed form [Act 1960/Sched. 12/14(1)].

The licence holder's record must contain the prescribed particulars, and the driver must carry with him a work ticket showing the name and address of the licence holder, time, date and route of the journey, and name and address of the organiser. Alternatively, a combined work ticket and record in the prescribed form may be used [1503/60].

The driver must produce the work ticket for inspection if required to do so by any police constable or an examiner appointed by the Traffic Commissioners [Act 1960/12th Sched./14(3)].

The p.s.v. licence holder must keep the record for 6 months and produce it on demand to any person authorised by the Traffic Commissioners [Act 1960/12th Sched./14(4)].

HIRE OR REWARD AND FARES

A vehicle is treated as carrying passengers for hire or reward if payment is made for, or for matters which include, the carrying of passengers, irrespective of the person to whom the payment is made.

A payment for carrying a passenger is treated as a fare, even though it is made in consideration of other matters in addition to the journey and irrespective of the person by or to whom it is made.

A payment is treated as made for the carrying of a passenger if made in consideration of a right to be carried, whether for one or more journeys and whether or not the right is exercised.

In any case where one or more passengers are being carried for hire or reward otherwise than in the course of a business of carrying passengers the vehicle is treated as carrying passengers at separate fares [Act 1960/118(3)].

Agricultural workers may be carried to and from their work in vehicles, without the p.s.v. authorisations that would otherwise be necessary if such passengers were carried for hire or reward. This concession is operative for 6 months from June 1 each year [Act 1960/118(6)].

It follows, therefore, that regular operation, or any other journeys not falling within the above categories, need to be under the authority of a road service licence if any question of separate payment by passengers arises.

P.S.V. LICENCES

Before using a motor vehicle as a stage, express or contract carriage (except as provided in following sections), the operator must obtain a public service vehicle licence [Act 1960/127(1)]. A vehicle licensed as a stage carriage may be used as either an express or contract carriage [127(2)] and a vehicle licensed as an express carriage may also be used as a contract carriage [127(3)]. An express carriage may be used on a stage carriage service if the Traffic Commissioners give consent in writing [127(4)].

A p.s.v. licence applied for on or after January 1, 1978 will be either a standard licence or a restricted licence depending on the size of vehicle and kind of service operated. To obtain a standard licence the operator has to possess specified qualifications. These are given overleaf on page 192.

A p.s.v. licence may be refused, suspended or revoked if, having regard to the conduct of the applicant or holder of the licence or to the manner in which the vehicle is being used, it appears to the Traffic Commissioners that he is not a fit person to hold such a licence [127(7)].

In considering his previous conduct, they must have regard to it in relation to any trade or business, using vehicles, of which he was the owner, a director or an employee. The Traffic Commissioners must also be satisfied about his arrangements for securing that drivers' hours are not exceeded; that he has and can use maintenance facilities effectively; and that he will use, or has used, his vehicles properly. His financial resources can also be taken into account. Representations from prescribed trade unions or associations, the police and local authorities must be considered by the Commissioners [Act 1968/35(1), (2)].

Except in relation to a vehicle with fewer than 8 seats, a p.s.v. licence is not granted unless a certificate of fitness is in force in respect of the vehicle [Act 1960/129(1)]. The fee for a certificate is £6·50 [32/69], and its life may be up to seven years, but the area certifying officer by whom the certificate is issued may, if he thinks fit, reduce the period to a minimum of one year [Act 1960/129(4)]. Any certificate may be revoked [129(5)] and the p.s.v. licence may be suspended if on inspection the vehicle is found to be unfit [133(1)]. Provision is made for 48 hours' grace to be allowed for remedying any defects not involving danger to the public [133(1)].

The normal validity period of a public service vehicle licence is one year [Act 1960/127(9)], and the fee is £12·50 [32/69]. A refund of one-sixth of the fee paid can be obtained from the Traffic Commissioners in respect of every two months unexpired at the date of surrendering the licence if the vehicle has been disposed of [1118/57/3]. A p.s.v. licence, when issued, is valid in every traffic area [Act 1960/127(8)]. Duplicate licences or backings lost, damaged or defaced can be obtained from the Traffic Commissioners for 25p [32/69]. A certificate of fitness is not invalidated by change of ownership of the vehicle [900/52/26].

Once a vehicle is licensed as a p.s.v. it may be operated as a contract carriage without any further licence (although the driver must, of course, hold a p.s.v. driver's licence). For the operation of a service of stage or express carriages, however, a road service licence is necessary.

This applies to every kind of service including excursions, long-distance tours, 'all-in' holiday tours and even up to the port of departure for tours abroad operated from this country by public service vehicles. Road service licences are dealt with on page 196.

OPERATORS' QUALIFICATIONS

Public service vehicle licences applied for on or after January 1, 1978 are divided into two classes—

(a) standard licences which relate to passenger service vehicles and which are used on public passenger transport services, and
(b) restricted licences which relate to vehicles which are not passenger service vehicles or which are passenger service vehicles but are not used for providing public passenger transport services [1461/77/3].

A passenger service vehicle, for these purposes, is defined as a motor vehicle constructed to carry more than eight passengers, exclusive of the driver [2(1)].

Public passenger transport services are defined as services provided for the public, or for specified categories of users, in return for payment by the passenger or by a person who arranges the transport, but not including such a service if it is provided by vehicles constructed to carry not more than 16 passengers (a) otherwise than in the course of a business of carrying passengers or (b) by a person whose main occupation is not the provision of road passenger transport services [2(1)]. It is difficult to see what kind of non-business activity a 9 to 16 seat minibus can be engaged in to come within the scope of a restricted licence and still require a p.s.v. licence.

A standard licence may authorise the use of a passenger service vehicle for the provision of public passenger transport services on (a) both national and international transport operations or (b) on national transport operations only [3(2)]. If a person causes or permits a passenger service vehicle to be used for providing a public passenger transport service he commits an offence unless (a) he holds a standard p.s.v. licence for the vehicle or (b) he is deemed to be the holder of such a licence by virtue of a permit issued under Regulation 20 of the P.S.V. (Licences and Certificates) Regulations 1952. If the holder of a standard licence restricted to national transport operations uses a vehicle on international work he commits an offence [3(5)(6)]. These penal provisions do not apply to the use of a vehicle authorised in a p.s.v. licence or permit applied for before January 1, 1978 [3(7)].

An application for a standard licence must be refused by the Traffic Commissioners unless they are satisfied that—

    (a) the applicant is of good repute,

    (b) the applicant has appropriate financial standing, and

    (c) the applicant is himself professionally competent or will, throughout the currency of the licence, have a transport manager who is of good repute and is professionally competent [6].

To determine whether or not a person is of good repute regard must be had to the existence and number of relevant convictions relating to him during the preceding five years [10(2)]. Relevant convictions are defined as—

    (a) a conviction of the person in question, or his servant or agent, of contravening any law relating to

        (i)   the maintenance of road vehicles in a fit and serviceable condition,

        (ii) speed and weight limits,

        (iii) driver licensing;

    (b) a conviction of the person in question of contravening p.s.v. legislation or forgery or making false statements in relation to p.s.v. documents;

    (c) a conviction of the person in question, or his servant or agent, of contravening, in relation to a p.s.v., drivers' hours and records law;

    (d) a conviction of the person in question, or his servant or agent, of contravening the law relating to bus fuel grants or new bus grants;

    (e) a conviction of the person in question, or his servant or agent, of contravening waiting restriction orders;

    (f) a conviction of the person in question, or his servant or agent, of contravening the Public Service Vehicle Operators (Qualifications) Regulations 1977 [1461/77/2(1)].

A person will be regarded as having appropriate financial standing if he has or will have available to him sufficient financial resources to ensure the proper administration of his road passenger transport undertaking including, if new, its launching [10(3)].

Only an individual can be professionally competent so that, in the case of a company, a transport manager who is of good repute and is professionally competent must be employed [10(4)(5)]. In the case of a partnership it is sufficient if one of the partners is professionally competent and he has effective responsibility for the management of the transport operations of the partnership [10(6)].

An individual will be regarded as professionally competent if

(a) he was engaged in road passenger transport operations between December 31, 1969 and January 1, 1975;

(b) if he holds a certificate issued by an approved body to the effect that he possesses the skills required appropriate to his class of licence; or

(c) he holds any other certificate of competence, diploma or other qualification recognised by the Secretary of State [10(7)].

An individual whose employment in road passenger transport operations commenced between January 1, 1975 and January 1, 1978 will be regarded as professionally competent till January 1, 1980 but after that date he will cease to be so regarded unless before then he has (i) been engaged in such operations for at least two years or (ii) has become the holder of a certificate mentioned in (b) or (c) above [10(8)].

A person will be regarded as being in road passenger transport operations if he is (1) the holder or joint holder of a p.s.v. licence, (2) the holder of a permit by virtue of which he is deemed to hold a p.s.v. licence, or (3) in responsible road transport employment, [2(2)]. Responsible road transport employment means employment in a position where the individual has effective responsibility for the management of transport operations of public service vehicles [2(1)]. The Passenger Transport Division of the Department of Transport will maintain a record of individuals, other than licence holders, who have established their professional competence by producing evidence of their responsible road transport employment.

The body approved by the Secretary of State for the purpose of issuing certificates of competence is the Royal Society of Arts. The Society will hold examinations for certificates of competence in national and international operations. The syllabus for the national examinations covers drivers' hours and records, driving licences, traffic regulations, accident procedure, vehicle and passenger insurance, vehicle weights and dimensions, vehicle selection, mechanical condition, p.s.v. and road service licensing, financial management, costing and charging, commercial conduct of a business, structure of law, company law, social legislation, taxation and p.s.v. conduct regulations. The international syllabus covers the framework of regulations and control, hours and conditions of work, tachographs, common rules for international passenger transport, insurance abroad, customs practice and formalities, financial aspects of operation, route planning, traffic regulations abroad and accident procedure.

The other qualifications accepted by the Secretary of State as proof of professional competence for national and international operations are (i) Fellow or Member of the Chartered Institute of Transport (road transport sector); (ii) Member or Associate Member of the Institute of Traffic Administration (road transport sector); and (iii) Member or Associate Member of the Institute of Road Transport Engineers. For national transport operations only they are (i) Licentiate of the Chartered Institute of Transport (road passenger transport sector) and (ii) Associate of the Institute of Road Transport Engineers (by examination).

STANDARD LICENCES

In addition to any other requirements, in his first application for a standard licence after 1977 an applicant must submit to the Traffic Commissioners, together with his licence application, a declaration containing

- (a) particulars of relevant convictions made against him in the preceding five years (relevant convictions are listed on page 193);
- (b) a statement that the applicant has adequate financial resources for the purpose of operating his undertaking;
- (c) if he relies on his own professional competence, particulars of his qualifications;
- (d) if he does not rely on his own professional competence, the name, address, place or intended place of work of his transport manager together with details of his professional qualifications and relevant convictions in the preceding five years [1461/77/4 (2)].

In the case of an applicant who was engaged in road passenger transport operations between December 31, 1969 and January 1, 1978, or a partnership one of whose partners was so engaged, previous convictions of himself and, where appropriate, the transport manager are required for the preceding 12 months and not five years [4(4)].

In any subsequent application for a standard licence the applicant must either (i) include in his application a statement that there has been no change in or addition to the declared particulars or (ii) submit a further declaration stating the changes that have occurred and giving any further particulars [4(3)].

A licence holder must notify the Traffic Commissioners within 28 days if any of the following events occurs

- (a) a relevant conviction of the licence holder or his transport manager,
- (b) the licence holder's bankruptcy or liquidation, sequestration of

his estate or appointment of a receiver, manager or trustee of
his undertaking,
(c) any change in the membership of a partnership,
(d) any change of transport manager [5(1)].

The holder of a standard licence restricted to national operations may
on surrendering it be granted a licence to cover both national and
international operations for the unexpired period of the surrendered
licence [8(2)]. The holder of a restricted licence may on surrendering
it be granted a standard licence [8(1)]. When a licence is so exchanged
the applicant must meet the qualification requirement appropriate to
the type of licence applied for [8(3)].

If it appears to the Traffic Commissioners that the licence holder is
not of good repute, does not have appropriate financial standing or is
not professionally competent and does not employ a transport manager
who is of good repute and is professionally competent they must
revoke the licence [7(1)]. Before doing so they must notify the holder
of their intentions, specify the grounds for their action and a time
within which written representations may be made by the licence
holder. They must consider such representations made within the time
allowed [7(2)].

In the event of the death or physical or mental incapacity of a standard licence holder or a transport manager, or in the event of a transport manager for other reasons ceasing to be employed by the licence
holder, the Commissioners may suspend revocation of the licence for a
reasonable time to enable the undertaking's licence to be transferred or
enable a new transport manager to be appointed [7(4)].

A refusal to grant, and the revocation of, a standard licence under
these provisions is to be treated as if done under Section 127(7) of the
1960 Act [6(2) and 7(3)]. This gives a right of appeal.

ROAD SERVICE LICENCES

Except in Passenger Transport Areas set up under the Transport Act
1968 or in the Greater London area applicants for road service licences
are required to submit to the appropriate area Traffic Commissioners
particulars of the type or types of vehicle to be used and, in the case of
regular services, the time-tables and fare-tables. For other than regular
services (e.g. excursions and tours) the particulars must be such as the
Commissioners require [Act 1960/140(1)]. Particulars of interests,
financial or otherwise, in other passenger transport concerns must also
be given [Act 1960/140(2) and 1506/60].

Among the matters to which the Traffic Commissioners are obliged
to have regard are:

Any transport policies or plans of the local authorities concerned which have been drawn to the Commissioner's attention by those authorities.

The transport requirements of the area as a whole (including an adjoining traffic area if relevant) and of particular communities in the area.

The need to provide and maintain efficient services to meet those requirements.

The suitability of the routes.

The convenience of disabled persons.

Representations made by persons already providing transport on or near the routes or by a local authority in whose area any part of the route is situated [Act 1960/135(2A)(2C) and Act 1978/Sched. 2].

If the licence is granted, the Traffic Commissioners may attach to it such conditions as they think fit with regard to the above matters and in particular for securing that the fares shall not be unreasonable; that where desirable in the public interest the fares shall be so fixed as to prevent wasteful competition with alternative forms of transport; that copies of the timetable and fare-table shall be carried and be available for inspection in vehicles used on the service; that picking-up or setting-down restrictions shall be imposed where necessary; in appropriate cases passengers are enabled to continue their journey by another means of transport and, generally, for securing the safety and convenience of the public [Act 1960/135(4)]. The Traffic Commissioners may from time to time vary the conditions of a licence in such manner as they think fit [135(5)]. Additional powers are given to the Commissioners with regard to the fixing of maximum or minimum fares [135(6)].

Traffic Commissioners must not grant a road service licence if they think, from the particulars given on the application form, that legal speed limits are likely to be contravened [135(2)].

BACKINGS

If a service operates in more than one traffic area, the operator must hold a road service licence in respect of each area affected. Licences granted in other areas after the first are described as 'backings', and in dealing with an application for a backing the Traffic Commissioners may impose any condition which they might have imposed had they been granting the licence, and they are empowered to vary any condition attached to the licence by the Traffic Commissioners who granted it. All the terms of the Act apply, in fact, to backings in the same way as to licences [Act 1960/137(1), (2)].

Wilful or frequent breaches of the conditions of a road service licence (or backing) may lead to revocation or suspension of the licence [136(1)].

Notwithstanding the provisions as to backings, no separate application need be submitted in respect of any 'corridor area', and a licence may be granted to cover both the originating area and a 'corridor area' as if it had been backed. A 'corridor area' is a traffic area in which passengers will not be taken up or set down or permitted to alight for the purpose of sightseeing or for any other purpose requiring a halt of more than 15 minutes [Act 1960/138(1)]. Before granting such a licence, the Commissioners concerned must consult the Commissioners of the corridor area as to the route to be followed [138(2)].

VARIATIONS

Before varying the licence or backing conditions, either at the instigation of a licence holder or of the Commissioners, notice must be given by the Commissioners to other persons affected or by way of publication in *Notices and Proceedings*. Objections to, or representations about, the application or proposal must be lodged, together with the licence or backing, with the Commissioners within 14 days [123/57/3(7)].

No such notification is necessary, however, for an application for a variation of licence or backing conditions for up to 8 weeks in circumstances which could not reasonably have been foreseen and which the Commissioners feel it expedient to grant. Decisions in such cases must still be published in *Notices and Proceedings* [2128/61/2(2)].

PROCEDURE

Applications for licences and backings should be sent together to the Traffic Commissioners for the primary, or originating, area. Such applications must be sent in at least 8 weeks before it is desired to commence the service or, on a renewal, 8 weeks before the existing licence or backing expires. Traffic Commissioners, however, have discretion to deal with applications for licences and backings received after the prescribed date [900/52/38]. Copies of applications are available for inspection at the Commissioners' offices [40] and copies of *Notices and Proceedings*, containing details of all applications, public sittings, and decisions, may also be inspected free of charge [41] or purchased at 12½p each [32/69], post free. Objections or representations (under Section 135 of the 1960 Road Traffic Act) must be in writing and must state the specific grounds of objection and the conditions which it is desired should be attached to the licence or backing if granted. Such objections must be submitted to the Traffic Commissioners not later than 21 days after publication of the application in *Notices and Proceedings*. A copy of the objection must at the same time be sent to the applicant [43].

In a case of urgency the Traffic Commissioners may dispense with the usual time-of-submission requirements, and a licence for a special occasion or a period not exceeding 8 weeks may be granted at a fee of 25p [47]. For a service to be operated on not more than 3 consecutive days, the licence fee is 10p a day [44]. Otherwise the fee for a road service licence is £1 a year [44] and the normal validity period is 3 years for licences covering either stage [414/37] or express services [747/38]. A short-term licence lasting up to six months may be granted [Act 1960/139A and Act 1978/Sched. 2].

HIRING OR SALE

If an operator lets out one of his vehicles on hire to another operator for use as a stage or express carriage, the hirer is responsible for ensuring that the vehicle bears a notice stating 'On hire to ——' either on the front or near side of the vehicle [900/52/20].

When a vehicle passes out of the possession of a licence holder, except under a hiring agreement, he must forthwith notify the appropriate Commissioners [21]. The issuing Traffic Commissioners must be notified when an authorised service is ended and the licence and backing, if any, returned for cancellation [48].

APPEALS

An 'aggrieved' applicant, licence holder, or objector may appeal to the Minister of Transport against the Traffic Commissioners' decision. This refers to the granting, refusal or variation of a road service licence, or in the case of a refusal to vary the licence in a way desired, an appeal by the holder, local authority or person providing transport facilities along or near the route or part of route; the revocation or suspension of a public service vehicle licence; the refusal of a certifying officer to remove the suspension of a p.s.v. licence; the refusal of a certifying officer to issue a certificate of fitness; the limitation of duration of a certificate; or the revocation of a certificate. Such appeals must be made in the prescribed manner within one month of the decision being made known (or publication of the decision in *Notices and Proceedings* where road service licences are concerned) and the Minister's decision is binding upon the Traffic Commissioners or certifying officer [Act 1960/143 and 123/57/3(3)].

A person should not seek an order of certiorari to quash the commissioners decision without first following the statutory appeal procedure. In *R. v. Traffic Commissioners for the North Western Traffic Area ex.p. British Rail* an application for certiorari was refused where an objector had not had an appeal lodged under Section 143 disposed of.

PERMITS

Traffic Commissioners can grant a permit, instead of a road service licence, for a vehicle to be used as a stage carriage or for school buses to be used as such as stage or express carriages [Act 1968/30(1) and Act 1978/Sched. 2]. Permits for non-school buses will not be issued unless the Commissioners are satisfied that there are no other transport facilities available to meet public need on the proposed route. School bus permits will allow passengers other than pupils to be carried only to the extent to which the passenger accommodation is not, and is not likely to be, required for pupils [30(2), (3)].

Permits, which may be revoked if any conditions are frequently not complied with, have a normal validity period of 3 years but can be less [30(5), (6)]. The fee for a permit is £1 per annum. Duplicate permits, marked as such, cost 25p [32/69].

MINIBUS PERMITS

The Minibus Act 1977 provides for the issue of permits to bodies using minibuses for non-profit making activities and for their exemption from public service vehicle licensing.

If a vehicle adapted to carry more than seven but less than sixteen passengers is used for carrying passengers for hire or reward it is not to be treated as a public service vehicle as long as (a) it is specified in a permit issued under the Act; (b) the vehicle is not used to carry members of the public at large nor for profit nor incidentally to an activity which is carried on for profit; and (c) the use of the vehicle is in accordance with conditions of the permit [Act/1(1)].

Permits may be granted (i) by the traffic commissioners to any body appearing to them to be concerned with education, religion, social welfare or other activity for the benefit of the community and (ii) by a designated body to itself or any other body to whom it is entitled to issue a permit [1(2)]. The Secretary of State may by order designate bodies appearing to him to be concerned with education, religion, social welfare or other activity of benefit to the community. In such an order he must specify the classes of bodies to whom the designated body may grant a permit; he may impose restrictions on the grant of a permit and may require conditions to be attached to it; and may require the designated body to make returns regarding permits granted by it [1(3)]. Whilst a minibus used under Section 1(1) is not a public service vehicle it is still to be treated as one for the purposes of any local Act which regulates the use of private hire vehicles and excludes public service vehicles from its scope [1(5)].

Traffic Commissioners and designated bodies may attach to a permit such conditions they consider appropriate [2(2)]. A permit cannot be varied so as to substitute another body for the body to whom it was issued or another vehicle for the one to which it relates but, apart from these restrictions, a permit may be varied or revoked by the body which granted it or by the traffic commissioners [2(3)]. A permit remains in force till it is revoked or, in the case of a permit issued by a designated body, till that body ceases to be designated [2(4)]. A permit may be granted to a named individual on behalf of a body rather than to the body itself [2(5)].

The Secretary of State may make regulations which prescribe

(a) the form of the permits and matters appropriate for conditions,
(b) the permit fees to be charged by Traffic Commissioners,
(c) the documents, plates and marks to be carried by vehicles used under permits,
(d) the conditions to be met by persons driving vehicles used under permits,
(e) the conditions of fitness to be met by vehicles used under permits.

The exemption from p.s.v. licensing given in Section 1(1) will not apply to the use of the vehicle at a time when a contravention of regulations made under (c) to (e) above occurs [3(2)].

The fee for a permit issued by the Traffic Commissioners is £7 and it must be paid in advance [1708/77/4]. A driver's notice must be fixed inside the vehicle so that it is easily readable by the driver without interfering with his control of the vehicle [5(2)]. The driver's notice identifies the vehicle, states the conditions attached to the permit and describes the classes of passengers which can be carried [Sched. 1]. A minibus disc which gives details of the vehicle, the issuing authority and date of issue, the operator's name and the classes of passengers must be fixed inside the minibus so that it does not interfere with the driver's control of the vehicle and so that it is easily readable from outside the vehicle [5(3)]. If a permit, driver's notice or disc is lost, destroyed or defaced the permit holder must notify the Traffic Commissioners or the body who issued it and obtain a replacement [7].

To drive a minibus under these provisions a person must be 21 years of age and hold a full, ordinary driving licence [6].

The conditions of fitness for minibuses used under this Act are given on page 180.

The bodies appearing to the Secretary of State to be concerned with education, religion, social welfare or other activities for the benefit of the community have been designated and the classes of bodies to whom they may issue permits specified [1709/77/3 & Sched.]. They include the councils of counties; non-metropolitan counties; metropolitan districts; inner and outer London boroughs; the City of London; the Scottish regions; the Orkney, Shetland and Western islands; the Inner London Education Authority; and 54 charitable bodies.

Every permit granted by a designated body must contain a condition that the minibus is not to be used to carry children between their home and school without the consent of the local education authority and the Traffic Commissioners of the area [5].

Within one month after granting a permit a designated body must send a copy of it to the Traffic Commissioners of the area and, in January each year, send a return to the Secretary of State giving details of permits granted, varied or revoked in the preceding calendar year [6].

COMMUNITY BUSES

Traffic Commissioners may grant (a) a road service licence under the Road Traffic Act 1960 authorising a vehicle to be used as a stage or express carriage or (b) a permit under Section 30 of the Transport Act 1968 authorising a vehicle's use as a stage carriage, in either case, to provide a community bus service using volunteer drivers [Act 1978/5(1)]. The only vehicles which can be used are those adapted to carry at least 8 and at most 16 passengers [5(2)]. The bus service may extend to the provision of excursions and tours [5(3)].

A licence or permit must not be granted unless the Traffic Commissioners are satisfied that the applicants (a) are a body of persons concerned for the social and welfare needs of one or more communities and (b) propose to provide the bus service without profit either to themselves or to anyone else. In the case of an application for a permit under Section 30 of the 1968 Act the Commissioners must also be satisfied that no other transport facilities are available to meet the reasonable needs of the proposed route [5(4)].

A vehicle used to provide a community bus service does not require a p.s.v. licence and the driver does not require a p.s.v. driver's licence [5(5)]. But the driver must be a volunteer and, if not the holder of a p.s.v. licence, comply with prescribed conditions. The vehicle must, unless authorised on a p.s.v. licence, comply with prescribed conditions of fitness. A specified disc or document must be displayed on the vehicle [5(6)]. A volunteer, for these purposes, is a driver who is not paid for driving the vehicle on the particular journey disregarding any payment of reasonable expenses incurred in making himself available to drive and any payment for earnings lost by making himself available in exceptional circumstances [5(7)].

Traffic Commissioners may grant a road service licence or permit for a community bus service to be provided wholly or partly in Greater London. But before granting or renewing such a licence or permit the Commissioners must ensure that the application is approved by the London Transport Executive and before varying a licence or permit must consult that Executive [5(8)].

A road service licence or Section 30 permit may be granted to authorise the use of a community bus as a contract carriage [6(1)]. Here a community bus is described as a vehicle adapted to carry at least 8 and at most 16 passengers which, whether or not belonging to the holder of the licence or permit, is used on a regular basis on the service [6(2)]. A licence or permit authorising use as a contract carriage will not be granted unless the Commissioners are satisfied it is reasonable with a view to financial support of the service [6(3)]. The provisions of Section 5(5) and (6) above, regarding exemption from p.s.v. licensing and alternative requirements, also apply to a community bus used as a contract carriage [6(4)].

Councils of non-metropolitan counties and non-metropolitan districts may make grants to persons providing community bus services [1(5)].

MUNICIPAL TRANSPORT UNDERTAKINGS

Any local authority already operating (under a local Act or Order) public service vehicles may, as part of that undertaking, use any of them as contract carriages on any road within its district [Act 1930/101 and Act 1968/36(1)]. Such an authority may resolve to operate contract carriages between places within and outside their district and, if requisite to other services, between places outside their district [36(2)]. The need for the Minister's consent to these operations was removed by the Local Government Act 1974.

Any local authority, already running public service vehicles, may acquire by agreement any p.s.v. undertaking or dispose of its own undertaking by way of sale, lease or exchange or, in Scotland, excambion [37(1)].

A local authority may make such charges for the carriage of passengers and parcels on its public service vehicles as it thinks fit [Act 1930/104(1)]. If the authority so desires, it may carry on its public service vehicles small parcels not exceeding 56 lb in weight, and dogs in the care of passengers; no other goods or animals may be carried [104(2)]. Joint working agreements may be made between local authorities or between a local authority and any other person [105].

Where such concessions were in force by November 30, 1954, local authorities may grant free or reduced charge travel concessions to certain classes of persons [Act 1955/1]. Within designated areas, local authorities must enter into arrangements with the Executive over concessionary fares [Act 1968/138].

PASSENGER TRANSPORT AREAS

The licensing provisions of the 1960 Road Traffic Act are altered materially by the Transport Act 1968, in so far as operations are conducted in areas (outside Greater London) known as passenger transport areas or, officially, as 'designated areas'. The Minister of Transport has power to designate any area and to provide a Passenger Transport Authority and a Passenger Transport Executive for that area [Act 1968/9(1)]. Before making an order designating a passenger transport area, however, the Minister must consult every local authority in or adjacent to the area. He must also give an opportunity to stage carriage operators in the proposed area to make representations [9(2)].

A Passenger Transport Executive can submit to the Passenger Transport Authority and obtain the Authority's approval of, among other things, any proposal for a major reorganisation of any transport services provided within or to and from the area [15(1)] and the Executive must obtain the Authority's approval for any alteration in the general level of charges [15(2)].

Within 12 months of its establishment the Authority and the Executive must publish a statement setting out in general terms the policies they intend to follow [18(1)]. Within 2 years, the Executive must prepare and the Authority must publish proposals for the future development of the passenger transport system in the area [18/2].

EXISTING SERVICES WITHIN P.T.A.

When the Minister has received this statement from the Authority he can order that certain provisions be applied to the area [Act 1968/19(1)]. These are that, in a designated area, no person other than the Executive or a subsidiary may provide a bus service in that area except under an agreement with the Executive. Existing services may be continued only with the Executive's consent [19(2)]. An existing operator must, within a prescribed period, apply to the Executive for consent to continue a service and, unless he has contravened any condition of his road service licence during the previous 6 months or has entered into an agreement with the Executive, his application must be granted and the Executive must attach exactly the same conditions to the road service licence or backing as obtained before his application relative to the picking up and setting down of passengers in the designated area [6th Sched./2, 3, 14]. An existing operator who has applied for a consent can continue his service before he is notified of the grant or refusal. He can also continue while he is entitled to appeal against any condition attached to the consent or of its refusal, and, if an appeal is lodged, until it is determined [6th Sched./4].

An application for a variation of a condition attached to a consent must not be unreasonably refused by the Executive. The Executive can, by giving written notice to the operator, make any reasonable variation without having received an application. In no case, however, can a variation affect the carriage of passengers except those carried wholly within the designated area [Act 1968/6th Sched./5].

REVOCATION OF CONSENT

A consent may at any time be revoked by the Executive if the operator has contravened any condition attached to it or if the Executive discovers any such contravention which it was not aware of when it granted the consent [Act 1968/6th Sched./7]. But contraventions will not lead to revocation unless they are committed wilfully or to the danger of the public involved in the breach [8].

COMPENSATION TERMS

By giving at least 9 months' notice, the Executive can at any time revoke any consent it has granted. In its notice, it must state a date— not less than 6 months—by which the operator concerned may claim compensation for any diminution in the value of the assets of his business and any expenditure (excluding income tax, capital gains tax or corporation tax) incurred in winding up all or part of his business. The operator can require the Executive to purchase his relevant business [6th Sched./10(1), (2)]. 'Assets' includes goodwill [10(3)]. Compensation payable for diminution of value is the difference between the market value of the relevant business immediately before and immediately after the revocation. Market value is defined as the amount which the assets would have fetched if sold in the open market by a willing seller to a willing buyer [11(1), (3)].

When the Executive is required to purchase an operator's relevant business, compensation is to be a sum which it might have been expected to realise if the consent had not been revoked and if the business had been sold as a going concern (on the revocation date) in the open market. The sum must not be less than the amount by which the value of the assets, other than goodwill, exceeds the total liabilities [Act 1968/6th Sched./12].

If any compensation terms are not agreed between the Executive and the operator within 6 months, they must be determined by an arbitrator (or, in Scotland, an arbiter) appointed on the application of either party by the Minister [6th Sched./13(1)].

ROAD SERVICE LICENCES AND P.T.A.

No road service licence is needed for any bus service operated wholly within a designated area. Where such a licence is granted for a service operated partly in a designated area, no conditions can be attached concerning passengers who are both picked up and set down in the area.

Any road service licence which is in force immediately before the date of designating an area ceases to be effective to the extent that it relates to the operation of a service and to the licence conditions about picking up and setting down passengers wholly in the area [Act 1968/19(3)].

The Executive is given a right to make representations to the Traffic Commissioners when they are considering the grant, backing or refusal of a road service licence in respect of which part of the route lies in a designated area. The Executive can also appeal against the Commissioners' decision [21(1)].

NATIONALISED BUS COMPANIES

Power is given to public authorities, known as the National Bus Company and the Scottish Transport Group to carry passengers by road and other means inside and outside their respective countries and to undertake other work such as hiring out vehicles, conducting travel agencies or any other activity authorised by the Minister [Act 1968/25, 26].

GREATER LONDON

It is the general duty of the Greater London Council to control transport in the Greater London area [Act 1969/1] and to do this to constitute a public authority called the London Transport Executive [4]. The duty of the Executive, in conjunction with the Railways Board and the National Bus Company, is to provide public passenger transport services meeting the needs of Greater London and with due regard to efficiency, economy and safety [5]. Only the Executive, its subsidiaries, persons operating in agreement with the Executive, or under a consent may provide a London bus service [23(2)]. Consents were granted to existing operators when the Act came into effect and can be renewed, varied, transferred to successors or be cancelled by the Executive [23(2) and Sched. 4]. Appeals can be made by the operator to the Metropolitan Traffic Commissioners against the Executive's decisions and an appeal procedure is laid down [Act 1969/Sched. 4 and 1269/72].

A London bus service is a service for which a road service licence would be required but excluding excursions, tours and express feeder services [Act 1969/23(7)]. A road service licence is not required for a London bus service [23(2)(a)].

Section 21 of the Transport Act 1968—which deals with the functions of Traffic Commissioners in passenger transport areas—applies to Greater London with minor amendments [23(6)].

EXPERIMENTAL AREAS

The Passenger Vehicles (Experimental Areas) Act 1977 provides for the designation of experimental areas in which local authorities can authorise the use of passenger vehicles for hire or reward without them being subject to licensing as public service vehicles.

The Secretary of State may designate experimental areas which consist of the whole or any part of the area of a local authority. If requested by the local authority he must designate the area [Act/1(2)]. A designation order may have effect for a period not over two years but may be extended or further extended for periods of up to two years. If requested by a local authority the Secretary of State must extend the period [1(3)(4)].

In an experimental area the local authority concerned may grant authorisations for vehicles used to carry passengers for hire or reward, whether or not at separate fares, (a) within the area or one or more parts of it or (b) within the area and also on journeys falling partly inside and outside the area, including journeys falling partly within the area of another local authority [2(3)].

An authorisation may be either

> (a) a general authorisation applying either
> > (i) to private vehicles generally or
> > (ii) to private vehicles adapted to carry a specified number of passengers being a number less than sixteen; or
> (b) a special authorisation issued to a specified person and applying

to such private vehicles or commercial vehicles as may be specified in it [2(3)].

For these purposes a commercial vehicle is a motor vehicle adapted to carry not more than five passengers which is, apart from this Act, used to carry passengers for hire or reward in the course of a passenger transport business. (Most taxis and private hire cars would come within this definition.) A private vehicle is a motor vehicle adapted to carry not more than 16 passengers which, apart from the Act, is not used to carry passengers for hire or reward in the course of a passenger transport business [2(9)].

A special authorisation granted by a local authority to cover journeys into the area of another authority shall be of no effect in that area unless granted with that other authority's consent [2(5)]. An authorisation may be granted only in accordance with the particular or general approval of the Secretary of State [2(6)].

Where the use of a private or commercial vehicle on a journey is covered by an authorisation the vehicle is to be treated as not being a public service vehicle for the purposes of (a) the Road Traffic Act 1960 and (b) any other enactment relating to public service vehicles where a p.s.v. is defined by reference to the 1960 Act [2(8)].

The Schedule to the Act prescribes conditions which may be attached to authorisations, provides for the grant and revocation of an authorisation and the resolution procedure for local authorities. The main points are given here.

The following conditions are attached to every general authorisation:

(a) An authorised journey must not be made in conjunction with or in extension of a service provided under a road service licence if the vehicle is owned, hired or made available by the holder of the licence or any person who receives remuneration in connection with that service;

(b) an authorised journey must be made without previous advertisement to the public;

(c) vehicles used under an authorisation must not stand or ply for hire;

(d) the carriage of passengers must be as a result of arrangements made before the journey began.

When granting a special authorisation the local authority may attach such conditions as they think fit in respect of any of the following:

(i) the persons by whom the specified vehicles may be used under the authorisation;

(ii)   the routes on which specified vehicles are to be used;
(iii) the timetables to be observed on specified journeys;
(iv)   the advertisement of services;
(v)   the points where passengers may board and alight;
(vi)   the fares to be charged;
(vii) any other matter which appears to the authority to be appropriate having regard to local circumstances.

In deciding whether to grant or revoke a special authorisation the local authority must have regard to the fitness for use of the vehicle and the suitability of persons who use the vehicle under the authorisation.

The local authority may revoke an authorisation at any time and must do so if directed by the Secretary of State. A general authorisation is revoked by a resolution of the council concerned and a special authorisation is revoked by giving notice of revocation to the person specified in it.

Before (a) passing any resolution to grant, vary or revoke a general authorisation or (b) to grant or revoke a special authorisation a local authority must give notice of the matter in one or more local newspapers. At least 21 days notice of its intention to consider a resolution or grant a special authorisation must be given and at least 56 days notice of its intention to revoke a special authorisation. Before passing the resolution or granting or revoking the special authorisation the local authority must take into account any representations made to them in relation to it. After passing a resolution and after the Secretary of State makes an order to revoke a general authorisation the local authority must give notice of the fact in a local newspaper and the grant, variation or revocation is not to take effect till such notice is given.

Three areas in Devon and four in North Yorkshire have been designated as experimental areas [1554/77].

INTERNATIONAL SERVICES

The European Communities Act 1972 amended Sections 160 and 239 of the Road Traffic Act 1960 and gave the Secretary of State power to make regulations in connection with international services operated under E.E.C. rules. He can exempt from road service licensing any international service authorised under Community provisions; require associated documents to be kept and produced; and appoint persons to enforce E.E.C. provisions. It is an offence not to keep or produce any document required under such regulations. The Road Transport (International Passenger Services) Regulations 1973 have been made under these powers.

Common rules for the international carriage of passengers by bus or coach, contained in E.E.C. Regulation 117/1966, apply to all international road passenger transport operations which begin or end in a Member State and on which vehicles with a capacity for more than 8 passengers (exclusive of the driver) are used. The operations are divided into three broad categories: regular services, shuttle services and occasional services. Whilst the Regulation defines what regular and shuttle services are, it does not state what requirements apply to them. These rules should have been formulated by 1968 but the E.E.C. countries have not reached agreement on them.

The rules in Regulation 117, therefore, apply only to occasional services and since Article 3 states that occasional services are those which are not regular or shuttle services one must look at the definitions of these services to see what services are involved. Article 1 states that regular services are services which provide for the carriage of passengers at specified intervals along specified routes, passengers being picked up and set down at predetermined stopping points. Regular services for special categories of passengers, such as workers or schoolchildren, are included. The fact that a service may be varied according to needs does not affect its classification as a regular service. These services appear to be comparable to stage and express services under British p.s.v. law and to include some services which might now be outside p.s.v. law.

Shuttle services are services consisting of repeated outward and return journeys on which previously formed groups of people are carried from one point of departure to one destination. Each group of passengers which has made an outward journey must subsequently be carried back to the point of departure. Passengers must not be picked up or set down during a journey. The first return journey and the last outward journey have to be made unladen. These services do not have any British counterpart. When common rules on shuttle services are agreed some exemptions from the conditions may be made.

Article 3 states that an occasional service is a service which is not a regular or shuttle service. Three types of occasional service are given. These are (a) closed-door tours where the same vehicle is used to carry the same group of passengers throughout the journey and bring them back to the place of departure; (b) services which carry passengers on the outward journey and return unladen; and (c) all other services. Unless authorised by a Member State passengers must not be picked up or set down during a journey. Though these services are termed 'occasional' they may be operated with some degree of frequency without ceasing to be occasional.

Article 5 says that occasional services of the types described in (a) and (b) above will not require any authorisation by a Member State other than by the State where the vehicle is registered. The 'other services' of (c) above are similarly exempt from authorisation by States other than that of registration provided that a number of conditions are met. These are: (1) The outward journey is made unladen and all the passengers are taken up in the same place; (2) The passengers consist of groups formed under contracts of carriage made before their arrival in the country where they are to be picked up, or are passengers making the return trip of the service at (1) above; or (3) The passengers have been invited to travel to another Member State at the expense of the person issuing the invitation. If these conditions are not met the service may have to be authorised by Member States.

The circumstances under which works-owned buses will not need authorisation when carrying employees to and from work are set out in Article 6. It is unlikely that British operators will be affected by these provisions. Such services are subject to certification instead of authorisation.

A control document must be carried on a vehicle which is on an occasional service and must be produced when required by an inspecting officer. The control document will be supplied by the Member State in which the vehicle is registered or by an authorised agent. The form the control document must take and the rules about its use are the subject of E.E.C. Regulation 1016/1968. Article 2 of this Regulation states that the control document shall consist of passenger waybills in duplicate in books of 50. The book is to be of a prescribed size and have a green paper front cover on which is to be recorded the book number, the issuing State, the carrier's name, the date and place of issue and the signature and stamp of the issuing authority. Instructions on the use of the book are to be printed inside the front cover and the top copy of a waybill must be carried on the vehicle throughout the journey.

On the three types of 'other' occasional service on which an authorisation is not required there must be carried on the vehicle a document showing that the journey comes within one of the three prescribed classes.

On the waybill a list of passengers' names must be given or be attached to it. Member States can agree between themselves to dispense with the list of names. Details of the vehicle, operator and driver must be given on the waybill together with a day-to-day journey schedule. The wording on the front cover and the front of each waybill must be in the language of the Member State where the vehicle is registered. On the back of the top copy of a waybill there must be a translation in the other official E.E.C. languages of the wording on the front of the waybill. A book of waybills is not transferable and it will be the duty of the operator to ensure that individual sheets are properly completed.

SPECIAL TYPES VEHICLES

Highways Act 1959
Motor Vehicles (Authorisation of Special Types) General Order, **1101/73**
Motor Vehicles (Authorisation of Special Types) (Amendment) Order, **No. 1779/74**
Motor Vehicles (Authorisation of Special Types) (Amendment) Order, **No. 323/76**

Motor vehicles and trailers which do not comply in all respects with the Motor Vehicles (Construction and Use) Regulations 1978 can be used on a road if they come within a class of vehicle specified in the Motor Vehicles (Authorisation of Special Types) General Order 1973. If a vehicle can be authorised under the Order the operator must comply with conditions which may be attached to the movement by the Order. The Order is of a permissive nature in that failure to comply with conditions of movement is not an offence in itself but such a failure removes the protection given by the Order and the operator will become liable for any contraventions of the Construction and Use Regulations which arise—see *Siddle C. Cook* v. *Arlidge*, [1962] 1 W.L.R. 203, n.

ABNORMAL INDIVISIBLE LOADS

Heavy motor cars and trailers specially designed and constructed for the carriage of abnormal indivisible loads and locomotives and motor tractors specially designed and constructed to draw such trailers and which do not comply in all respects with the Construction and Use Regulations can be used on a road provided they comply with specified C. and U. requirements and with other specified conditions [1101/73/20].

An abnormal indivisible load is defined as a load which cannot without undue expense or risk of damage be divided into two or more loads for the purpose of carriage on roads, and cannot, owing to its size, be carried by a heavy motor car or trailer or a combination of both complying with all the requirements of the Construction and Use Regulations, or which, owing to its weight, cannot be carried by a heavy motor car or trailer or a combination of both with a total laden weight of under 24,390 kg and complying with all the C. and U. requirements [19]. A vehicle carrying 12 beams each 51 ft 6 in long could not be authorised under the Order because the load was divisible into 12 separate beams—*Smith* v. *North Western Traffic Area Licensing Authority*, [1974] R.T.R. 236.

In addition to specified C. and U. Regulations applying, the main conditions of movement are as follows:

The overall width of a heavy motor car must not exceed 2·9 metres unless a load can be carried safely only on a wider vehicle [20(g)]. The width of a trailer must not exceed 2·9 metres unless it is drawn by a locomotive or motor tractor and a load can be carried safely only on a wider trailer [20(i)]. The width of a locomotive or motor tractor must not exceed 2·9 metres unless drawing a trailer which exceeds that width, as above [20(h)]. But the overall width of any vehicle or load must not exceed 6·1 metres [20(j), (k)].

The overall length of a vehicle must not exceed 27·4 metres and the length of a load, including the vehicles on which it rests, must not exceed 27·4 metres, except that when a load is carried by a motor vehicle and trailer the length of the motor vehicle is disregarded [20(1)].

A vehicle's tyres must be pneumatic or made of soft or elastic material [20(n)].

The total laden weight of the vehicles carrying the load must not exceed 152,400 kg and except for heavy motor cars first registered or trailers constructed before January 1, 1952, the weight transmitted to a road by any wheel must not exceed 11,430 kg. For this purpose any two wheels are counted as one if the distance between the centres of the areas of contact between such wheels and the road surface is less than 610 mm.

In the case of wheels not fitted with pneumatic tyres, the total weight on any wheels in line across the vehicle must not average more than 765 kg per 25 mm width of tyre in contact with the road.

Limits are also placed on the weight bearing on a strip of road at right angles to the vehicle. A weight of 45,720 kg is allowed on a strip of road surface up to 610 mm wide; thereafter up to a width of 2·13 metres weight is allowed at the rate of 30,000 kg per metre and thereafter at the rate of 10,000 kg per metre [20(o)].

A vehicle or combination of vehicles cannot carry more than one abnormal indivisible load at any one time except (a) as long as the vehicle's Construction and Use weight limits are not exceeded more than one such load of the same character can be carried or (b) more than one load can be carried if the total laden weight of the carrying vehicles does not exceed 76,200 kg, the carriage of more than one load does not cause the vehicle's overall length to exceed 18·3 metres or the overall width to exceed 2·9 metres and the loads carried are loaded at the same place and carried to the same destination [20(p)].

If a load consists of engineering plant from which parts have been detached the load and parts can be carried on the same vehicle provided (i) the detached parts do not protrude further than the load; (ii) the load and parts are loaded at the same place and have the same destination; and (iii) the total weight of the vehicles carrying the load and parts does not exceed 76,200 kg [1101/73/20(q) and 323/76].

On ordinary roads the speed of an authorised vehicle must not exceed 12 m.p.h. but it may go up to 20 m.p.h. if the vehicle is unladen, does not exceed 2·9 metres wide and complies with specified construction requirements [23(f)].

If the overall width of the vehicle, including the load, exceeds 3·5 m the overall length of a vehicle, including the load, but excluding a load-bearing drawing unit, exceeds 18·3 metres; the overall length of a combination of vehicles, including the load, exceeds 25·9 metres; the length of a forward projection of the load exceeds 1·83 metres or the length of a rearward projection of the load exceeds 3·05 metres then one person, in addition to the driver, must be employed to attend to the vehicle and load. If three or more such vehicles are travelling in convoy this requirement applies to the foremost and rearmost ones [24].

If the load projects more than 1·83 metres to the front or rear, marker boards must be fitted to it in the manner set out in the C. and U. Regulations (see page 230) and if a load projects to the rear more than 1·07 metres but not over 1·83 metres it must be made visible to other road users [25]. An end marker board is not required if the load is fitted with reflective rear markings [25(5)].

If the overall width of vehicle together with its load exceeds 4·3 metres the prior approval of the Secretary of State, on Form V.R. 1, must be obtained [26]. The V.R. 1 must be carried on the vehicle while on the authorised journey [26(2)(b)].

If a vehicle, including the load, has an overall width over 2·9 metres or an overall length over 18·3 metres (excluding a load-bearing drawing unit); or a combination of vehicles has an overall length over 25·9 metres; a forward or rearward projection of the load is over 3·05 metres; or the load-carrying vehicle's gross weight exceeds 76,200 kg then two days' notice of the movement of the load must be given to the chief officer of each police area through which the vehicle passes. The police can vary the time, date or route of the vehicle, and, while on a journey, cause it to halt in the interests of road safety or to avoid traffic congestion [27]. The form the notice must take is set out at the end of this chapter.

A highway and bridge authority must be given six days' notice of the movement of a vehicle which exceeds 76,200 kg gross weight and two days' notice in any other case when a C. and U. axle or gross weight is exceeded. An indemnity must also be given to highway and bridge authorities before using such a vehicle on a road [28]. The authority may dispense with some particulars in the notice [28] but may not dispense with a notice entirely—*George Cohen 600 Group, Ltd.* v. *Hird*, [1970] 2 All E.R. 650; [1970] 1 W.L.R. 1226. The form the notice and indemnity must take are set out on pages 196 to 198.

A vehicle carrying an abnormal indivisible load must not be driven on to a bridge at the same time as another such vehicle and must not be parked on a bridge except in circumstances beyond the driver's control [29]. If a vehicle exceeding 32,520 kg (laden or unladen) stops on a bridge it must be moved off it as soon as practicable and if it is necessary to jack-up the vehicle on a bridge the advice of the bridge authority must be sought as to the use of spreader plates [30].

LOAD OVER 4·3 METRES WIDE ON NORMAL VEHICLE

A load over 4·3 metres wide can be carried on a vehicle which otherwise complies in all respects with the Construction and Use Regulations provided specified conditions are complied with. These conditions are that the vehicle's speed does not exceed 20 m.p.h. [23]; an attendant is employed [24]; the approval of the Secretary of State has been obtained on form V.R. 1 which is carried on the vehicle [26]; and police notice is given [27].

ENGINEERING PLANT

Engineering plant is defined as movable plant or equipment being a motor vehicle or trailer specially designed and constructed for engineering operations and which cannot comply with certain requirements of the Construction and Use Regulations or the Track-Laying Regulations and which is not constructed primarily to carry a load other than a load being excavated material raised from the ground by apparatus on the motor vehicle or trailer, or materials which the vehicle or trailer is specially designed to treat while carried thereon, or a mobile crane which does not comply with certain of the requirements of the same two sets of Regulations [1101/73/19].

Such vehicles can be used on a road subject to conditions contained in Article 21, other relevant Articles and specified C. and U. Regulations being complied with.

A mobile crane may be used on a road only to get from one place to another and not for lifting or carrying goods except when actually engaged in engineering operations. Other engineering plant can be used on a road only to travel between engineering operation sites, and must carry no load except necessary gear or equipment. Engineering plant actually engaged on road work can carry material which can be treated while carried on the vehicle or which has been raised from the ground by apparatus on the vehicle [21(a), (b)].

A motor vehicle over 7·93 metres long must not draw a trailer other than a broken-down vehicle [21(n)]. A mobile crane must not draw a trailer and engineering plant must not draw a trailer other than engineering plant, a living van or office used in connection with road works [21(c), (d)].

The same weight restrictions apply to engineering plant as apply to vehicles authorised to carry abnormal indivisible loads [21(k), (o), (r)].

Engineering plant (other than gritting machines) which is not fitted with pneumatic or soft or elastic tyres must have smooth tyres with the edges rounded to a radius of from 12 to 25 mm [21(j)].

Gritting machines can have some or all tyres consisting of equal-sized diagonal cross-bars, not less than 1 in wide, with spaces not greater than the width of the bars [21(j)].

Except in the case of a steamer with a reversible engine every motor vehicle must be equipped with an efficient brake. On motor vehicles registered on or after January 1, 1952, this brake must be capable of acting also as a parking brake unless another brake is available for that purpose [21(l)].

A trailer must have an efficient brake or suitable scotches or other similar devices [21(m)].

A vehicle must not exceed 27·4 metres overall length or 6·1 metres overall width [21(p), (q)].

A vehicle authorised under Article 21 must not exceed 12 m.p.h. [23(2)].

An attendant, police notice, highway and bridge authority notice and indemnity are required in the same circumstances as apply to the carriage of abnormal indivisible loads [24, 27, 28].

If a special appliance or apparatus fitted to the vehicle projects over 1·83 metres forward or over 3·05 metres rearward it must be fitted with marker boards. If it projects over 1·07 metres rearwards but not over 3·05 metres steps must be taken to make it visible to other road users [25].

If engineering plant weighing over 32,520 kg is caused to stop on a bridge it must be moved off it as soon as practicable and the advice of the bridge authority must be sought as to the use of spreader plates before jacking-up the vehicle on a bridge [30].

If a vehicle exceeds 4·3 metres wide special approval for the movement must be obtained from the Secretary of State on Form V.R. 1 and this form must be carried on the vehicle on the journey [26].

OUTSIZE DUMPERS

Subject to certain conditions, heavy motor cars or trailers or articulated vehicles constructed primarily for use in private premises for moving excavated material and fitted with a tipping body or movable platform and which do not conform to certain requirements of the Construction and Use Regulations can be used on roads only to go to and from the private premises, or between private premises and a port or vice versa. No load other than the vehicle's 'necessary gear or equipment' must be carried.

Requirements are laid down as to axle and gross weights, length, speed, attendants needed and notice to police and highway authorities [1101/73/16].

OTHER VEHICLES

The Order also authorises the use of many specialised vehicles subject to conditions laid down for each type of vehicle. The types of vehicle include track-laying vehicles [1101/73/5]; military vehicles [6]; tracked lifeboat vehicles [7]; grass cutting machines and hedge trimmers [8, 9, 10]; pedestrian-controlled road maintenance vehicles [11]; vehicles on trial [12]; straddle carriers [13]; harvesting machines [14]; balers [15]; vehicles for export or on test [17]; and vehicles fitted with movable platforms [18].

LIABILITY FOR DAMAGE

If a highway authority is obliged to incur extraordinary expense in repairing a road as the result of the passage of excessive weight or other extraordinary traffic, the additional expense as compared with normal repair costs may be recovered from the person responsible. The operator and highway authority may, however, agree in advance on the payment of a sum by way of composition of such liability, and in this event no proceedings for the recovery of damages can be taken. Proceedings must, in any case, be begun within 12 months of the damage or not later than 6 months after the completion of the work occasioning the damage [Act 1959/62(1), (2)].

FORM OF NOTICE TO POLICE
The Motor Vehicles (Authorisation of Special Types)
General Order, 1973

In pursuance of Article 27 of the above-mentioned Order I/We ....
.... of ....
being the owner(s) of the undermentioned vehicle(s) to which the Order applies
hereby give notice that it is my/our intention to use the said vehicle(s) on the
roads specified below from ....
to .... starting at approximately .... a.m./p.m. on the ....
day of .... and completing the journey at
approximately .... a.m./p.m. on the ....
day of ....
The route proposed to be followed is: Department of the Environment
.... to ....   Classification No. ....
.... to ....   „   „   ....

Note—Any further particulars of route necessary to define it clearly are to
be given overleaf, and where a road is unclassified sufficient information is to be
given to enable it to be identified.

PARTICULARS
(to be given in respect of each vehicle)
1. Vehicle(s) to which the Order applies.
    Index mark and registration number (if any) ....
    Operator's licence number (if any) ....
    Type ....
    Description of load (if any) ....
    Dimensions of vehicle(s) and of load (if any)—
    Maximum height of vehicle(s) or of vehicle(s) and load ....
    Overall width of vehicle(s) inclusive, where a load is to be carried having a
        lateral projection, of the width of any such projection ....
    Overall length of vehicle(s) ....
    Length of any projection of special appliance or apparatus or load—
        Forward projection ....
        Rearward projection ....
    Distance between vehicles where load is to be carried by more than one
        vehicle ....
    Overall length of any combination of vehicles (inclusive of load)................
    Total weight of vehicle(s) (inclusive of load, if any) ....
2. Other vehicle(s) (if any) drawing or drawn by the above-mentioned vehicle(s).
    Index mark and registration number (if any) ....
    Operator's licence number (if any) ....
    Type ....
    Laden weight ....
    Date............................... Signed ....

FORM OF NOTICE TO
HIGHWAY AND BRIDGE AUTHORITIES

The Motor Vehicles (Authorisation of Special Types)
General Order, 1973

In pursuance of Articles 16, 17 and 28 of the above-mentioned Order
I/We ....
of..
being the owner(s) of the undermentioned vehicle(s) to which the Order applies
hereby give notice that it is my/our intention to use the said vehicle(s) on the
roads specified below from ....
to .... starting at approximately .... a.m./p.m. on the ....
day of.. and completing the journey at
approximately .... a.m./p.m. on the ....
day of ....
The route proposed to be followed is: Department of the Environment
.... to ....   Classification No. ....
.... to ....   ,,   ,, ...

Note—Any further particulars of route necessary to define it clearly are to
be given overleaf, and where a road is unclassified sufficient information is to be
given to enable it to be identified.

PARTICULARS
(to be given in respect of each vehicle)

1. Total number of vehicles to be used including not only vehicles the use of
   which is authorised only by the Order, but also other vehicles to be used in
   conjunction therewith ....
2. Number of such vehicles, the use of which is authorised only by the Order
   ....
3. Vehicle(s) to which the Order applies.
      (Particulars to be given in respect of each vehicle. All particulars in respect
   of an articulated vehicle should be included as if it were a single vehicle.)
   Index mark and registration number (if any) ....
   Operator's licence number (if any) ....
   Type ....
   Description of load (if any) ....
   Overall dimensions of vehicle(s)
         (inclusive of load, if any)—Maximum height...
                                          Maximum width ....
                                          Maximum length ....
   Weight of vehicle(s) (inclusive of load, if any)..
   Spacing and weight of load-carrying axles—
      (a) first load-carrying axle:
            (i) number of wheels ....
            (ii) approximate weight on axle...
            (iii) distance to second load-carrying axle ....
      (b) second load-carrying axle:
            (i) number of wheels ....
            (ii) approximate weight on axle...
            (iii) distance to third load-carrying axle..
   Repeat for all load-carrying axles.

In the case of track-laying vehicles a dimensioned sketch plan is to be attached showing the number and disposition of all wheels (if any) and tracks in contact with the road surface indicating the weights transmitted by the wheels or tracks of the vehicle(s).

4. Other vehicle(s) (if any) drawing or drawn by the above-mentioned vehicle(s).

Index mark and registration number (if any) ....

Operator's licence number (if any) ....

Type ....

Laden weight ....

FORM OF INDEMNITY

I/We hereby agree to indemnify you and each and every highway or bridge authority responsible for the maintenance and repair of any road or bridge on the journey to which the above notice relates in respect of any damage which may be caused to any such road or bridge:

(a) by (any of) the above-mentioned vehicle(s)—
    (i) by reason of the construction of or weight transmitted to the road surface by (any of) the said vehicle(s); or
    (ii) by reason of the dimensions, distribution or adjustment of the load carried by (any of) the said vehicle(s); or

(b) by any other vehicle by reason of the use of (any of) the above-mentioned vehicle(s) on the road or, as the case may be, the bridge, except to the extent that the damage was caused or contributed to by the negligence of the driver of the other vehicle

provided that any claim in respect of damage so caused by any vehicle shall be made in writing within twelve months from the date on which the vehicle is last used on the journey to which the above notice relates, stating the occasion and place of the damage.

Date........................ Signed..

Note—Paragraph (a) (ii) above only applies where vehicles are carrying an abnormal indivisible load and in other cases should be omitted.

SPEED LIMITS

Road Traffic Regulation Act 1967
Road Traffic Act 1972
Motor Vehicles (Variation of Speed Limits) Regulations, **No. 747/73**
Motor Vehicles (Speed Limits on Motorways) Regulations, **No. 748/73**
Motorways Traffic (Speed Limit) Regulations, **No. 502/74**
Port Talbot By-Pass (Speed Limit) Regulations, **No. 1855/74**
70 m.p.h., 60 m.p.h. and 50 m.p.h. (Temporary Speed Limit) Order 1977

GENERAL LIMITS

On restricted roads (as denoted by appropriate signs authorised by Section 75 of the Road Traffic Regulation Act 1967) the normal maximum speed limit is 30 m.p.h. [Act 1967/71(1)] but lower or higher speeds may be permitted by Order [71(2)]. On unrestricted roads in England, Scotland and Wales, the limit is 70 m.p.h. on dual carriageways and 60 m.p.h. on other roads but many such roads have lower limits applied to them [1977 Order].

A restricted road is defined as a road on which street lamps are placed not more than 200 yd apart [Act 1967/72(1)] but a trunk or classified road is not deemed to be a restricted road because it has lamps within the distance mentioned unless that system of lighting was provided before July 1, 1957 [72(2)]. Sections of restricted roads, furnished with the frequency of lamps mentioned, can be specified as unrestricted roads and, likewise, sections of unrestricted roads can be specified as restricted roads [72(3)].

There is a speed limit exemption covering fire-brigade, ambulance and police vehicles whenever the observance of this limit would hinder the execution of their duties [Act 1967/79]. Military vehicles are not exempt from this requirement, but (apart from service regulations) they are not required to observe any other speed limits; this applies to specified classes of motor vehicles owned by the Ministry of Defence, and used for naval, military or Air Force purposes, or vehicles so used while being driven by persons for the time being subject to the orders of any member of the Forces of the Crown [2192/47].

PARTICULAR LIMITS

Class of vehicle	*m.p.h.*

PASSENGER AND DUAL-PURPOSE VEHICLES

1. A p.s.v. over 3 tons unladen or adapted to carry more than 7 passengers	50
2. A vehicle not over 30 cwt unladen, adapted to carry more than 7 passengers and which is not a p.s.v.	50
3. A vehicle over 3 tons unladen or adapted to carry more than 7 passengers and not falling in 1 or 2 above	40
4. When one trailer is drawn by a motor car adapted to carry not more than 7 passengers or by a vehicle not over 30 cwt unladen adapted to carry more than 7 passengers	
(a) where the conditions of paragraph 25 of this Schedule are met	50
(b) in any other case	40
5. A vehicle drawing one trailer not within 4 above	
(a) in the case of a p.s.v. over 3 tons unladen or adapted to carry more than 7 passengers	40
(b) a vehicle not within (a)	30
6. A vehicle drawing more than one trailer	20
7. Vehicles without pneumatic tyres	20

GOODS VEHICLES

1. Generally (except in 2 or 3 below)	40
2. A vehicle not over 30 cwt unladen and not drawing a trailer	50
3. A motor car not over 30 cwt unladen drawing a trailer where the conditions of paragraph 25 of this Schedule are met	50
4. A heavy motor car drawing a trailer (not including artics)	30
5. A motor car drawing a goods trailer over 5 cwt unladen or other trailer (not being a living van or goods trailer) over 15 cwt unladen (not including artics)	30
6. Vehicles drawing more than one trailer	20
7. Certain vehicles not fitted with pneumatic tyres	20
8. Vehicles without soft tyres	5

MOTOR TRACTORS

1. Generally (except in 2. and 3. below)	20
2. Vehicles fitted with wings, springs, pneumatic tyres, and dual-braking system	30
3. As in 2. above when drawing a trailer fitted with wings, springs, pneumatic tyres and certain brakes	30
4. Vehicles drawing two or more trailers	12
5. Vehicles without soft tyres	5

LOCOMOTIVES

1. Generally (except in 2. and 3. below)	12
2. Vehicles with pneumatic tyres, wings, springs and dual-braking systems	20
3. As in 2. above when drawing a trailer with pneumatic tyres, wings, springs, certain brakes and subject to a gross train weight limit	20
4. Vehicles drawing two or more trailers	12
5. Vehicles not fitted with soft tyres	5

The conditions of paragraph 25 are
(a) the kerbside weight of the drawing vehicle must be marked outside the vehicle on its nearside or inside the vehicle;
(b) the maximum gross weight of a living van trailer or non-goods trailer must be marked on its nearside;
(c) the above weights may be in imperial units or kilograms but the same units must be used for the vehicle and trailer;
(d) a '50' plate of prescribed form is fitted to the rear of the trailer;
(e) the following weight ratios must be observed:
   (i) the maximum gross weight of a living van trailer, the laden weight of a braked goods trailer and the maximum gross weight of any other kind of braked trailer must not exceed the kerbside weight of the drawing vehicle;
   (ii) the laden weight of an unbraked goods trailer and the maximum gross weight of any other unbraked trailer (not being a living van) must not exceed 60 per cent of the kerbside weight of the drawing vehicle.

[Act 1967/78, Sched 5 and 747/73]

A vehicle falling within two or more of the above descriptions is restricted to the lowest of those limits [Sched. 5(13)].

If an employer issues a time-table or schedule, or gives any directions that a journey is to be completed in a specified time, and it is not practicable to complete the journey in the time laid down without exceeding a speed limit the time-table, schedule or directions shall be evidence that the employer procured or incited the employee to commit the offence [Act 1967/78A, Act 1972/203].

MOTORWAYS

On a motorway the speed limit for all vehicles is 70 m.p.h. [502/74]. Vehicles of the following classes are subject to the lower limits shown:

1. Goods vehicles over 3 tons unladen (except in 3. below) — 60 m.p.h.

2. Any vehicle drawing a trailer (excluding artics) if the trailer has less than 4 wheels or has 4 close-coupled wheels, except when falling in 3. below — 50 m.p.h.

3. A vehicle not over 30 cwt unladen drawing a two-wheeled or close-coupled four-wheeled trailer in circumstances where the speed limit for the vehicle on ordinary roads under Schedule 5 of the 1967 Act is 40 m.p.h. or less — 40 m.p.h.

[748/73]

'Close-coupled' means that the distance between the centres of the wheels on one side of the trailer is not over 33 ins.

On a specified section of the M4 motorway and on four of its slip roads in London; the Mancunian Way A57(M) in Manchester; part of the M1 at Hendon; parts of the Acton Expressway and Gravelly Hill interchange, Birmingham; parts of the Leeds South East Urban Motorway; Glasgow Inner Ring Road; and Port Talbot By-Pass there is a limit of 50 m.p.h. for all vehicles. On the southern motorway approaches to Blackwall Tunnel, London, there is a limit of 60 m.p.h. [502/74, 1855/74].

USE OF VEHICLES

Highways Act 1959
Road Traffic Act 1960
Weights and Measures Act 1963
Road Traffic Regulation Act 1967
Roads (Scotland) Act 1970
Highways Act 1971
Road Traffic Act 1972 as amended by *Road Traffic Act 1974*
Heavy Commercial Vehicles (Controls and Regulations) Act 1973
International Road Haulage Permits Act 1975
Agriculture (Avoidance of Accidents to Children) Regulations, **No. 366/58**
London Traffic (Misc. Prohibitions and Restrictions) Regulations, **No. 659/58**
Fixed Penalty (Offences) Order, **No. 1599/60**
Fixed Penalty (Offences) (Scotland) Order, **No. 1196/62**
Various Trunk Roads (Prohibition of Waiting) (Clearways) Order, **No. 1172/63**
Traffic Signs (Temporary Obstructions) Regulations, **No. 1474/66**
Quarry Vehicles Regulations, **No. 168/70**
Fixed Penalty (Areas) (England and Wales) Order, **No. 1194/70**
Fixed Penalty (Areas) (Scotland) (No. 3) Order, **No. 1610/70**
Weights and Measures (Amendments of Schedules 5 & 7) Order, **No. 1708/70**
Cubic Measures (Sand, Ballast and Agricultural Materials) Regulations, **No. 1712/70**
Functions of Traffic Wardens Order, **No. 1958/70**
'Zebra' Pedestrian Crossing Regulations, **No. 1524/71**
Road Vehicles Lighting Regulations, **No. 694/71**
Motor Vehicles (Third Party Risks) Regulations, **No. 1217/72**
Traffic Signs (Temporary Obstructions) (Amendment) Regulations, **No. 49/75**
Road Traffic (Owner Liability) Regulations, **No. 324/75**
Road Traffic (Owner Liability) (Scotland) Regulations, **No. 706/75**
Fixed Penalty (Increase) Order, **No. 1153/75**
Traffic Signs Regulations and General Directions, **No. 1536/75**
Goods Vehicles (International Road Haulage Permits) Regulations, **No. 2234/75**
Goods Vehicles (Authorisation on International Journeys) (Fees) Regulations, **No. 2062/76**
Motor Vehicles (Construction and Use) Regulations, **No. 1017/78**

ACCIDENTS

If an accident occurs owing to the presence of a vehicle on a road and
personal injury is caused to any person other than the driver of that

vehicle, or damage is caused to any vehicle other than that vehicle or its trailer, or damage is caused to any animal other than one carried in that vehicle or trailer, or to any property forming part of the land on which the road runs or adjacent land, the driver of that vehicle must stop. A policeman or any person having reasonable grounds may demand the driver's name and address and also the name and address of the owner and the registration number of the vehicle [Act 1972/25(1)]. 'Animal' means any horse, cattle, ass, mule, sheep, pig, goat or dog [25(3)].

If in the event of any such accident the driver, for any reason, does not give his name and address to any such person, then he must report the accident at a police station or to a police constable as soon as reasonably practicable—but in any case not later than 24 hours after the accident [25(2)]. If a driver does not report the accident as soon as reasonably practicable though it is inside the maximum 24 hours allowed he commits an offence—*Bulman* v. *Bennett*, [1974] R.T.R. 1.

Similarly, accidents involving personal injury to a third party must be reported within 24 hours unless the relevant certificate of insurance was produced at the time of the accident to a police constable or to some person who, having reasonable grounds, required its production then [Act 1972/166(1)].

In *Harding* v. *Price*, [1948] 1 K.B. 695; [1948] 1 All E.R. 283 it was held that a driver who was unaware that his vehicle had been involved in an accident could not be convicted of failing to stop and report.

Any failure in or damage to a public service vehicle of a nature calculated to affect the safety of passengers or other persons using the road must be reported without delay to the Traffic Commissioners for the area in which the incident occurred [Act 1960/132(1)].

Any contract for the conveyance of a passenger in a public service vehicle is declared to be void so far as it purports to avoid any liability for injury to or death of a passenger while being carried in, entering, or alighting from the vehicle [Act 1960/151].

In *Wilkie* v. *London Passenger Transport Board*, [1947] 1 All E.R. 258 it was held that a free pass issued to an employee was a licence to travel and was not a contract so that conditions attached to it excluding liability were valid. But in *Gore* v. *Van der Lann*, [1967] 2 Q.B. 31; [1967] 1 All E.R. 361 a free pass granted to a pensioner was held to be a contract since she had to apply for it and all the elements of a contract were present. In that case conditions excluding liability were invalid.

Any antecedent agreement to restrict or negative a person's liability under the third party insurance requirements has no effect [Act 1972/148(3)].

ATTENDANTS

Basically, two persons must be employed in driving and attending a locomotive and, if the vehicle draws a trailer, an attendant must be employed for each trailer drawn in excess of one. A road roller rolling a road is exempt [Act 1972/34(1)]. However, two persons are not required to drive or attend a locomotive propelled by an internal combustion engine or electrical power [1017/78/138(2)].

When a vehicle, other than a locomotive, is drawing a trailer one person must be employed, in addition to the driver, to attend to the trailer [Act 1972/34(2)]. There is no need for a second man to be present in the following cases: an articulated vehicle; land locomotive or land tractor drawing a land implement or land implement conveyor; land tractor drawing an agricultural trailer; motor car drawing a trailer with not more than two wheels; motor car drawing a four-wheeled trailer with two close-coupled wheels on each side; motor tractor drawing a special meat-carrying trailer between docks and railway stations or between wholesale markets and docks or railway stations; motor tractor drawing a machine or implement for road repair, maintenance or cleansing; motor tractor drawing trailer designed and used solely for street cleansing, refuse collection, or gully or cess-pool emptying; works truck drawing a works trailer when the unladen weight of each does not exceed 1525 kg; a vehicle drawing a trailer fitted only with a parking brake and overrun brakes; a motor vehicle drawing a broken-down vehicle, whether or not in consequence of a breakdown, which cannot be steered by its own steering; a road roller; any Ministry of Defence vehicle drawing a trailer fitted with brakes which the driver can apply; a vehicle used for the statutory removal of another vehicle; a vehicle drawing a towing implement; or any vehicle drawing a trailer(s) fitted with power brakes which can be operated by the driver (if two or more such trailers are drawn one attendant is required) [1017/78/138(1)].

An attendant is not required for a trailer which is an agricultural vehicle not constructed to carry a load or a trailer carrying water for the drawing vehicle [Act 1972/34(3)].

For the carriage of attendants on exceptional loads see the Long, Wide or Projecting Loads' section in this chapter, page 230.

BREAKDOWN SIGN

A portable traffic sign in the prescribed form of a triangle with a red border (each side about 20 in long) may be placed by anyone on any part of any motorway or any other road, footway or verge to warn traffic of a temporary obstruction. The sign must be at least 50 yd away from the obstruction on the same side of the road as the obstruction [1474/66 and 49/75].

CHILDREN ON FARM VEHICLES

Children who have not attained the age of 13 years may not ride on any of the following vehicles while they are being used in agricultural operations or while they are going to or from the place of such operations: tractors; self-propelled agricultural machines; trailers; conveyor trailers; machines mounted on tractors or vehicles or towed or propelled by them; and binders or mowers drawn by animals [336/58/ 3(1)]. But a child may ride in a trailer if he rides (a) on the floor or (b) on a load provided the trailer has 4 sides each higher than the load [3(2)]. A child must not drive a tractor, self-propelled vehicle or machine while it is being used for agricultural operations or is going to or from the place of such operations [4]. A child must not ride on implements mounted wholly or partly on tractors or vehicles or implements towed or propelled by vehicles or on animal-drawn rollers [5]. The expression 'trailer' does not include horse-drawn vehicles [2].

DRAWING A TRAILER

A locomotive may not draw more than three trailers; a motor tractor, one laden or two unladen trailers; and a motor car or heavy motor car, one trailer [1017/78/137(1)]. An agricultural trailer not constructed to carry a load and a trailer carrying water for the drawing vehicle are not counted as trailers for these purposes [137(3)(a)]. A broken-down articulated vehicle is classed as one trailer when being drawn following the breakdown but only if it is unladen [137(3)(b)].

A composite trailer comprising a dolly convertor and semi-trailer is treated as one trailer for the purpose of Regulation 137 [3(6A)].

A motor car or heavy motor car may draw two trailers if one of them is a towing implement and the other is a vehicle which rests on or is suspended from the towing implement [137(2)]. A towing implement is described as a device on wheels to enable a motor vehicle to draw another vehicle with that other vehicle resting on or suspended from the device so that some but not all of the wheels on which the other vehicle runs are raised from the ground [3(1)]. A towing implement which is attached only to the vehicle drawing it is exempt from most construction requirements provided specified conditions are met [4(12)].

A solo motor cycle may not draw a trailer other than a broken-down motor cycle [1017/78/130] and any other motor cycle may not draw a trailer over 254 kg unladen or over 1·5 metres wide [131]. A straddle carrier may not draw a trailer [132].

A trailer must not be used to carry passengers for payment, except a broken-down vehicle drawn at not over 30 m.p.h. and which, if the vehicle is constructed to carry more than 7 persons or is carrying more than 8 persons, is attached by a rigid drawbar [133]. A living van trailer with two wheels or four close-coupled wheels must not carry a passenger, except when tested by its maker, or by a repairer, distributor or dealer [134]. A p.s.v. may not draw a trailer but (a) an empty p.s.v. may draw another empty p.s.v. in case of emergency and (b) a trailer may be drawn if permitted on the vehicle's road service licence or it is on a London bus service and the drawing of a trailer by the p.s.v. and its means of attachment have been approved by a certifying officer [135].

When a trailer is drawn by means of a rope or chain the distance between vehicles must not exceed 4·5 metres [128(1)]. When a trailer is drawn by any means and the distance between vehicles exceeds 1·5 metres steps must be taken to render the means of attachment clearly visible to other road users [128(2)].

If a motor vehicle is drawing one trailer the overall length of the combination of vehicles (not including any load) must not exceed 18 m, unless the trailer is constructed and normally used to carry long loads or is a broken-down vehicle [136(1)]. When a motor vehicle is drawing two or more trailers, or one trailer constructed and used to carry long loads, the overall length of the drawing vehicle must not exceed 9·2 metres and, unless police notice is given and an attendant employed, the overall length of the combination of vehicles (not including the load) must not exceed 25·9 metres [136(2)]. If a vehicle is drawing two trailers only one of them may exceed 7 m in length and if three trailers are drawn none of them may exceed 7 m [136(3)].

Except in the case of a trailer fitted with overrun brakes and a trailer which is a broken-down vehicle which cannot be steered, the brakes of a trailer must be capable of being applied by the driver of the drawing vehicle unless another person is in a position to apply them [126]. When a trailer is detached from the drawing vehicle and parked at least one of its wheels must be prevented from moving by setting a brake or using a chain [127].

INSURANCE

A person must not use, or cause or permit another person to use, a motor vehicle on a road unless the use of the vehicle is covered by a policy of insurance or security in respect of third-party risks specified in the Act [Act 1972/143(1)]. It is a defence for an employee-driver charged with using a vehicle without insurance to prove that the vehicle did not belong to him and that he did not know or have reason to believe that the use of the vehicle was not insured [143(2)].

Third-party insurance is not compulsory in the case of vehicles owned by county and local authorities; vehicles owned or used under the direction of the police; salvage vehicles used under the Merchant Shipping Act 1894; vehicles used under directions of the armed forces; vehicles owned and operated by the London Transport Executive; or to vehicles owned and controlled by a person who has deposited £15,000 with the Supreme Court [144].

The policy must be issued by authorised insurers who are members of the Motor Insurers' Bureau and must insure persons specified in the policy in respect of (a) any liability which may be incurred by him in respect of death or injury to any person due to the use of the vehicle on a road and (b) any liability for the payment of emergency treatment. The policy is not required to cover death or injury to an employee of the policyholder being carried in the course of his employment or any contractual liability [145].

A policy of insurance is of no effect for these purposes until the insurers deliver a certificate of insurance to the insured [147(1)]. A certificate of insurance must be issued by the insurers not later than 4 days after the date of issue or renewal of the policy [1217/72/6]. If a policy is cancelled the certificate must be returned to the insurers not later than 7 days after the cancellation [Act 1972/147(4)].

LONG, WIDE OR PROJECTING LOADS

A load over 4·3 metres wide cannot be moved under the Construction and Use Regulations [1017/78/140(1)]. Apart from loose agricultural produce, a load which projects over the side of a vehicle more than 305 mm or the overall width of which exceeds 2·9 metres cannot be carried unless (a) the load is indivisible, (b) it is not reasonably practicable to comply with the measurements above, (c) the police are given two clear days' notice of movement of the load and (d) if the load exceeds 3·5 m wide, an attendant is employed [140(2)].

A load cannot be carried on a vehicle or vehicles if the overall length of the vehicle(s) including the distance between them, together with any forward or rearward projection of the load exceeds 27·4 metres (the length of a load-carrying drawing unit is excluded) [140(3)].

A load cannot be carried on a vehicle or vehicles if the overall length of the vehicle(s), including the distance between them, together with any forward or rearward projection of the load exceeds 18·3 metres unless the police are notified of movement and an attendant is employed. The length of a load-carrying drawing unit is excluded [140(4)(a)].

A load cannot be carried on a trailer or trailers drawn by a motor vehicle where the overall length of the combination of vehicles, including distances between vehicles and projections of the load, exceeds 25·9 metres unless police notice is given and an attendant is employed [140(4)(b)].

If an articulated vehicle not over 15 m long and not normally used to carry indivisible loads of exceptional length carries a load and the overall length thereby exceeds 16·8 m the police must be notified of the movement [140(6)(e)].

If a vehicle has a special appliance of apparatus, or carries a load, which has

(a) a rearward projection over 1·07 metres but not over 1·83 metres, steps must be taken to make the projection visible to other road users;

(b) a rearward projection over 1·83 metres but not over 3·05 metres, an end marker board must be fitted to the projection;

(c) a forward projection over 1·83 metres but not over 3·05 metres, an attendant must be employed and marker boards fitted; or

(d) a forward or rearward projection over 3·05 metres, police notice must be given, marker boards fitted and an attendant employed [140(5), (6)].

Special provisions are made for a projecting load consisting of a racing row-boat and a load carried by a straddle carrier [140(6) proviso, (7)–(9)].

If the weight of a load rests on more than one vehicle (such as an artic) a projection is to be measured from the front of the foremost vehicle and the rear of the rearmost vehicle [139(d)(ii)]. Where a load carried on a vehicle projects over (but is not borne by) a pulling or pushing vehicle the projection, for marker-board purposes only, is to be measured from the front or rear of the pulling or pushing vehicle, as the case may be [140(10)].

None of these requirements applies to vehicles used for fire, ambulance, police or defence purposes or to a vehicle used for moving a traffic obstruction [140(11)].

When police notice is required in any of the foregoing circumstances it must be given to the chief officer of each police area in which the vehicle travels at least two clear days (excluding Sundays and bank holidays) before the movement takes place. The form of notice is not prescribed but it must contain the time, date and route together with details of length, width and projections, as appropriate. Unless the journey is varied by the chief police officer, and apart from delays caused by the vehicle being stopped by a constable to avoid congestion or in the interests of road safety, the vehicle must be used only in accordance with the notified particulars and none of the notified measurements may be exceeded [1017/78/Sched. 8(1)]. The police can accept shorter notice and fewer particulars and will generally do so by telephone provided written confirmation is sent.

When an attendant is required he must be additional to the driver but he can be the same person as a trailer mate if one is required. His duties are to warn the driver of the vehicle and any other person of any danger likely to arise from the use of the vehicle. If three or more vehicles requiring an attendant travel in convoy it is sufficient if only the foremost and rearmost vehicles have an attendant [Sched. 8(2)].

An end marker board is in the form of an isosceles triangle with a base and height of at least 610 mm. Side marker boards are in the form of a right-angled triangle, 610 mm by 1520 mm. Both types must be made up of alternate 100 mm wide red and white stripes surrounded by a 50 mm wide red border. An end marker board must not be fitted more than 0·6 metres from the end of the projection, more than 2·5 metres above ground level and must face squarely to the front or rear, as the case may be. On projections over 3·05 metres to the rear or 1·83 metres to the front a side marker board must be fitted to each side of the projection not more than 0·9 metres away from the end marker board, not more than 2·5 metres above ground level and must face squarely to the side. If a forward projection exceeds 4·5 metres or a rearward projection exceeds 5·1 metres additional side marker boards must be fitted so that the distance between the end of the vehicle and a side marker or between side markers does not exceed 2·4 metres on a forward projection or 3·6 metres on a rearward projection. Marker boards must be lit by indirect light at night [Sched. 8(3)].

The movement of abnormal indivisible loads is dealt with in the chapter on special types vehicles, pages 212 to 220.

In London the use of all roads within a 3-mile radius of Charing Cross and of many other roads beyond that area is subject to special daytime restrictions. Except under a written permit issued by the police, the following prohibitions apply to the scheduled roads between 10 a.m. and 7 p.m. on any weekday:

No load may exceed 8 ft 6 in in width or 36 ft in length or project more than 8 ft 6 in beyond the rearmost part of the vehicle (excluding tailboard), whilst a *motor* vehicle may not carry a load longer than one and three-quarter times its own length (excluding tailboard).

Fire-brigade vehicles are exempt from these provisions [659/58/15, 16].

MASCOTS

A motor vehicle first used on or after October 1, 1937, must not carry a mascot in a position likely to strike a person with whom the vehicle collides unless the mascot has no projections likely to cause injury [24/73/132].

NOISE

It is an offence to use on a road any vehicle or trailer which causes excessive noise.

A good defence to any proceedings in this connection is to prove that the noise was temporary or accidental and could not have been prevented with due diligence, and in the case of proceedings against the driver—other than an owner-driver—it is a good defence to prove that the noise arose through the fault or negligence of some other person whose duty it was to keep the vehicle in good condition or to pack or adjust the load properly [1017/78/114].

Causing noise by failing to exercise reasonable care is an offence on the part of the driver [115].

It is an offence to use or cause or permit to be used on a road a vehicle first registered on or after January 1, 1931, or a trailer, which emits a noise in excess of prescribed sound levels expressed in decibels. The limits are set out on the following page.

This Regulation does not apply to any motor vehicle going, by appointment, to be noise tested or mechanically adjusted for noise or a motor vehicle returning after such testing or adjustment. Nor does it apply to a vehicle when stationary for such purposes as using its power take-off or to a vehicle first used before November 1, 1970, if using an exhaust brake with which it is fitted [1017/78/116 and 9th Sched.].

The engine must always be stopped for the prevention of noise when a vehicle is stationary, other than in a traffic stop, for testing purposes, or when machinery or plant is driven through a power take-off from the engine [117].

Excluding motor cycles, maximum sound levels in decibels are:

Class of vehicle	First used	
	Before Nov. 1, 1970	On or after Nov. 1, 1970
1. Plated goods vehicle exceeding 3560 kg gross weight	92	92
2. Plated goods vehicle first used before Jan. 1, 1968, with 50% and 25% brake efficiencies	92	—
3. Motor tractors, locomotives, land tractors, works trucks and engineering plant	92	92
4. Passenger vehicles for more than 12 passengers	92	92
5. Any other passenger vehicles	87	87
6. Goods vehicles which are motor cars, other than (1) and (2)	88	88
7. Any other vehicle not listed above	92	88

NOTICE OF PROSECUTION

A person who is prosecuted for dangerous, careless or inconsiderate driving; failure to comply with specified traffic signs or the directions of a constable on traffic duty; leaving a vehicle in a dangerous position; or speeding cannot be convicted of the offence unless (a) he was warned at the time of the offence that a prosecution would be considered, or (b) within 14 days of the offence a written notice, specifying the offence, its time and place and indicating that a prosecution was being considered, was served on him or the registered keeper of the vehicle, or (c) within 14 days of the offence a summons for the offence was served on him [Act 1972/179]. A notice is not required for an offence if at the time or immediately thereafter an accident occurs owing to the presence of the offending vehicle [179(3A)].

The place of the offence must be sufficiently specified in the notice—*Young* v. *Day* (1959), 123 J.P. 317.

A written notice is deemed to be served if sent by registered post or recorded delivery to the accused's last known address, even if it is returned or not received by him [179(2)]. In *Nicholson* v. *Tapp*, [1972] 3 All E.R. 245; [1972] 1 W.L.R. 1044 it was held that the requirement had not been complied with when a notice was sent by recorded delivery on the 14th day after the offence and consequently could not be received by the accused within the stipulated 14 days. The requirement to give notice is deemed to have been complied with unless the contrary is proved [179(3)] and failure to give notice in 14 days will not prevent conviction if failure was due to the accused's or registered keeper's identity not being known or was due to the conduct of the accused [179(4)].

PARKING

A person must not cause or permit a vehicle to remain at rest on a road in a position, condition or circumstances likely to cause danger [Act 1972/24]. A person in charge of a vehicle must not cause or permit it to stand on a road so as to cause unnecessary obstruction [1017/78/122]. Leaving a vehicle on a road for a reasonable time, although it amounts to an obstruction, does not amount to an unnecessary obstruction—*Solomon* v. *Durbridge*, (1956) 120 J.P. 231. A person who, without lawful authority or excuse, wilfully obstructs the free passage along a highway commits an offence and can be arrested [Act 1959/121]. A vehicle must not be driven on common land or moorland unless it is done within 15 yd of a road for the purpose of parking the vehicle. A vehicle must not be driven on a footpath or bridleway [Act 1972/36].

Parking a heavy commercial vehicle (i.e. a goods vehicle over 3 tons unladen) on the verge of a road, on land between carriageways or on a footway is an offence. But it is a defence to prove that the vehicle was parked (a) with the permission of a uniformed policeman, (b) to save life, fight fire or other like emergency or (c) to load or unload, could not be parked elsewhere to do so and was not left unattended [Acts 1972/36A and 1973/2].

It is an offence to leave on a road a vehicle unattended by a licensed driver without stopping the engine (except for fire-engines, vehicles used for police or ambulance purposes or vehicles with engine-driven ancillary equipment) and applying the parking brake [1017/78/124].

Whenever a vehicle is stationary on a road during the hours of darkness it must, unless otherwise permitted by a uniformed policeman, be parked with its nearside against the edge of the road. There are exceptions which cover the operation of vehicles used in connection with building or demolition, repair of any other vehicle, removal of traffic obstructions, road repair or maintenance, laying or maintenance of gas, electricity, water or telephone services. Nor does the restriction apply to the use of one-way streets, parking places, hackney carriage stands and bus stops or to vehicles in use for fire-brigade, ambulance, police or defence purposes if its application would hinder the use of such vehicles [123].

When a trailer is detached from its drawing vehicle, at least one wheel must be prevented from revolving by setting the brake or using a chain [127].

Except in traffic stops or when picking up or setting down passengers, the headlamps of all vehicles, other than breakdown vehicles or tower wagons in use, must always be switched off when the vehicles are stationary [694/71/13].

No person must open, or cause or permit to be opened, any door of a vehicle on a road so as to cause injury or danger to any person [1017/78/125].

When a vehicle is stationary its horn must not be sounded but this restriction does not apply to police, fire-brigade or ambulance vehicles or if the horn is a theft alarm, to summon assistance on a p.s.v. or is used in a case of danger due to the presence of another vehicle [118].

No waiting or parking is allowed on any main carriageway forming part of trunk roads as indicated by 'Clearway' traffic signs without authority from a police constable in uniform [1172/63/4]. Exceptions are vehicles used: in connection with building or demolition; for the removal of any traffic obstruction; for roadworks; for mains and other services; for fire-brigade, ambulance or police purposes; for postal vans; and for the collection by or for a local authority of refuse or cleaning cess-pools [5]. A vehicle must not wait on a verge or lay-by adjacent to a clearway carriageway for the purpose of selling goods from the vehicle but exemption is made for selling and delivering to premises [6].

PEDESTRIAN CROSSINGS

The driver of a vehicle must give precedence to a pedestrian who is within the limits of an uncontrolled zebra crossing [1524/71/8].

If the area of road at either side of a zebra crossing is marked with alternating diagonal white lines in the centre and edges of the carriageway that area is a 'zebra controlled area' [71/5]. The driver of a vehicle in a zebra controlled area who is travelling towards the crossing must not overtake (a) the nearest to the crossing of any moving vehicles or (b) the nearest to the crossing of any vehicles which have stopped to allow persons to use the crossing [10]. If a broken white line is marked across the carriageway, 1 m from the crossing, the driver should stop at this line while giving precedence [5(2)]. In a one-way street a zebra crossing which is divided by a street refuge is treated as two crossings and a vehicle approaching one part of the crossing can overtake a vehicle which has stopped at the other part [11]. A vehicle must not stop in a zebra controlled area except (a) to allow persons to cross the road or because it is illegal to overtake a vehicle stopped for this purpose, (b) when prevented from going ahead by circumstances beyond the driver's control or by accident, (c) when engaged on specified emergency, maintenance, building or repair work, (d) if making a left or right turn, or (e) a stage or express carriage picking up or setting down passengers having passed over the crossing [12, 14, 15].

Except in circumstances beyond the driver's control or to avoid an accident, a vehicle must not stop on a zebra crossing [9(1)].

QUARRY VEHICLES

A quarry vehicle must be equipped with a horn when used in a quarry and when such a vehicle is used in a quarry during the hours of darkness there must be provided sufficient artificial light, whether on the vehicle or not, to enable the vehicle to be used safely [168/70/3]. A quarry vehicle is described as a mechanically propelled vehicle, including plant, which forms part of the equipment of the quarry, but excluding pedestrian-controlled vehicles, motor cycles and vehicles for use on rails or a ropeway [2(1)].

A quarry vehicle or trailer with a tipping body must not be used unless devices are provided for preventing the body from collapsing when raised. The device can be on the vehicle but must be independent of the tipping mechanism [4(1)]. The quarry owner or manager must take steps, including the provision of stop blocks, anchor chains or similar devices, at places where a vehicle is tipped to prevent it causing injury by running away, falling or overturning [4(2)]. A person who uses a tipping quarry vehicle must use the safety devices provided [5].

A person in charge of a quarry vehicle must not leave it unless it is so placed or secured that it cannot accidentally move or be set in motion [6]. A person who drives a quarry vehicle in a quarry without due care and attention commits an offence [7]. A person must not drive a quarry vehicle unless (a) he is authorised to do so by the owner or manager and he is 17 years of age or (b) he is similarly authorised to receive driver-training and he drives under the close supervision of an authorised competent person [9(1)]. The owner or manager must ensure that when a learner drives a quarry vehicle prominent signs to that effect are shown at the front and rear of the vehicle [9(2)]. Overhead structures or cables which could obstruct a vehicle must be signed [10].

REVERSING

A vehicle must not be reversed for a greater distance or time than may be requisite for the safety or reasonable convenience of the occupants of that vehicle or of other traffic on the road [1017/78/120]. Road rollers and other plant engaged on roadworks are exempt.

A driver who, after checking to the rear, reverses into a parked vehicle is not ipso facto guilty of careless driving—*Hume* v. *Ingleby*, [1975] R.T.R. 502.

ROAD HAULAGE PERMITS

For laden British haulage vehicles to enter or travel through most European countries an authorisation or permit is required. A limited number of authorisations are given by the Council of Ministers of the European Conference of Ministers of Transport, and, in relation to E.E.C. countries, under Regulation 2892/72 of the Council of the European Communities. The bulk of continental journeys is made on permits issued under bilateral road transport agreements between the United Kingdom government and the governments of individual European countries. The agreements are treaties made under Crown prerogative and therefore are not law. The Department of the Environment issues to British operators the journey permits supplied by foreign governments under the treaties. To enable the Crown to charge for this service Section 56 of the Finance Act 1973 enables the Minister for Transport to make regulations fixing fees for issuing permits and E.C.M.T. and E.E.C. authorisations.

These regulations provide that the fees payable for E.C.M.T. and E.E.C. authorisations are £95 per year or £24 per quarter. The fee for a journey permit is £2·50 and for a period permit it is £45. If a journey permit covers more than one return journey it is charged for at the rate of £1·50 for each return journey[2062 /76/3, 4, 5].

The International Road Haulage Permits Act 1975 enables the Secretary of State to make regulations providing that goods vehicles registered in the United Kingdom, trailers drawn by such vehicles and unattached trailers in the U.K. may not be used on international haulage or own-account transport unless a prescribed document is carried on the vehicle or by the person in charge of it. If a person, without reasonable excuse, uses a vehicle in contravention of the regulations he can be fined up to £200 [1(3)].

If it appears to a traffic examiner that a prescribed document should be carried on a vehicle he may

(a) require the driver to produce it and permit him to inspect and copy it;

(b) detain the vehicle for the above purpose;

(c) at any reasonable time, enter premises where he believes a vehicle to which the regulations applies is kept; and

(d) at any reasonable time, enter premises where he believes a prescribed document is to be found and inspect and copy any such document he finds there.

[1(2)]

A driver who wilfully obstructs an examiner, or without reasonable excuse, fails to produce the required documents can be fined up to £100 [1(4)]. Any other person who wilfully obstructs an examiner acting under Section 1(2)(d) can be fined up to £100 [1(5)].

If it appears to an examiner that the driver of a vehicle on an international journey has, without reasonable excuse, refused or failed to comply with a requirement under Section 1(2) he may prohibit the removal of the vehicle out of the United Kingdom [2(1)]. Written notice of the prohibition must be given to the driver specifying the reason for the prohibition, whether it applies absolutely or for a specified purpose and whether it is for a specified period or is indefinite. The prohibition has immediate effect [2(2)]. The prohibition may be removed by written notice when an examiner is satisfied that the vehicle is not being used on a journey to which the regulations apply or a prescribed document is carried on the vehicle [2(3)]. As soon as reasonably practicable after a notice has been given under Section 2(2) or (3) the examiner who gave it must take steps to inform the vehicle operator of its contents [2(4)]. A person who, without reasonable excuse, takes a vehicle out of the U.K. in contravention of a prohibition, or causes or permits such removal, can be fined up to £200 [2(6)].

The 'user of a vehicle' has the same meaning as in operators' licensing law [1(8)]. There is a rebuttable presumption that a vehicle which displays a licence or trade plates issued under the Vehicles (Excise) Act or corresponding Northern Ireland provisions is registered in the United Kingdom [1(6)].

An international road haulage permit has been added to the list of documents specified in Section 169 of the 1972 Act which it is an offence, with intent to deceive, to forge, alter, use, lend or allow to be used by another person. It is also an offence under Section 170 of that Act to knowingly make a false statement to obtain a permit. If a police officer or examiner has reason to believe an offence under Section 169 or 170 has been committed in relation to a permit he has power under Section 173 to seize the document [Act 1975/3]. The definition of international road haulage permits includes E.E.C. authorisations [3(5)].

The Goods Vehicles (International Road Haulage Permits) Regulations 1975 apply to goods vehicles registered in the United Kingdom, trailers drawn by such vehicles and unattached trailers for the time being in the United Kingdom. Such a vehicle may not be used on a journey to which the Regulations apply unless an international road haulage permit issued by the Secretary of State for that journey and vehicle is carried on the vehicle or, in the case of a trailer, on the drawing vehicle or by the person in charge of it.

The Regulations apply to haulage and own-account journeys to

Austria, France, West Germany and Italy, including journeys passing through any part of those countries. A number of exceptions from the Regulations are provided and these follow the exemptions given in the bilateral transport agreements between Great Britain and the four countries and in certain E.E.C. directives.

SAND, BALLAST AND READY-MIX VEHICLES

Before a road vehicle laden with ballast commences a journey the person in charge of it must be given a conveyance note containing prescribed particulars [Act 1963/Sched. 5]. It must be produced to a weights and measures inspector if required [30(1)]. The conveyance note must be handed to the buyer before the vehicle is unloaded or, if he is absent, left for him [Sched. 5(9)]. A vehicle carrying ready-mixed cement mortar or concrete must also have with it a conveyance note when laden [Sched. 7]. 'Ballast' includes sand, gravel, shingle, ashes, clinker, chippings (including coated materials), hardcore, aggregates and other materials known as ballast [Sched. 5(1)].

If the body of a vehicle is used as a cubic measure of ballast it must conform to specified calibration and marking requirements [Sched. 5(4)]. A calibration strip, complying with prescribed technical details, must be fitted inside the body on two opposite sides near to the centre of the side [1712/70/7(2)]. The body of a vehicle may be used to measure both metric and imperial quantities but if this is done separate pairs of metric and imperial calibration strips must be used, one of each pair on opposite sides of the body and not more than 20 cm apart. On a vehicle the imperial strips must be nearer to the rear or offside than the metric strips [7(9)]. When a vehicle body is used as a measure its maximum content must be marked on its nearside [9(1)]. When measuring ballast against a calibration mark the vehicle body must be filled in all parts and levelled off. If a person carrying out a measurement fails to level off the ballast when it is loaded or causes or permits a heaped load to be sent out he commits an offence [Sched. 5(5)]. These calibration and measuring requirements also apply to the body of a vehicle used as a measure for agricultural lime or salt, or inorganic fertilisers [Sched. 7].

SECURING CRANE GEAR

When a mobile crane is travelling on a road, any crane hook or similar 'implement' which is suspended from a crane or jib must be secured either to the main appliance or to some part of the vehicle so that it does not cause danger to any person on the vehicle or on a road [1017/78/144].

SKIPS

A builder's skip must not be deposited on a highway without permission of the highway authority [Act 1971/31(1)]. In giving permission the highway authority can impose conditions as to the siting of the skip, its dimensions, marking to make it easily visible, care and disposal of its contents, its lighting and guarding and its removal [31(2)]. In any case where permission is given the owner must ensure that the skip is properly lit at night; it is marked with owner's name and telephone number or address; it is removed when filled; and the authority's conditions are complied with [31(4)]. Where an offence is due to the fault of a person other than the owner that other person may be prosecuted even if the owner is not [31(5)]. It is a defence for a person charged under this section to prove that the offence was due to the fault of another and he could not prevent it [31(6)], but notice of the identity of the person responsible must be given to the prosecution 7 days before the hearing [31(7)]. A defence is provided for a person charged, under any other legislation, of failing to light a skip at night [31(8)]. If a person is charged with obstructing the highway with a skip it is a defence for him to prove that it was deposited in accordance with a permission [31(9)].

A builder's skip is described as a container to be carried on a vehicle and placed on roads for the storage of builders' materials, or the removal and disposal of builders' rubble, waste, household and other rubbish or earth. A person who hires a skip for more than one month is regarded as an 'owner' [31(11)].

Even though a skip may be deposited with permission, a highway authority or constable in uniform can require the owner to remove or reposition it or do so themselves [32(2), (4)].

Similar provisions are in force in Scotland [Act 1970/22, 23].

SOUNDING OF HORN

An audible warning instrument must not be sounded when a vehicle is stationary on a road, other than when danger arises due to another moving vehicle or when used as a theft alarm or to summon assistance and it must not be sounded on a moving vehicle on a restricted road between 11.30 p.m. and 7 a.m. [1017/78/118]. No person may use an instrument emitting a sound similar to a two-tone horn, gong, bell or siren [118(2)]. The above restrictions do not apply to vehicles of specified emergency services if it is necessary or desirable to indicate the urgency of the vehicle's use or to warn other road users of its presence [118(3)].

An instrument, other than a two-tone horn, may be used on a vehicle to inform the public that it is carrying goods for sale, provided it is used only for that purpose and, when on a restricted road, it is not sounded between 11.30 p.m. and 7 a.m. [118(5)]. Loudspeakers fitted to vehicles must not be used between 9 p.m. and 8 a.m. nor at any other time for advertising any entertainment, trade or business, except between 12 noon and 7 p.m. to announce that perishable food is for sale [Noise Abatement Act 1960].

TELEVISION SETS

No television set must be installed or used in a motor vehicle if all or any part of the screen is visible, either directly or reflected, to the driver while in the driving seat. Nor must the controls, other than the one for sound volume and the main switch, be within his reach. Further, no set must be used in a vehicle in such a way that it could distract the driver of any other vehicle on the road [1017/78/143].

TICKET FINES

The fixed penalty procedure applies to offences committed in respect of a vehicle (a) parked without lights or reflectors at night, (b) obstructing a road, or being left, parked, waiting, loaded or unloaded in a road, and (c) non-payment of a parking meter charge [Act 1967/80(1)]. The fixed penalty procedure applies throughout England, Wales and Scotland [1610/70 and 1194/70]. Offences of obstruction and leaving a vehicle in a dangerous position have been excluded from the system [1599/60 and 1196/62].

A person who commits an offence to which the system applies may be given a notice by a constable or traffic warden, or it may be affixed to the vehicle, and if he pays the fixed penalty he cannot be convicted of the offence. After a fixed penalty notice has been issued no proceedings may be taken in respect of that offence in the next 21 days [Act 1967/80(3)]. Once a notice has been attached to a vehicle it must not be removed or interfered with by any person other than the driver or person in charge of the vehicle [80(8)]. The fixed penalty is now £6 but it can be reduced or increased by the Secretary of State provided it does not exceed one-half of the penalty which may be imposed on first conviction for the offence concerned [80(9) and 1153/75].

TICKET FINES—OWNER'S LIABILITY

Owner-liability provisions of the Road Traffic Act 1974 apply where a fixed penalty notice has been given for parking without lights or reflectors, contravening a parking prohibition (except obstruction), non-payment of a parking meter charge or failing to display a current excise licence and the penalty has not been paid within 21 days or any longer period stated on the notice [Act 1974/1(1)].

In proceedings for an offence brought against a person as owner of the vehicle there is a conclusive presumption that the owner was the driver at the material time [1(2)]. But the presumption does not apply unless a prescribed notice is served on the owner in the six-month period following the date of the fixed penalty notice [1(3)]. Neither does the presumption apply if the person served with the prescribed notice was not the vehicle owner at the material time and he supplies a statutory statement of ownership to that effect [1(4)] or if the vehicle was used without the owner's consent or if the accused was not the owner of the vehicle and he has a reasonable excuse for not complying with the prescribed notice [1(5)].

The prescribed notice must be in the given form [324 or 706/75], give particulars of the offence and the fixed penalty concerned and provide that unless the fixed penalty is paid in the appropriate period the person on whom the notice is served (a) is required before the end of that period to supply a statutory statement of ownership and (b) is invited to supply a statement of facts [1(6)].

The statutory statement of ownership is to be signed by the person making it and state (a) that he was the owner of the vehicle at the material time or (b) if he was not the owner, the name and address of the owner if the information is in his possession. A statement of facts states who the driver was at the material time [Act 1974/Sched. 1].

Where a prescribed notice has been served and the fixed penalty has not been paid in the appropriate period the person on whom the notice has been served is liable to a £100 fine if, without reasonable excuse, he fails to supply a statutory statement of ownership [1(7)]. If a person served with a prescribed notice supplies a statement which is false and does so recklessly or knowing it to be false he is liable to a £400 fine [1(8)].

Payment of the fixed penalty before the day on which proceedings are begun against a person under section 1(7) discharges his liability for that offence. The conviction of a person for the offence stated in the prescribed notice discharges any other person's liability for that offence and for an offence under section 1(7). Conviction of a person under section 1(7) discharges the liability of any person for the offence given in the prescribed notice [1(9)].

The 'appropriate period' referred to above means the period of 14 days from the date of the prescribed notice under Section 1(6) is served or such longer period as may be allowed [5(1)].

Owner-liability provisions in respect of excess parking charges are contained in section 2 and are in identical form to those in Section 1 above.

Section 3 contains supplementary provisions relating to hired vehicles and applies where a prescribed notice served under section 1(6) or 2(6) is served on a vehicle-hire firm and at the relevant time the vehicles and applies where a prescribed notice served under Section ing a hire-purchase agreement) for a fixed period of less than 6 months. It is a sufficient compliance with the prescribed notice if the vehicle-hire firm supplies the person who served the notice with a statement that at the relevant time the vehicle was hired and supplies a copy of the hiring agreement and a copy of a statement of liability signed by the hirer under that agreement [3(2)]. A statement of liability is a statement made under the hiring agreement by which the hirer acknowledges that he will be liable as owner of the vehicle for the fixed penalty offences subject of Section 1(1) and excess parking charges subject of section 2(1) during the currency of the hiring agreement [3(3)].

Where a vehicle-hire firm complies with Section 3(2) any reference in Section 1 or 2 to the owner of the vehicle is to be read as the hirer of the vehicle and a statement of ownership as a statement of hiring [3(4)]. The vehicle-hire firm can be required, in the six-month period after it received the prescribed notice, to produce the originals of the copy-documents it supplied under Section 3(2) and if, without reasonable excuse, it fails to do so it will be treated as not having complied with the prescribed notice [3(5)].

For the purposes of these owner-liability provisions the owner of a vehicle shall be taken to be the person by whom the vehicle is kept and in any proceedings brought under the above sections it shall be presumed that the owner at any time was the registered owner [5(3)]. But it is open to the defence to prove that the registered owner at a particular time was not the person by whom the vehicle was kept and it is open to the prosecution to prove that the vehicle was kept by some other person [5(4)]. A prescribed notice under Section 1(6) or 2(6) may be served on a person by delivering it to him or leaving it at his proper address or by sending it to him by post [5(5)].

TRAILER PLATES

A trailer plate of approved design and consisting of a white triangle with red reflectors of not less than 19 mm diameter, must be displayed vertically on the back of every trailer at a height of not more than 1·22 metres, and fixed either on the centre line or to the off-side. The need for a plate does not apply to a trailer which is drawn by a motor car or dual-purpose vehicle with not more than 7 passenger seats, or to a semi-trailer which forms part of an articulated vehicle, or is specially constructed for the carriage of round timber; nor does the requirement apply to broken-down vehicles, land implements, land implement conveyors, agricultural trailers, water carts drawn by road rollers or any trailer carrying two obligatory reflectors to comply with the Road Vehicles Lighting Regulations and bearing the approved markings [1017/78/81].

A '50' plate must not be displayed on the rear of a trailer when the speed limit of the drawing vehicle at the time is less than 50 m.p.h. [96].

TRAFFIC SIGNS AND SIGNALS

A person driving a motor vehicle on a road must stop when required to do so by a constable in uniform [Act 1972/159]. Drivers must obey the directions of a constable engaged in the regulation of traffic [22] and a traffic warden in uniform so engaged [Act 1967/81(6) and 1958/70]. A direction given by a policeman for the purpose of a traffic survey is regarded as given in the regulation of traffic and section 22 applies to traffic survey direction signs [Act 1972/22A]. A traffic survey direction must not be used to cause unreasonable delay to a person unwilling to provide survey information [22A(4)].

Between 8 a.m. and 5.30 p.m. when children are on their way to or from school and are crossing or seeking to cross the road, the driver of a vehicle must stop when a uniformed school crossing patrol exhibits the prescribed sign [Act 1967/25].

Drivers must obey the red 'stop' signal of traffic lights; 'stop', 'give way', 'keep left' and 'no entry' signs. In daylight hours the 'stop—weight check' sign displayed by a person authorised to weigh vehicles must be complied with. Drivers of large vehicles (over 55 ft long, 9 ft 6 in wide or 32 tons) must stop and telephone for permission before driving on to an automatic half-barrier level crossing [Act 1972/22].

Where a road is marked along the centre with a continuous white line alongside a continuous or broken white line a vehicle must not stop (at either side of the lines) except to enable a person to get on or off the vehicle; to enable goods to be loaded or unloaded; to enable the vehicle to be used in connection with building, maintenance or repair work; vehicles used for fire, police or ambulance purposes; a vehicle required by law to stop, or to avoid an accident or in circumstances beyond the driver's control; or if done with the permission of a uniformed constable. When a continuous line is to the left of a broken or continuous line a vehicle must be driven so that the continuous line is on the right-hand side of the vehicle, except that a vehicle may cross or straddle the white line to gain access to a road or premises adjacent to the road or if it is necessary to do so to pass a stationary vehicle, or owing to circumstances beyond the driver's control, to avoid an accident, or to comply with the directions of a uniformed constable [Act 1972/22 and 1536/75/23].

VEHICLES ON FOOTPATHS

Certain local authority appliances or vehicles are allowed to be used on footpaths, footways and bridleways provided they do not travel at more than 5 m.p.h. [2126/63].

VIEW TO THE FRONT

No driver must be in such a position, when driving, that he cannot have proper control of his vehicle and cannot retain a full view of the road and traffic ahead [1017/78/119].

WEIGHT

The owner must cause the unladen weight to be painted or otherwise conspicuously marked on the nearside of a locomotive, motor tractor and registered heavy motor car [1017/78/80].

VEHICLE EXCISE LICENSING

Vehicle and Driving Licences Act 1969
Vehicles (Excise) Act 1971
Finance Act 1971
Motor Vehicles (International Circulation) Order, **No. 1074/57**
Visiting Forces and International Headquarters (Application of Law) Order, **No. 1536/65**
Motor Vehicles (Production of Test Certificate) Regulations, **No. 418/69**
Goods Vehicles (Production of Test Certificates) Regulations, **No. 560/70**
Vehicle and Driving Licences Act 1969 (Commencement No. 7) Order, **No. 244/71**
Vehicle and Driving Licences (Transfer of Functions) (Appointed Date) Order, **No. 377/71**
Road Vehicles (Registration and Licensing) Regulations, **No. 450/71**
Road Vehicles (Registration and Licensing) (Amendment) Regulations, **No. 1865/72**
Motor Vehicles (International Circulation) (Amendment) Order, **No. 869/71**
Motor Vehicles (Third Party Risks) Regulations, **No. 1217/72**
Road Vehicles (Registration and Licensing) (Amendment) Regulations, **No. 1089/75**
Road Vehicles (Registration and Licensing) (Amendment) Regulations, **No. 1680/76**

Any person who uses or keeps on a public road any mechanically propelled vehicle (apart from one of an exempted class) for which an excise licence is not in force commits an offence [Excise Act/8(1)]. A person 'keeps' a vehicle on a road if he causes it to be on a road for a period, however short, when it is not in use there [38(2)]. An employer was held liable for using an unlicensed vehicle though he had not authorised his employee to use it on a road—*Richardson* v. *Baker*, [1976] R.T.R. 56.

APPLICATIONS

On April 1, 1971, the functions of levying excise duty on vehicles, licensing and registration of vehicles and licensing of drivers were transferred to the Secretary of State for the Environment from local authorities [Act 1969/1, 244/71, 377/71]. But until all vehicle files

247

have been transferred to the new licensing centre at Swansea local authorities will continue to exercise the above functions as agents for the Secretary of State.

Applications for excise licences can be dealt with at local vehicle licensing offices and applications should be made not more than 14 days before the licence is to have effect [450/71/4]. Head post-offices can issue renewal licences within 14 days after the expiry of the last licence only if: (a) the application is made on the renewal notice Form V.11, (b) any change in ownership or address has been recorded in the registration document, and (c) no alteration has been made to the vehicle or change made in its use which could result in a different rate of tax being paid.

All applications, except for trade licences, must be accompanied by the appropriate certificate of insurance [1217/72/9] and, in the case of vehicles subject to test procedure and three or more years old, by the relevant test certificate or declaration [418/69/4], or, in the case of a goods vehicle over 30 cwt unladen which requires a goods vehicle test certificate, that certificate, a declaration or a certificate of temporary exemption [560/70/4].

The holder of an excise licence may surrender it at any time during its currency and apply for a refund of duty [450/71/5]. For each complete and unexpired month on the licence a refund, calculated as follows, is payable; in the case of a trade licence taken out for three months only, one-third of the duty paid; and in the case of any other licence, one-twelfth of the annual rate of duty for that licence [Excise Act/17 and Sched. 7, Pt. I, 13].

The owner of a vehicle can apply for a duplicate licence or registration book if the original is lost, destroyed, damaged or illegible. A charge of £2 is made for a duplicate unless the illegibility or colour fading is due to no fault of the applicant. If the original licence or book is found it must be returned to the issuing authority [450/71/6 and 1680/76].

DURATION OF LICENCE

A vehicle licence may be taken out for any period of 12 months; for a calendar year; for four months if the annual rate of duty is over £18; for any seven consecutive days in the case of a Special Types Vehicle over 11 tons unladen [Excise Act/2 and Sched. 7]. Duty on a licence for 12 months is payable at the annual rate; for four months at eleven-thirtieths of the annual rate; and for seven days at one-fifty-second of the annual rate plus 10% [2(4)].

RATES OF DUTY

Contained in Vehicles (Excise) Act 1971 and are as follows:

Hackney carriages
Hackney carriages   £25
                         with an extra 50p for each person
                         above 20 for which the vehicle has
                         seating capacity   [Schedule 2]

In calculating the seating capacity, 16 in per person must be allowed in the case of continuous seats; otherwise the basis is one seat per person, not counting the driver's seat [450/71/42].

The expression 'hackney carriage' means, in this context, a mechanically propelled vehicle standing or plying for hire, and includes a mechanically propelled vehicle let for hire by a person whose trade it is to sell such vehicles or let them for hire (but not under hire-purchase) [Act, 38(1)].

Tractors, etc.

(1) Agricultural machines, defined as being locomotive   £8·50
    ploughing engines, tractors, agricultural tractors, and
    other agricultural engines which are not used on
    public roads for hauling any objects except as follows:

    (a) for hauling their own necessary gear, threshing
        appliances, farming implements, a living van for
        accommodation of persons employed in connec-
        tion with the vehicle, or supplies of water or fuel
        required for the purposes of the vehicle or for
        agricultural purposes
    (b) for hauling from one part to another part of a
        farm, agricultural or woodland produce of or
        articles for the farm
    (c) for hauling, within 15 miles of a farm occupied
        by the licensee, agricultural or woodland produce
        of that farm or land occupied with that farm, or
        fuel required for any purpose on that farm or for
        domestic purposes by the occupier's employees
    (d) for hauling articles required for a farm by the
        licensee, being either the owner or occupier of

the farm, or a contractor engaged to do agricultural work on the farm by its owner or occupier,
or for hauling articles required by that person for
land occupied by him with a farm
(e) for hauling within 15 miles of a forestry estate
occupied by the licensee, agricultural or wood-
land produce of that estate, or fuel required for
any purpose on that estate, or for domestic purposes by persons employed by the occupier, or
for hauling articles required for such a forestry
estate by the occupier
(f) for hauling within 15 miles of the holder's farm
material to be spread on roads to deal with ice,
frost or snow, or hauling a snow-plough or
similar contrivance.
[The term 'tractor', in this definition, does not
include a vehicle not designed for use on land or
one capable of exceeding 25 m.p.h. on the level
under its own power [Finance Act 1971/6(1)].

(2) Vehicles designed, constructed and used for the   £8·50
purpose of trench digging or any kind of excavating
or shovelling work which are used on public roads
only for that purpose or for proceeding to and from
such work, and when so proceeding neither carry nor
haul any load other than what is necessary for their
propulsion or equipment
(3) Mobile cranes used on public roads only, either as   £8·50
cranes in connection with work being carried on on a
site in the immediate vicinity, or for the purpose of
proceeding to and from a place where they are to be
used as cranes and when so proceeding neither carry
nor haul any load other than such as is necessary for
their propulsion or equipment
(4) Works trucks, being goods vehicles designed for use   £8·50
in private premises and used on public roads for
carrying goods between two premises or between
premises and a vehicle, or in connection with roadworks
(5) Mowing machines   £8·50
(6) Vehicles (other than the above) constructed and used
solely for haulage and not for carrying or having
superimposed on them any load except such as is
necessary for their propulsion or equipment—

(a) Being haulage vehicles registered in the name of a travelling showman and used solely by him for the purpose of his business and for no other purpose—

Not exceeding 7¼ tons unladen	£84
Exceeding 7¼ but not exceeding 8 tons	£101
Exceeding 8 but not exceeding 10 tons	£118
Exceeding 10 tons, for each ton or part of a ton in excess	£18

(b) Other haulage vehicles—

Not exceeding 2 tons unladen	£100
Exceeding 2 but not exceeding 4 tons	£180
Exceeding 4 but not exceeding 6 tons	£260
Exceeding 6 but not exceeding 7¼ tons	£340
Exceeding 7¼ but not exceeding 8 tons	£415
Exceeding 8 tons	£415
plus £70 for each ton or part of a ton in excess up to 10 tons	
Exceeding 10 tons	£555
plus £80 for each ton or part of a ton in excess	

[Schedule 3]

Goods vehicles

(1) Goods vehicles registered in the name of a person engaged in agriculture (defined in 4th Sched./9(1) under title of 'farmer's goods vehicle') and used on public roads solely for conveying the produce of or articles required for the purpose of the agricultural land he occupies, and for no other purpose. Vehicles used by a contractor to cut and remove grass on farmland were not farmers' goods vehicles because the contractor did not 'occupy' the land—*Howard* v. *Grass Products, Ltd.*, [1972] 3 All E.R. 530; [1972] 1 W.L.R. 1323. In *McKenzie* v. *Griffiths, Ltd*, [1976] R.T.R. 140 a vehicle used by a farmer to transport manure from a racing stable to a mushroom grower was held not to be a farmer's goods vehicle. Section 18(7) of the Act, however, authorises the licensee of a farmer's goods vehicle to carry the produce of or articles required for another farmer, provided that (a) the vehicle is so used only occasionally, (b) that the goods carried for another farmer represent only a small proportion of the total load carried and (c) that no payment or reward is made or given—

Unladen weight of vehicle		Initial rate	Rate per annum additional for each ¼ ton or part of a ¼ ton in excess of the weight in col. 1
Exceeding	*Not exceeding*		
		£	£
—	12 cwt	30	—
12 cwt	16 cwt	32	—
16 cwt	1 ton	35	—
1 ton	3 tons	35	4
3 tons	6 tons	67	3
6 tons	10 tons	103	2
10 tons		135	4

(2) Goods vehicles registered in the name of a travelling showman, used solely for his business, and fitted permanently with a living van or some other special type of body or superstructure—

Unladen weight of vehicle		Initial rate	Rate per annum additional for each ¼ ton or part of a ¼ ton in excess of the weight in col. 1
Exceeding	*Not exceeding*		
		£	£
—	12 cwt	30	—
12 cwt	16 cwt	32	—
16 cwt	1 ton	35	—
1 ton	3 tons	35	4
3 tons	6 tons	67	3
6 tons	10 tons	103	4
10 tons		167	6

(3) Electrically propelled goods vehicles and tower wagons whether electrically propelled or not—

Unladen weight of vehicle		Initial rate	Rate per annum additional for each ¼ ton or part of a ¼ ton in excess of the weight in col. 1
Exceeding	*Not exceeding*		
		£	£
—	12 cwt	40	—
12 cwt	16 cwt	44	—
16 cwt	1 ton	50	—
1 ton	4 tons	50	5
4 tons	6 tons	110	6
6 tons	10 tons	158	5
10 tons	—	238	8

(4) Goods vehicles, other than those chargeable with duty under (1), (2) and (3) above—

Unladen weight of vehicle		Initial rate	Rate per annum additional for each ¼ ton or part of a ¼ ton in excess of the weight in col. 1
Exceeding	*Not exceeding*		
		£	£
—	16 cwt.	50	—
16 cwt.	1 ton	56	—
1 ton	4 tons	56	14
4 tons	10 tons	224	25
10 tons		824	30

(5) Additional duty for drawing a trailer—
    (i) Vehicles used by travelling showman   £30
    (ii) Other goods vehicles—
        Unladen weight of drawing vehicle—
          Not exceeding 1½ tons   £30
          Exceeding 1½ but not exceeding 3 tons   £40
          Exceeding 3 but not exceeding 4 tons   £67
          Exceeding 4 tons but not exceeding 6 tons   £90
          Exceeding 6 tons   £112

                                 [Schedule 4]

For the purposes of the above paragraph an articulated vehicle is treated as one vehicle and not a vehicle drawing a trailer [Sched. 4/6(1)]. A goods vehicle for these purposes is a mechanically propelled vehicle constructed or adapted for use *and used* for the conveyance of goods or burden of any description, whether in the course of trade or otherwise [9(1)].

Other vehicles
Vehicles not dealt with in Schedules 1 to 4 (Schedule 1 deals with bicycles and tricycles)
    (a) Electrically propelled vehicles★ and other vehicles
        not exceeding 7 h.p. and first registered before
        Jan. 1, 1947   £36

    (b) Vehicles not included above   £50
                                   [Schedule 5]

★ A vehicle is not deemed to be electrically propelled unless the electrical motive power is derived either from a source external to the vehicle or from an electrical storage battery which is not connected to any source of power when the vehicle is in motion [Excise Act/38(3)].

EXEMPTIONS

Under the Vehicles (Excise) Act 1971, Section 4, no duty is payable on fire-engines, on vehicles kept by a local authority while they are used for the purposes of its fire-brigade service, on ambulances, or on road rollers. Vehicles used for no purpose other than the haulage of lifeboats and their necessary gear are similarly exempted.

No duty is payable on invalid carriages not exceeding 8 cwt unladen.

Exemption has also been granted for road construction vehicles used on a road to carry built-in road construction machinery (with or without articles or material used for that machinery), and for vehicles constructed and used solely for carrying machinery for spreading grit or other materials on roads affected by ice or snow.

Local authority watering vehicles (for cleansing or watering roads or cleansing gullies) used by a local authority or a contractor are exempt as also are tower wagons used solely for street lighting purposes. In *Anderson and Heeley, Ltd.* v. *Paterson*, [1975] 1 All E.R. 523; [1975] 1 W.L.R. 228 a platform truck fitted with a Hiab loader and used for carrying and installing street lighting columns was held not to be a tower wagon.

Vehicles used for clearing snow from public roads by means of a plough or similar contrivance need not be taxed for carrying out such work [7(3)].

Road-gritting attachments, farm implements not constructed or adapted for the carriage of goods or burden of any description and drawn by farmers' goods vehicles, gas-producer trailers, snow-ploughs and road-construction vehicles are not regarded as trailers for trailer tax purposes [Sched. 4/9(2)]. Local authority watering vehicles and tower wagons which are trailers are exempt from trailer tax [Sched. 4/6(2)].

In the case of a vehicle used mainly as a goods vehicle, and taxed as such, which is also used to carry employees of the user of the vehicle (without charge) in the course of their employment, no extra duty is chargeable [18(6)].

A goods vehicle not used for carrying goods for hire or reward or in connection with a trade or business is not treated as a goods vehicle for taxation purposes [Sched. 4/3(d)].

A mechanically propelled vehicle being taken to, brought away from, or during a previously arranged compulsory test is exempt [5(1)].

For any vehicle which is to be used exclusively on roads not repairable at the public expense, a declaration must be made in the same way as if the owner were going to apply for a licence. No licence will be issued by the council but a registration book will be given to the owner [450/71/25].

Subject to the approval of the Secretary of State no tax is payable on a vehicle which uses public roads only in passing from land in the owner's occupation to other land in his occupation for distances not exceeding a total of 6 miles in any week. Cases of this kind are dealt with by special application to the appropriate vehicle taxation licensing office [Act 1971/7(1)].

No licences are issued for vehicles belonging to the Crown but every such vehicle must carry a certificate of Crown ownership [450/71/24].

No excise duty is chargeable for any vehicle in the service of a visiting force or headquarters [1536/65/8(4)].

Certain civil defence vehicles are exempt [450/71/27].

Vehicles brought temporarily into Great Britain by persons resident outside the United Kingdom or vehicles registered in the Isle of Man and brought into Great Britain by a person resident outside the United Kingdom are exempt [1074/57/5, 869/71].

It may be noted that as the Finance Acts do not apply to the Crown the cars of Her Majesty the Queen are exempt. Exemption for the vehicles of foreign diplomats of certain rank and the representatives of Dominion Governments is a matter of diplomatic privilege arranged between sovereign powers.

Declarations in respect of some exempt vehicles have to be made to the appropriate authority [450/71/26].

Certain vehicles exempt from purchase tax are not subject to excise duty [Excise Act/6].

CHANGE OF USE

If a vehicle is used in an altered condition or a different manner from that for which it was taxed, a higher rate of duty may become payable; for this to be so, however, the alteration (of condition or use) must be such as to satisfy all the conditions which bring a vehicle into that higher tax category [Act 18(1), (5)]. Any such alterations must be notified in writing by the owner to the council with which the vehicle is registered and the registration book must also be sent to the council for amendment [450/71/11].

If a goods vehicle taxed at the private rate is used for drawing a trailer for carrying goods in connection with a trade or business extra tax is payable. In *James* v. *Davies*, [1953] 1 Q.B. 8; [1952] 2 All E.R. 758 the High Court held that a Land-Rover, taxed as a private car and used for towing a trailer in which goods were carried, must be licensed as a goods vehicle and trailer.

MOBILE PLANT

Vehicles carrying no load other than built-in machinery and articles used in connection therewith are taxable as goods-carrying vehicles, but the weight of the machinery may be deducted in calculating the unladen weight [Act 1971/4th Sched./5(1)].

A mobile concrete mixer, used wholly as such, is, however, subject to a special excise tax allowance. The first 30 cwt of the weight of the built-in mixing plant must be included in the unladen weight of the vehicle leaving any weight in excess of 30 cwt to be regarded as part of the load [5(2)].

UNLADEN WEIGHT

The Sixth Schedule to the Vehicles (Excise) Act 1971 states that, for the purposes of that Act, the unladen weight of a mechanically propelled vehicle shall be taken to be the weight of the vehicle inclusive of the body and all parts (the heavier being taken where alternative bodies or parts are used) which are necessary to or ordinarily used with the vehicle when working on a road but exclusive of the weight of water, fuel or accumulators used for the purposes of the supply of power for the propulsion of the vehicle, and of loose tools and loose equipment [Para. 1].

If a vehicle has a body which is constructed or adapted for being lifted on or off the vehicle with goods inside and is from time to time used for that purpose the weight of that body is disregarded in calculating the vehicle's unladen weight [Para. 2]. The onus of proving that these conditions are met rests on the user of the vehicle [2(3)].

In calculating the unladen weight of a goods vehicle, for the purposes of Schedule 4, there must be included the weight of a receptacle, being an additional body, used for carrying goods if goods are loaded into it, carried in or unloaded from it without it being removed from the vehicle; provided that the weight of the receptacle is not to be included (a) unless it was placed on the vehicle by, or on behalf of, the registered owner, or (b) if it is constructed or adapted for being lifted on or off the vehicle with goods inside and is from time to time used for that purpose, (c) if the receptacle is specially constructed or adapted for carrying livestock and is used solely for that purpose [Para. 3]. In proviso (b) the burden of proof rests on the user of the vehicle [3(2)] and in proviso (c) agricultural produce or requisites can be carried on a journey of which the main purpose is the carriage of livestock or on an outward or return journey to or from carrying livestock [3(3)].

For the purposes of Schedules 3 and 4 the weight of towing attachments is disregarded but subject to a maximum allowance of 1 cwt for any attachment at one end of a vehicle and 2 cwt if the vehicle has attachments at both ends [Para. 4].

REGISTRATION MARKS AND BOOKS

When a vehicle is licensed for the first time it is allocated a registration mark which must be displayed on it, and on any vehicle drawn by it, in a prescribed manner [Excise Act/19].

The registration mark must be exhibited at the front and at the rear of every mechanically propelled vehicle (except works trucks and agricultural machines), the size of lettering to be as prescribed

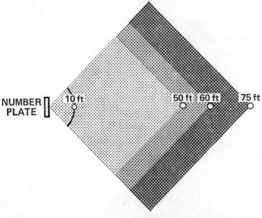

How the test of number plate visibility applies. The shaded areas cover all points from which every letter and figure of the identification mark must be 'easily legible', The 50 ft line applies to the rear plates of motor cycles, pedestrian-controlled vehicles, and invalid carriages during the hours of darkness; the 60 ft line to the rear plates of motor cycles, pedestrian-controlled vehicles, and invalid carriages in daylight and to the rear plates of all other classes of vehicle at night; and the 75 ft line to both front and rear plates of all vehicles (except motor cycles, pedestrian-controlled vehicles, and invalid carriages) during daylight. The 10 ft line is the minimum distance from which observations are to be made.

[450/71/18]. These markings must be on a flat rectangular number plate or flat surface [Sched. 2/9]. Registration numbers on works trucks and agricultural machines can be either on both sides or on the back only [21]. In the case of invalid carriages and pedestrian-controlled vehicles, it is permissible to exhibit the front identification mark on both sides of the vehicle in a vertical position on a flat, unbroken surface or on both sides of the front mudguard [18(3)]. A motor cycle requires a number plate at the rear only [1089/75].

On vehicles first registered before October 1, 1938, the mark must be displayed in a vertical position and be 'easily distinguishable', but for vehicles registered for the first time on or after that date the mark, which must be 'easily legible', need not necessarily be vertical; instead, it must comply with the conditions as to visibility indicated in the diagram above [450/71]. The test of being 'easily legible' applies 'in the absence of fog' during the hours of darkness (except to works trucks which do not need to have their registration numbers illuminated) [19], and also during 'normal' daylight [18].

When a trailer (including a broken-down vehicle) is drawn, the mark of the drawing vehicle must appear on the rear of the trailer except in the case of a trailer drawn by an agricultural machine when the mark of another such machine owned by the same person may be displayed [22].

Number plates made of reflex reflecting material must be marked with the appropriate British Standard specification number, namely B.S. AU 145:1967.

Number plates of reflex reflecting material must be fitted on vehicles first registered on or after January 1, 1973, except vehicles over 3 tons unladen which are fitted with reflective rear markings; stage carriages; pedestrian-controlled vehicles; works trucks; agricultural machines; and trailers [1865/72].

The size and form of registration marks is contained in Schedules 2 and 3 of the Road Vehicles (Registration and Licensing) Regulations 1971.

Registration marks must not be obscured or allowed to become not easily distinguishable [Excise Act/22(2)] but it is a defence for a person to prove that he took all reasonable steps to prevent such an occurrence.

Before issuing a registration book for a vehicle the Secretary of State can require the vehicle to be produced in order to check that the particulars supplied by the owner are correct [450/71/8(1)]. The owner of a vehicle must produce the registration book when required, at any reasonable time, by a police officer or person acting for the Secretary of State [8(2)]. The Secretary of State can require a book to be surrendered to him for correction purposes [8(3)]. Except for persons authorised, it is an offence to deface or mutilate any registration book, or alter or obliterate any entry in it, or, except for a new owner entering his name and address in it, to make any entry or addition in the book [8(4)].

HACKNEY CARRIAGE PLATES

If as the result of taxing a vehicle at the hackney carriage rate of duty the tax paid is less than would have been payable at the private car rate, the vehicle must carry the prescribed hackney carriage plate at the rear. If the vehicle is licensed to ply for hire and carries a distinguishing mark to that effect the plate need not be displayed. Nor need a plate be displayed on a vehicle with seating for 20 or more passengers or on a hackney carriage temporarily adapted to carry goods [Excise Act/21 and 450/71/41].

LICENCES

When a vehicle chargeable with duty under the Act is used or kept on a public road a licence must be displayed on it in the prescribed manner [Excise Act/12(4)]. The licence must be in a holder to protect it from the weather [450/71/16(2)] and, in the case of a vehicle with a windscreen extending to the nearside, must be displayed on the nearside of the windscreen or, on any other vehicle with a driver's cab with a nearside window, on that window, or otherwise on the nearside of the vehicle in front of the driver's seat [16(3)].

It is an offence to alter, deface, mutilate or add anything to a licence or to display a licence so tampered with or on which the particulars have become illegible or the colour altered by fading. To exhibit anything which is intended to be or could be mistaken for a licence is also an offence [450/71/7].

FORGERY AND FRAUD

It is a serious offence to forge or fraudulently alter or use, or fraudulently lend or allow to be used, any registration mark, hackney carriage plate, licence or registration document [Excise Act/26].

TRADE LICENCES

A motor trader or vehicle tester can apply to the Secretary of State for a trade licence. In the case of a motor trader the licence covers vehicles temporarily in his possession and recovery vehicles kept by him for dealing with disabled vehicles. In the case of a vehicle tester it covers vehicles submitted to him for testing and, in the case of a motor trader who is a manufacturer, it covers vehicles kept by him for research and development [Excise Act/16(1)]. A trade licence cannot be used on more than one motor vehicle at a time (except when a recovery vehicle draws a disabled vehicle), it can be used only for prescribed purposes and it does not authorise a vehicle to be kept on a road if it is not being used [16(1)].

A motor trader is a manufacturer or repairer of, or dealer in, mechanically propelled vehicles and a person is regarded as a dealer if his business is mainly one of collecting and delivering mechanically propelled vehicles [16(8)]. A recovery vehicle is a vehicle on which there is mounted, or which is drawing, or which is carrying as part of its equipment, apparatus designed for raising a disabled vehicle wholly or partly from the ground or for drawing a disabled vehicle when so raised, and which is not used for the conveyance of goods other than a disabled vehicle wholly raised by that apparatus, and which carries no other load than articles required for the operation of, or in connection with, that apparatus or otherwise for dealing with disabled vehicles [16(8)]. In *E. Pearson & Son (Teesside), Ltd.* v. *Richardson*, [1972] 3 All E.R. 277; [1972] 1 W.L.R. 1152 it was held that an artic drawing unit kept for breakdowns and equipped with jacks and tow bar was a recovery vehicle. But in *Scott* v. *Gutteridge Plant Hire, Ltd.*, [1974] R.T.R. 292 an articulated low loader fitted with a winch and carrying a defective tracked shovel was held not to be a recovery vehicle. The court did not decide the case on the construction of the vehicle but on the fact that the tracked shovel had been driven on under its own power and had not been raised by any apparatus. In *Robertson* v. *Crew* [1977] R.T.R. 141 it was held that a car with its rotar arm removed was not a disabled vehicle.

A trade licence may be taken out for one calendar year or, except for a trade licence for motor cycles, a period of three months beginning on the first day of January, April, July or October [16(4)]. The annual rate of duty is £25 (motor cycles, £5) and the rate for three months is eleven-fortieths of the annual rate (taken to the nearest 5p) [16(5)]. A person may hold more than one trade licence [16(6)].

The purposes for which a mechanically propelled vehicle may be used by a motor trader under a trade licence are as follows:

(a) for its test or trial or the test or trial of its accessories or equipment in the ordinary course of construction or repair or after completion;

(b) for going to or from a public weighbridge for registration purposes;

(c) for its test or trial for the benefit of a prospective purchaser, and connected journeys;

(d) for its test or trial for the benefit of a person interested in promoting publicity in regard to it, and connected journeys;

(e) for delivering it to the place where the purchaser intends to keep it;

(f) for demonstrating its operation or that of its accessories or equipment when being handed over to the purchaser;

(g) for delivering it between his own premises or premises of another motor trader;

(h) for going to or returning from a workshop in which a body or a special type of equipment or accessory is to be or has been fitted to it or in which it is to be or has been painted or repaired;

(i) for going from the premises of a motor trader to a place from which it is to be transported by train, ship or aircraft, or the reverse;

(j) for going to or returning from any garage, auction room or other place at which vehicles are usually stored or usually or periodically offered for sale and at which the vehicle is to be or has been stored or is to be or has been offered for sale;

(k) for going to or returning from a place where it is to be or has been tested, or to a place where it is to be broken up or dismantled; or

(l) in the case of a recovery vehicle—

(i) for going to or returning from a place where assistance is to be, or has been, rendered to a disabled vehicle,

(ii) for going to or returning from a place where it is to be, or has been, held available for rendering assistance to a disabled vehicle, or

(iii) for carrying a disabled vehicle, or for towing such a vehicle (whether with the assistance of a trailer or not), from the place where it has broken down or from such other place where it is parked to a place for repair or storage or breaking up.

[450/71/35(4)]

Motor vehicles kept by a manufacturer for research and development can be used on a road under a trade licence for those purposes only [36].

A vehicle tester who is the holder of a trade licence may use the licence only for testing motor vehicles and trailers or their accessories or equipment in the course of his business as a vehicle tester [37].

A motor trader may not carry goods on a vehicle used under a trade licence except the following types of goods and only when on the authorised purposes specified:

(i) a load carried for demonstrating the vehicle or its equipment and which is returned (except in case of accident) to the place of loading on a journey mentioned in (a), (c), (d) or (f) above;

(ii) in the case of a recovery vehicle, the goods referred to in the definition of such a vehicle and including a disabled vehicle when on a journey mentioned in (l) above;

(iii) a load built in as part of the vehicle or permanently attached to it;

(iv) parts, accessories or equipment to be fitted to the vehicle and tools for fitting them when on a journey mentioned in (g), (h) or (i) above; or

(v) a load consisting of a trailer when the carrying vehicle is on a journey mentioned in (e), (h) or (i) above.

[450/71/38(1)]

A manufacturer's research and development vehicle used under a trade licence can carry only a load for testing the vehicle, its equipment or accessories and which (except in case of accident) is returned to the place of loading, or a load built in or permanently attached to the vehicle [38(2)]. The same type of load can be carried on a vehicle being tested by a vehicle tester [39]. For the purposes of Regulations 38 and 39 an articulated vehicle is regarded as a single vehicle [38(3)].

The only persons who may be carried on a vehicle used under a trade licence are as follows:

1. the driver, being the licence holder, his employee or any other person who has the licence holder's consent and is accompanied by him or his employee;

2. a statutory attendant;

3. a person carrying out a statutory inspection of the vehicle;

4. any person in a disabled vehicle being towed;

5. the licence holder or his employee if his presence is necessary;

6. an employee of the licence holder going to a place to drive vehicles in the course of his employer's business;

7. a prospective purchaser, his servant or agent, or any person he asks to accompany him (must be accompanied by the licence holder or his employee); or

8. a publicity promoter (must be accompanied by the licence holder or his employee).

[450/71/40]

If the Secretary of State refuses an application for a trade licence made by a motor trader or vehicle tester the applicant is given 28 days in which to ask the Secretary of State to review his decision. In reviewing his decision the Secretary of State must consider any written representations made to him by the applicant [Excise Act/25 and 450/71/29].

If a licence holder changes his business name or address he must forthwith notify the Secretary of State and return the licence for amendment [450/71/30]. Trade plates issued with a trade licence must be displayed in the same manner as a normal registration mark and the plate carrying the licence must be at the front of the vehicle [33]. If a plate is lost or damaged the licence holder must apply for a replacement. A charge of £3·25 per plate is made where two are replaced at the same time and, in any other case, £5·50 for a front plate and £4 for a rear plate [31(3) and 1680/76]. It is an offence to alter, deface, mutilate or add anything to a trade plate or to display a trade plate which has been so tampered with. It is also an offence to display anything which could be mistaken for a trade plate [32]. Trade plates remain the property of the Secretary of State and must be returned when the holder ceases to hold a licence [31(2)].

WEIGHT LIMITS

Motor Vehicles (Construction and Use) Regulations, **No. 1017/78**

LOCOMOTIVES

The total laden weight of a locomotive must not exceed 20,830 kg. But if each of its wheels is sprung and is fitted with a pneumatic or solid tyre the weight may be 22,360 kg if it has less than six wheels; 26,420 kg with six wheels; or 30,490 kg with more than six wheels. Except for road rollers and four-wheeled locomotives first used before June 1, 1955, the axle weight must not exceed 11,180 kg [1017/78/82]. On a four-wheeled locomotive first used before June 1, 1955, not more than three-quarters of its total weight may be on one axle [49].

There are no weight limits for solo motor tractors since such a vehicle would become a locomotive if its weight, apart from fuel, loose tools, etc., exceeded $7\frac{1}{4}$ tons.

The total laden weight of all trailers drawn by a locomotive must not exceed 40,650 kg [83].

GOODS VEHICLES

Goods vehicle weight limits are complicated and fall into three broad categories: those in force since before August, 1964; those introduced in August, 1964, and those introduced in June, 1972. They may also be reduced to the weight shown on a maker's plate or a Ministry plating certificate. Where the general limits do not coincide with plated limits the lower weight must be observed [95(7), 150(3)].

Rigid trucks and drawbar trailers

The basic weight limit for a four-wheeled heavy motor car, motor car or drawbar trailer (including a composite trailer) is 14,230 kg

[85(1), 86(2) and 3(6A)]. For a heavy motor car with six or eight wheels the limits are 20,330 kg and 24,390 kg respectively but in the case of such a vehicle first used on or after June 1, 1973, and to which Regulation 89 (below) does not apply these limits are reduced to 16,260 kg and 18,290 kg respectively [85(1)].

The basic axle weight limit for a heavy motor car, motor car or drawbar trailer (including a composite trailer) is 9,150 kg [85(1), 86(1) and 3(6A)].

The above limits also apply to artic drawing units.

The total laden weight of a trailer made before February 27, 1977, with no brakes other than overrun brakes and a parking brake must not exceed 3560 kg. But in the case of a trailer made on or after this date and which is fitted with overrun brakes, whether or not it is fitted with any other brake, the total laden weight must not exceed 3,500 kg [86(4)]. This last limit does not apply to certain agricultural trailers [86(5)].

In the case of

(a) a heavy motor car or motor car equipped with a maker's plate and which can achieve braking efficiencies of 50% and 25%,

(b) a temporarily imported heavy motor car or motor car which complies with specified construction requirements and can achieve 50% and 25% braking efficiencies, and

(c) a trailer equipped with a maker's plate or a temporarily imported trailer which complies with specified construction requirements in either case drawn by a vehicle at (a) or (b), and as if a motor tractor were included in (a) and (b), and while maintaining those brake efficiencies

the axle weight limit is 10,170 kg, provided it has twin wheels with their centres not more than 300 mm apart or is fitted with 300 mm wide tyres, and the gross weight limits are as follows:

Number of axles	Distance apart of outer axles	Gross weight kg
2	3·25 m but less then 3·65 m	15,250
2	3·65 m or more	16,260
3	5·48 m or more	22,360
4	7·01 m but less than 7·92 m	26,420
4	7·92 m or more	28,450

[85(2), 86(3) and Sched. 6]

These gross weight limits do not apply to a motor vehicle of type (a) or (b) which is drawing a trailer unless that trailer comes within (c) [85(2)]. Neither do they apply to vehicles forming part of an articulated vehicle [Sched. 6].

Regulation 89 applies to the same types of vehicle at (a), (b) and (c) above, except that plated axle weights must also be given on a temporarily imported vehicle. It also applies to a composite trailer consisting of a converter dolly and semi-trailer where both have makers' plates and which is drawn by a motor tractor, heavy motor car or motor car which, while drawing the trailer, has braking efficiencies of 50% and 25%. It does not apply to vehicles forming part of an artic. None of the foregoing limits, apart from the

Number of axles	Distance apart of outer axles	Maximum plated axle weight kg	Permitted gross weight kg
2	Less than 2·65 m (104·3 in) But if the vehicle is a trailer with two closely spaced axles (1·02 m to 2·5 m apart), the distance between the front trailer axle and the rear motor vehicle axle is at least 4·2 m and Regulation 89 applies to both vehicles	—	14,230
		—	16,260
2	At least 2·65 m (104·3 in)	—	16,260

Three-axled vehicle not to exceed 16,260 kg gross except:

3	At least 3 m (118·1 in)	—	18,290
3	At least 3·2 m (126 in)	Not over 8,130	20,330
3	At least 3·9 m (153·6 in)	Over 8,130	20,330
3	At least 3·9 m (153·6 in)	Not over 8,640	22,360
3	At least 4·6 m (181·1 in)	Over 8,640	22,360
3	At least 4·9 m (193 in)	Not over 9,400	24,390
3	At least 5·1 m (200·8 in)	Over 9,400	24,390

Four-axled vehicle not to exceed 18,290 kg gross except:

4	At least 3·7 m (145·6 in)	Not over 8,640	20,330
4	At least 4·6 m (181·1 in)	Not over 8,640	22,360
4	At least 4·7 m (185 in)	Not over 8,640	24,390
4	At least 5 m (196·8 in)	Not over 9,150	24,390
4	At least 5·6 m (220·5 in)	Not over 9,150	26,420
4	At least 6 m (236·2 in)	Not over 9,660	26,420
4	At least 5·9 m (232·4 in)	Not over 9,150	28,450
4	At least 6·3 m (248 in)	Not over 9,660	28,450
4	At least 6·3 m (248 in)	Not over 9,400	30,490
4	At least 6·5 m (256 in)	Not over 9,660	30,490

Maximum plated axle weight means the highest axle weight shown in column 2 of a Ministry plate or, if no such plate is fitted, the highest axle weight shown on a maker's plate.

[89(3) and Sched. 7, part I]

3560 kg and 3500 kg limits, applies to a vehicle to which this regulation applies [89(2)]. The gross weight limits are tabulated opposite.

In the case of a vehicle first used before June 1, 1973, these limits shall not reduce the 20,330 kg and 24,390 kg limits the vehicle could have been used at under Regulation 85(1) [89(3) proviso].

A heavy motor car or motor car which complies with the provisions of Regulation 89 and which is an artic drawing unit is subject to the weight limits shown in the table below [90].

Number of axles	Distance apart of outer axles	Intermediate axle weight kg	Permitted gross weight kg
2	Less than 2·4 m (94·5 in)	—	14,230
2	At least 2·4 m (94·5 in)	—	16,260
Vehicles with three or more axles not to exceed 18,290 kg except:			
3 or more	At least 3 m (118·1 in)	8,390	20,330
3 or more	At least 3·8 m (149·6 in)	8,640	22,360
3 or more	At least 4·3 m (169·3 in)	9,150	24,390

Intermediate axle weight means the highest weight shown in column 2 of a Ministry plate, or, if no such plate is fitted, on a maker's plate for any axle other than the foremost and rearmost.

[90 and Sched. 7, part II]

Articulated vehicles

The basic weight limits for an artic are 20,330 kg if the semi-trailer has two wheels and 24,390 kg if it has four or more wheels [88(1)].

But, in the case of an artic formed by (a) a semi-trailer fitted with a maker's plate or a temporarily imported semi-trailer (as previously referred to) and (b) a drawing unit fitted with a maker's plate or a temporarily imported vehicle and, in any case, when braking efficiencies of 50% and 25% can be achieved, the gross weight limits are as shown in the table overleaf.

Regulation 88 does not apply to a vehicle to which Regulation 91 applies [91(2)].

Regulation 91 applies to an artic formed by (a) a drawing unit to which Regulation 90 applies and (b) a semi-trailer equipped with a maker's plate or a temporarily imported trailer and when braking efficiencies of 50% and 25% can be achieved. The gross train weight limits are tabulated overleaf in the lower table.

Number of axles	Distance apart of outer axles	Permitted train weight kg
3	Under 5·48 m	20,330
3	5·48 m or more	24,390
4	Under 7·01 m	24,390
4	7·01 m but less than 7·92 m	26,420
4	7·92 m but less than 9·75 m	28,450
4	9·75 m but less than 11·58 m	30,490
4	11·58 m or more	32,520
Over 4	Under 7·01 m	24,390
Over 4	7·01 m but less than 7·92 m	26,420
Over 4	7·92 m but less than 8·99 m	28,450
Over 4	8·99 m but less than 9·75 m	30,490
Over 4	9·75 or more	32,520

[88(2) and Sched. 6]

Class of articulated vehicle	Inner axle spacing			Gross train weight Tons
		Metres	In	
Two axled motor vehicle with—				
1 axled trailer	Less than	2·1	82·68	20,330
1 axled trailer	At least	2·1	82·68	22,360
1 axled trailer	At least	3·1	122·1	24,390
2 or more axled trailer	Less than	2·9	114·2	24,390
2 or more axled trailer	At least	2·9	114·2	26,420
2 or more axled trailer	At least	3·1	122·1	28,450
2 or more axled trailer	At least	3·6	141·8	30,490
2 or more axled trailer	At least	4·2	165·4	32,520
Three or more axled motor vehicle with—				
1 axled trailer	Less than	2	78·7	22,360
1 axled trailer	At least	2	78·7	24,390
1 axled trailer	At least	2·7	106·3	26,420
1 axled trailer	At least	3	118·1	28,450
1 axled trailer	At least	4	157·5	30,490
1 axled trailer	At least	4·4	173·3	32,520
2 or more axled trailer	Less than	2	78·7	24,390
2 or more axled trailer	At least	2	78·7	26,420
2 or more axled trailer	At least	2·3	90·5	28,450
2 or more axled trailer	At least	3·2	126	30,490
2 or more axled trailer	At least	4	157·5	32,520

Inner axle spacing means the distance between the rearmost axle on the **drawing** unit and the foremost axle on the trailer.

[91 and Sched. 7, part III]

Road trains

The total laden weight of a drawbar trailer together with that of the motor tractor, heavy motor car or motor car drawing it must not exceed 22,360 kg. But, as long as all the wheels of the vehicles in the combination are wheeled (as opposed to being tracked) they may total 24,390 kg and, if the trailer is fitted with power-assisted brakes which the driver can operate, they may total 32,520 kg [87].

Distribution of weight

The weight transmitted by a heavy motor car, motor car or trailer to a strip of road at right angles to the length of the vehicle and less than 1·02 metres wide must not exceed 11,180 kg; 1·02 metres but less than 1·22 metres, 16,260 kg; and 1·22 metres but less than 2·13 metres, 18,300 kg [94]. These restrictions do not apply to a vehicle to which Regulation 92 applies [92(7)].

Bogie and axle weights

Regulation 92 applies to heavy motor cars, motor cars and trailers to which Regulation 89 applies, whether or not the vehicle forms part of an artic. It provides that *two closely spaced axles* (i.e. not less than 1·02 m and not more than 2·5 m apart) spaced at the distance given in the table below must not exceed the weight shown in column 2 but they may go up to the weight shown in column 3 if their plated weight permits and the plated weight of either axle does not exceed half the weight shown in column 3 [92(2), (3)].

MAXIMUM WEIGHTS FOR TWO CLOSELY SPACED AXLES				
Column 1 *Distance between axles*			Column 2 *Total weight* *kg*	Column 3 *Total weight* *kg*
	Metres	*In*		
At least	1·02		12,200	16,260
At least	1·05	41·34	15,260	17,280
At least	1·2	47·25	16,270	18,300
At least	1·35	53·15	17,280	18,800
At least	1·5	59·06	18,300	19,320
At least	1·85	72·85	19,320	20,340

[Sched. 7, part IV]

Three closely spaced axles which have an outer axle spread given in column 1 of the table overleaf must not each exceed the weight shown in column 2. Here 'closely spaced' means having an outer axle spread of not more than 3·25 m and none of the axles having a plated weight of more than 7630 kg. These limits do not require a vehicle first used

before June 1, 1973, to be used at a lower weight than it could have
been used under Regulation 94 [92(4)].

MAXIMUM WEIGHTS FOR THREE CLOSELY SPACED AXLES

Column 1 Distance between outer axles Metres	In	Column 2 Axle weight kg
Less than 1·4	55·12	3,720
At least 1·4	55·12	4,070
At least 1·5	59·06	6,100
At least 2	78·74	6,610
At least 2·55	100·4	7,120
At least 3·15	124	7,630

[Sched. 7, part V]

In addition, in the case of a semi-trailer to which Regulation 92
applies, if any one of *three adjacent axles* of the vehicle has a plated
weight over 7630 kg the weight transmitted by all the axles must not
exceed 18,290 kg except as follows:

Outer axle spread	Maximum plated weight of middle axle kg	Permitted total weight kg
At least 3 m (118·1 in)	8,390	20,330
At least 3·8 m (149·6 in)	8,640	22,360
At least 4·6 m (181·1 in)	9,150	24,390

[92(5) and Sched. 7, part VI]

These limits do not require a semi-trailer first used before June 1,
1973, to be used at a lower weight than it could have been under
Regulation 94 [92(5)].

The axle weights for a vehicle to which Regulation 92 applies
are contained in Regulation 93. They are that basically the weight
transmitted by a two-wheeled axle must not exceed 9150 kg but,
if the axle is fitted with twin wheels at 300 mm centre or 300 mm
wide tyres, it is allowed 10,170 kg [93(2) (3)].

If the vehicle has more than two wheels in line, such as on oscillating
axles, the limit on those wheels is 11,180 kg except if those wheels form
part of two closely spaced axles or part of three adjacent axles on a
semi-trailer when the limit is reduced to 10,170 kg [93(4)].

Makers' plated weights

Until a goods vehicle receives a Ministry plating certificate the weights given on its maker's plate must not be exceeded [95]. Once a Ministry plate is issued the maker's plated weights are not enforceable. The maker's plated weights on locomotives and tractors first used on or after April 1, 1973, must not be exceeded [95(3)].

Ministry plated weights

The weights shown in column 2 of a plating certificate must not be exceeded [150]. These weight limits take effect at the end of the month in which the vehicle is required to be plated.

COUNTING AXLES

Except for Regulation 108 (tyre mixing), in counting the number of axles of a vehicle and the weight transmitted by any one axle, any number of wheels which rest within a strip of road surface 1·02 metres wide at right angles to the length of the vehicle shall be counted as one axle [1017/78/3(6)].

PUBLIC SERVICE VEHICLES

Basically the total laden weight of a heavy motor car which is a public service vehicle must not exceed 14,230 kg and an axle weight must not exceed 9150 kg [1017/78/84(1)]. But in the case of a p.s.v. which is a heavy motor car or motor car with 50% and 25% braking efficiencies, or a similar temporarily imported vehicle, the following higher weights are permitted:

(a) 10,170 kg on an axle fitted with twin wheels with centres 300 mm apart or with 300 mm wide tyres.
(b) 15,250 kg gross weight if the outer axle spread is 3·25 metres but less than 3·65 metres, and
(c) 16,260 kg gross weight if the outer axle spread is 3·65 metres or more.

[84(2)]

INDEX

Printed in Great Britain by Butler and Tanner Ltd, Frome and London